Fever Dreams

Fever Dreams
New Work from Padua

PADUA
PLAYWRIGHTS
PRODUCTION

Padua Playwrights Press
Los Angeles

Produced by Sideshow Media LLC, New York, NY

Editorial director: Dan Tucker
Editorial assistant: Tessa Perliss
Cover and interior design: CoDe. New York Inc., Jenny 8 del Corte Hirschfeld and
Mischa Leiner
Supervising Padua editor: Guy Zimmerman

Padua Playwrigts Productions
840 Micheltorena St.
Los Angeles, CA 90026

Printed in the United States of America

Distributed in the United States and Canada by Theatre Communications Group,
520 Eighth Avenue, 24th Floor, New York, NY 10018-4156
ISBN: 978-0-9630126-9-2

Contents

Beauty in the Present Tense

by Guy Zimmerman

1.

When I moved from New York City to Los Angeles in the early 1990s, I thought I was saying goodbye to the challenging theater you could then find at places like The Kitchen, Performance Garage, St. Mark's in the Bowery, or PS1. After some thrashing around in arenas where playwriting was viewed as a bush-league version of film-and-TV writing, I encountered a group of artists practicing a brand of sharp-edged, literary theater that easily equaled what I had left in downtown New York. I'm talking about the Padua Hills Festival run by Murray Mednick, as well as the attendant playwriting workshops orchestrated by his like-minded colleagues, including John Steppling. If anything, this work was more grounded in literary and critical history than anything that survived the cultural chemotherapy of the gentrified 1980s in New York. Moreover, this approach to theater was alive to what might be called the vertical dimension of tragic drama—how the art form points effortlessly toward potent mysteries of being that are otherwise spoken of only within a religious context.

Mednick, along with Sam Shepard and María Irene Fornes, arrived in Southern California as part of the great diaspora of the early 1970s, when various cultural and economic forces brought the Off-Off Broadway era to a close. Although the explosion of theatrical innovation that rocked lower Manhattan in the 1960s seemed to dissipate quickly, one way to view the history of American theater in the four decades since is as a series of after-shocks from that seismic event. A perspective of that kind sheds light on the eleven plays assembled here. Together they amount to four generations in a distinct and robust lineage of theater writing that has roots in the New York aesthetic, but that has been sustained by the oddly generative semidesert culture of Southern California.

As a place to exhibit creative work in any art form, Los Angeles can't compete with New York. When it comes to assembling an audience for art of any kind, traffic congestion alone is a serious obstacle. But a strong case can be made that Los Angeles is a better place to create new work. Life is still cheaper in Los Angeles than in New York, and more importantly, living here forces the artist to grapple with an unidealized America defined by anxiety and greed, and by all the toxins in between. The friction between this alienated American landscape and the sources of artistic inspiration feed energy into the work and ground it in meaning. In the hothouse of Manhattan or of Williamsburg it's possible to imagine our collective life to be different than it actually is, and to avoid the unpleasant work of pondering what is actually taking place. In Los Angeles, the simple act of leaving the house entails encountering the middle-American mindset, which haunts the semi-urban landscape with its forlorn, fast-receding dream of an easy and perfectible happiness.

The rebellious idea that Los Angeles is, paradoxically, a superior place to create new work is even more convincing in the theater, for a complement of reasons. While there's never much of a theater-going audience in Los Angeles, and freeway traffic dampens nightlife across the basin, there's a wealth of gifted actors wanting to reconnect with the artistic aspect of their vocation. Also, theater rentals are cheap compared to those available in New York, and Actors' Equity allows actors to work on stage for almost nothing in Los Angeles. So theater happens in Los Angeles, and with fewer constraints, such that when the impulse to explore the form arises with sufficient strength and combines with natural talent, there's a good chance that a transformative new play will make itself known. The result is an extension of the authentic, playwrights-theater tradition that began at Theater Genesis and other Off-Off Broadway venues in New York, but that was uprooted by the rising cost of living, and by its own centripetal forces.

The Padua approach to the writing of plays, cultivated collectively in writing workshops, involves training rigorously in the formal aspects of the playwright's craft, and then neutralizing the conceptual mind in favor of a more open awareness in which listening constitutes the fundamental act. Padua workshops are run more like painting studios than like typical MFA-style writing workshops. Instead of simply discussing texts written elsewhere, the students actively compose new work. It is an essentially poetic approach that aims to deliver a higher grade of transformative capacity by reaching down past the discursive mind to that burnished, high-energy space where the true voices live. It's as if the play already exists and the playwright's job is to hear it. Well, that's not quite right—better, perhaps, to say that the playwright is creating the text in a highly charged dance with himself or herself, "following," as Mednick likes to say, "where you lead." The mind is trained to hear not only the words but also the spaces between the words, so that by the time they hit the page they bring the power of their own silence along for the ride. Whether we call this power "the unconscious," or whether we locate it in the elemental forces of nature or in the heavens, this process restores the theater to its place as the locus of transformative human encounters.

It's an approach perfected in Mednick's work, and his plays included here, *Clown Show for Bruno* and *Destruction of the Fourth World,* should be viewed as full-length dramatic poems. In this mode of working, it's the language itself, rather than plot or situation, that holds the stage front and center. Dramatic tension and character remain crucial, but the playwright's task is to find those elements in a more intimate encounter with voice itself, allowing the characters to form distinctly enough so that they announce their own "dramatic" situations.

John Steppling's two plays, *Phantom Luck* and *Spanish Angel,* show how this same basic approach can yield entirely different results when run through a West-coast sensibility. A Miles Davis figure to Mednick's Charlie Parker, Steppling combines an exact and cinematic ear with a deep feeling for the lyrical potential in the landscape of Los Angeles, and a deep knowledge in how this landscape has been depicted by others. In both of these new plays you can feel the playwright holding a character in awareness and letting the dramatic shape of the play unfold from there.

The rest of the playwrights assembled here, myself included, ring the changes on this same basic approach. In each case there is some inherent sensibility that can be traced to a certain way of hearing the world, and the play arises from the interaction of this sensibility with the elements of craft and the demands of the form. As in the work of Shakespeare or the Greeks, realistic sets and stage directions are almost entirely absent. The playwright listens and lets the world emerge from what the characters say as they bear up under the weight of their existence. These voices can be said to rise up out of the silence of the body, or, to descend from the larger world of others and history and time.

But Padua is not just a literary tradition; working directly with actors on stage is viewed as an equal part of the playwright's training, and a crucial aspect of meeting the demands of the vocation. The last step in the process of writing a play involves working with actors to bring that play to life in front of an audience. A reading is not enough; the playwright needs to stand behind the audience for multiple performances, watching as the actors enact that unique exchange night after night, the meaning of the text shifting and changing with the demands of each audience. Padua has always emphasized the primacy of language and the cultivation of a playwright's theater, but with the recognition that language for the stage is crafted first and always as a signpost for actors—so that they may know how to act in front of an audience. It is the audience that tells the writer if these actions are coherent, and no play may be considered complete until emerging from the crucible of this interchange.

2.

The following notes on the plays collected here are intended only as the most cursory introduction to these texts. Those considering the plays for production are strongly advised to assemble some skilled actors for a reading. This work is meant to be heard live much more than read on the page.

In *Clown Show for Bruno*, Mednick pays homage to the great Polish writer and artist Bruno Schulz. In 1939, when the Nazis occupied Poland, Schulz was driven into the Jewish ghetto and enslaved by a Nazi officer. The Nazi's house needed to be livened up, so Schultz was deployed to paint fairy tale figures on the walls of the children's bedroom. Caught in an escalating feud between his "protector" and another Nazi official, Schulz was shot dead on the streets of his hometown on November 19. Written in the fast-paced rhythms of the Yiddish theater, *Clown Show for Bruno* utilizes clowning, masks, and mime to celebrate creative genius and joy in the face of terror. In Mednick's *The Destruction of the Fourth World*, the ancient Native American trickster, Coyote, makes ready for the end of the world with his only accomplice—a thirteen-year-old boy from a dysfunctional Jewish family. Haunted by the death of his mother, the young boy, Bernie, investigates the meaning of prayer, an inquiry that quickly leads him into dangerous terrain. The playwright's ferociously energized rhythms combine with comedic wordplay to examine how creative and destructive aspects of human existence relate to each other, and what they imply about our common future.

Hotel Bardot is inspired by Freud, Jung, Lacan, the *Tibetan Book of the Dead*, and by Tantric texts, whose suggestion to "meditate on your own death" became Heidi Darchuk's mantra during the writing of the play. The action opens as the heroine, K, enters into an already broken afterlife in the form of a rotting hotel and manages to level it to the ground and then escape, in her way, destroying time. By doing so, K transcends a human life of victimhood to become a version of Kali, Indian Goddess of annihilation, time, and blackness. The writer here is operating as a lucid dreamer, navigating her nonsensical and surreal landscape with clear, open eyes, fully awake and unafraid.

Working on *The Empty Bed* as she entered her forties, Sharon Yablon here addresses the unresolved differences between children and their parents, and how these tensions change as we turn into adults and our parents nearly turn back into children. Ungainly at first, these characters seem to exist free of our squeamishness about who and what we actually are. More subversively, they're charming, finding their way into our affections even though we aren't quite sure we should trust them. Once inside, they start making trouble, drawing our gaze to those corners of our lives we'd prefer to ignore—our mortality, for example. Over time this honesty begins to lend them a quasi-heroic stature. The plays collected here, consequently, begin to shift from the comic toward the tragic. Meanwhile, like dreams we can't wake up from, the characters keep coming at us.

Head Trader is a goodbye to a New York City increasingly defined by the perpetual mania of the young urban professional as he is consumed by groundless anxieties. Death, again, is in the air, the action unfolding in a nighttime limbo between this world and the next. *The Inside Job*, meanwhile, is about demons and angels on the American scene in the age of George W. Bush and Enron. The play unfolds inside a suburban condo whose current tenants, Max and Victoria, are "downwardly mobile." The play opens as Max arrives home with a young woman named Heidi, whose name was the last word to leave Victoria's lips. As it turns out, Heidi knows more about Victoria's malaise than Max initially suspects, and what she reveals sheds light on an American landscape in which terror is active and at large. Taking place over the course of a single evening, the play interrogates the theatrical form to see what it can reveal about the "Tex-ification" of the American mind at the beginning of the twenty-first century.

Delving into another corner of the Texas state of mind, Hank Bunker roots *The Interview* in the incongruous juxtaposition of sunlit Dealey Plaza and the brutal imagery of JFK's murder. Bunker explores, in a darkly hilarious way, how existence can assert bewilderingly opposite truths in the same instant—and what might happen if we attempt to resist them. Connie feels the world has failed to acknowledge the reality of her inner thoughts and feelings, particularly as they concern her growing panic over being range-bound by Ronnie's success as a golfer. She digs in against this existential erosion with the best weapon at her disposal—the historical record—and finds to her regret that facts are no match for the truth.

In *Liddy,* Sissy Boyd investigates the mother-child relationship and the paralyzing self-loathing that can exist there. The play is infused with Boyd's droll, self-directed humor, and the muscular lyricism that is her poetic gift. In Boyd's work, the body vanquishes language. Sitting astride its usually dominant opponent, the body seems as surprised as anyone by its victory, which it knows to be temporary. The poetic utterances that emerge are muscular and yet awkward, as if questioning their own autonomy. One has the feeling they have floated up from oracular sources deep below. Before the normal state of affairs reasserts itself we have a chance to hear unusual truths.

A majestic meditation on randomness and fate, *Phantom Luck* came about out of Steppling's desire to write about gamblers and the existential aspects of their obsession. The play seeks to illuminate and amplify, rather than resolve, the contradictions in our attitudes toward games of chance, which covertly play a central role in the rituals of materialism. Those familiar with the playwright's work will sense the presence of central influences— the playwrights Buchner, Kroetz, and Beckett, the poets James Wright and Vallejo, and other figures from this history of Western thought, especially Adorno and Heidegger—as well as noir and pulp elements from Jim Thompson to Edward Bunker. *Spanish Angel* follows a hermetic shopkeeper as he is inexorably drawn back into a SoCal underworld defined by broken dreams and violent dysfunction. Widely known for the stripped-down minimalism of his early work, Steppling here reveals a capacity for deep feeling that brings with it an historical and social awareness steeped in the Marxist and Freudian critiques of bourgeois values.

In *A New World War,* Rita Valencia updates the Orwellian view of the totalitarian mind-set. In this not-too-distant future, political oppression is taken to be, at root, merely a social manifestation of an emotional dynamic common to us all. Antar's cyborg, the perfectly named "Gauloise," is a consumerist Pinocchio, highlighting in uncomfortable ways what is automatic in our behavior and what is not. From Gauloise's point of view, we humans are "need machines" longing for a contact with an Other that can never truly arrive. "Intimacy level 4," this illusion is called, and Antar is lost in her desire to experience it. The phrase has the perfect wistful irony to it, shedding light on the engine of desire fueling the consumerist paradise we have created.

3.

For the most part, these plays were written in Los Angeles in the first decade of the twenty-first century, a time, I am certain, that will come to be regarded as a low point in the country's political and cultural history. While only a few of these plays are overtly political, each of them represents an act of protest against a culture hurtling further into the small-minded darkness of American materialism. Written by professional playwrights at different stages of development, these plays rebel against the positivist vision of human reality that fuels our collective misadventure. They are dramas constructed to participate in an anarchic revolution in sensibility that is still in the process of articulating itself, and one way or the other they are a gas to perform and to witness. Together they suggest that the role of theater, and of the arts in general, is due for a revival, art being one of the avenues human beings have always taken as they seek to free themselves from discredited habits of mind, and reconnect to the open field of possible futures.

Clown Show for Bruno

by Murray Mednick

Clown Show for Bruno *was first produced by Padua Playwrights at ArtShare, Los Angeles under the direction of Guy Zimmerman, and with the following cast:*

Emilio Daniel Stein
Jacko Bill Celentino
Cleo Kali Quinn and Dana Weiluns

Characters

CLOWNS
Emilio
Jacko
Cleo

They play all the parts, using MASKS.

Bruno
Josephina (Juna)
Father
Mother
Landau
Gunther
Sophia

CHORUS *(in italics)*

Any of the clowns can say the chorus lines. Dialogue in parentheses are asides.

With drawings from the works of Bruno Schulz, a portrait of his friend, Romana Halpern, and the photo of Felix Landau on his horse, and with gratitude to Jerzy Ficowski and his book, Regions of the Great Heresy.

Scene

A bench on a stage.
A chair.

And so and so

Here we go
For Bruno
Gnome of gnomes

Shot twice in the head
In Dro-Ho-Bytz
On Mickewitz and Cyacky
See-Ah-Kee
Right on the corner

By a Kraut named Gunther

So.

Sex-obsessed libidinous
Jew Bruno Schulz
Like you and me
God bless the motherfucker

Set up by history

Yet another stupid human illusion

As the race propagates and multiplies
Itself to extinction

C'est la vie
Bring on the clowns!

Emilio   It's very appealing because
It's me
Also.
It's me
I am Bruno.
I am Bruno Schulz
Also.
At any rate I can identify
As they say
With him.
He was into kings and queens and gnomes
And sex.
Who knows if he ever got laid
Bruno
Except with an occasional whore
Who knows?

Jacko   I'll bet he did.

Cleo   I'll bet he didn't.
Ask me why.

Jacko   Why?

Cleo   Because he never does.

Jacko   Who's dat?

Cleo	Him. Emilio. Dis.
	It's so crass.
	It's so incredibly crass.
Jacko	Who's dat?
Cleo	Da Katzenjammer Kid
	Dat's who.
Emilio	Ha-ha.
	(They all crack up)
All	Okay.
	All right.
	Okay.
Emilio	That's enough.
Cleo	Fine and good.
Jacko	Why is dat?
Cleo	Why?
Jacko	Why, because he never.
Together	He's a gnome
	He's a gnome
	He's a little Jewish gnome
	And he never.
Jacko	He's kinda insecure, dat.
Cleo	Dat he is.
Jacko	So he never.
	He puts his arms around a lady
	And he kisses her
	On da nose!
Cleo	Oh, God, it's so crass.
Jacko	What about you, lady?
Cleo	Say again?
Jacko	I say, What about you, lady?

Cleo	I stink it's crass.
	(They crack up again)
Jacko	All's well.
	Fine and good.
	He should be ashamed.
Cleo	I'm sure he is.
	I'll bet he is.
	Are you?
Emilio	Yes, because I'm looking at dem.
	I can't stop lookin' at dem and dinkin'
	About dem.
Cleo	Say again?
Emilio	Thinking about them or it.
Cleo	It?
Emilio	You know, fornication and copulation.
Cleo	It's so crass.
Jacko	Give him a break, why don't you?
	Lighten up.
	Kind out.
	And by that I mean like
	Butt out or bug out.
Emilio	Or fuck off.

What is it anyway but biology
Biology as the rabbis say
Between the pisser and the asshole
Because the human stuff
(Or stiff)
Needs to procreate
And that's why.

Cleo	So what?
Jacko	It needs to procreate and replicate
	And duplicate.
Cleo	So what?
Jacko	So it can go on
	And keep going on.
	So I ax myself sincerely—
Cleo	What's dat?
Jacko	Going on for what?
	Is it to satisfy and gratify,
	Mortify and glorify,
	Horrify and multiply?
Cleo	Oh, stop.
Jacko	After all, a person can live without sex.
Together	Monks do it.
	Bruno did it.
	Emilio does it.
Emilio	We don't do it
	Me and Cleo,
	Cleo and I.
Cleo	We do too do it!
Emilio	That's what I said?
	Is that what I said?
Cleo	It's so crass.
Jacko	They live without
	And they don't complain.
	They don't suffer,
	They don't pine,
	They don't waste away.
Cleo	They don't sulk,

	They don't kill their lives.
	Wives.
Emilio	I know some stories you wouldn't believe. Jews in the mountains. They thought there was free love. Stories you wouldn't believe. We should do a show.
Cleo	Oh.
Jacko	No.
Cleo	Oh, no.
Emilio	We should do a show about that.
Jacko	Dis is it, eh?
	Dis is da show.
Emilio	"Lifetime Affairs"
	We'll call it.
	Where people made arrangements.
Cleo	No, Bruno.
Jacko	It's a true story.
Cleo	Bruno Schulz.
Emilio	Clowning for Bruno
	We should call it.
Cleo	No.
Jacko	I don't like it.
Cleo	No.
Emilio	Fine and good,
	Just as well,
	I won't tell you.
	Fine.
Jacko	Now he's pouting.
	He has his pout face on.
	Look at dat pout face.
	Isn't dat nice?

Emilio	No, I'm happy now.
Jacko	You see dat?
Emilio	I'm happy.
	I'm very happy now.
Jacko	You see dat?
	Dat's duh happy face.
	Youse see a difference dere?
Cleo	Ha-ha
	No *difference between the pouty face and the*
	happy face.
Emilio	In those days there was no di-vorces
	Ya know?
Cleo	Yeah, yeah?
Emilio	So Lily and Junie and Pookie and I don't know who else,
	they rented an apartment in Wonderland, and there
	they could meet with their true loves who was not their
	es-pouses.
Jacko	Don't tell me any stories okay?
Emilio	This was in da mountains in the turties and the forties,
	or the fifties…
	Let's go to Dro-Ho-Bytz in 1934.

(The BRUNO MASK and the JOSEPHINA MASK)

Bruno	There is a Jewish religion
	But it don't go
	deep.
Josephina	Deep?
Bruno	No. Of course, it's a beautiful religion.
Josephina	You, you should know.

	You should save more.
	You should shave more.
	Blend in better.
Bruno	I agree, definitely.
Josephina	You should slave more,
	You should try and sell more
	art more.
Bruno	I agree. Definitely.
Josephina	And stand up straight.
Bruno	Can we go back?
Josephina	Because you stoop already.
Bruno	Can we go back?
Josephina	Back?
Bruno	Five minutes ago,
	Or sooner.
	I kissed you
	and you ducked.
Josephina	Yes?
Bruno	You didn't like it?
Josephina	I liked it.
Bruno	Then why?
Josephina	Men—all they want is one
	thing.
Bruno	I'll worship you. I'll get down on my knees.
Josephina	Stand up, Bruno.
	Stand up.
	And be a man.
Bruno	I'll worship you.
	I worship you.
Josephina	Be a man.

	For what is life but to bear children
	And die?
	I am a Christian now.
	Converted.
Bruno	That's okay.
	Immortal?
Josephina	Yes, Darling.
Bruno	Good, good. Good, good, good.
Josephina	Good?
	Why Good?
Bruno	How could it be bad?
Josephina	I'm not sure I want to.
Bruno	What?
Josephina	Fornicate
	Or co-habitate.
Bruno	That's okay.
	That's fine.
Josephina	I think we should
	Wait.
Bruno	Fine and good.
Josephina	Don't you think?
Bruno	I do, I do,
	Very good.
Josephina	And you?
	Immortal?
Bruno	Who me? Not me.
Josephina	Oh.
Bruno	Jew, me.
Josephina	I know.
Bruno	Jew I am.

	Excuse me.
	I am a Jew.
Josephina	So?
Bruno	Immortality, no.
Josephina	No?
Bruno	No.
Josephina	What happens
	Then?
Bruno	We die.
Josephina	What happens then?
	And then?
Bruno	We stay.
Josephina	Oh.
	It's terrible.
Bruno	But I don't know
	Really.
	You?
Josephina	No.
Bruno	The blood survives.
Josephina	I see.
Bruno	The family line.
	The name, maybe.
Josephina	Schulz?
	(Laughter)
Bruno	Schulz, on and on.
Josephina	You have art.
	You have writing.
Bruno	My father.
	I feel remorse.
Josephina	What

	Your father?
Bruno	We should marry.
Josephina	I don't know.
	Your father?
Bruno	He don't feel good.
Josephina	You see?
Bruno	Otherwise.
Josephina	What?
Bruno	Is fine with him.
Josephina	I should go.
Bruno	Oh.
Josephina	I'll go.
Bruno	Go.
Josephina	No.
Bruno	He's sick.
Josephina	I know.
Bruno	Why wait?
Josephina	No way.
Bruno	Why not?
Josephina	Sex is for marriage only.
Bruno	So?
Josephina	I don't know.
Bruno	Come on.
Josephina	No.
Bruno	Why not?
Josephina	Bye, Bruno. *(End MASKS)*

And he fell into a sexual rage
Which stayed in the center of his chest
Growling as she left the café

He is a nonviolent fellow
After all.

Life seemed incomprehensible—
People were going on with their business—

Their meaningless and stupid activities—

As if nothing had happened to him
Bruno,
At all, nothing at all,
Just a moment in time
And that's all there is, he thought
A moment in time

A moment in time

While she

While she

She is walking down the street
And people are looking at her butt

Clowns   OY!

Her sexy little butt
It's just a wonderful thing to look at
Wonderful

A Bruno Schulz drawing here

Poor Bruno.

Clowns   In lust!

He had said one more extra thing
Too late and too useless and vain
And he knew it and ate it
Like the snail he was or is
Caught out of his house
His pride and well-being.

So.

Emilio   Revealed and destroyed.

Stepped on like the worm
He is or was.

Jacko   Say again?
Cleo   Say what?
Jacko   Revealed what?
Emilio   Pride revealed.
Jacko   Destroyed what?
Emilio   Well-being destroyed.
Cleo   You can't be was and is at da same time.
Jacko   AHA!
Cleo   Too loud.

Jacko	Excuse me?
Cleo	Too loud.
Emilio	No need to shout.
Cleo	And at the same time—
Jacko	What?
Cleo	And at the same time people—
Jacko	People?
Cleo	You know, like us.
Jacko	Okay, they were?
Cleo	Peoples was having ideas and making plans.
Jacko	Like us?
Cleo	Ideas about life and plans for the future.

It's disgusting in a way,
Wouldn't you say?

Which lead to a gunshot in the head.
End Bruno.

So.

(FATHER MASK and BRUNO MASK)

Bruno	Dada? Daddy? Papa? Father?
Father	We all come from afar.
	From a far land.
	Far away.
	Desert and mountain.
	The forest and the sea.
	We come.

	Jungle and prairie.
	Hill and savannah,
	We come from
	There.
Bruno	Okay.
Father	From there. *(End* MASK*)*
Bruno	Okay.
Cleo	So how ya doin'?
	How are ya,
	What's up?
Bruno	Say?
Cleo	How ya doin', how are ya, what's up?
Bruno	Fine.
Cleo	Good.
Bruno	Good, good, good.
Cleo	What are you taking now?
	Pills?
	You take pills?
Bruno	I do, because I'm sick.
Cleo	Why are you sick?
Bruno	I don't know.
Cleo	Is it the pills?
Bruno	I don't know. No.
Cleo	What's wrong with you? There's always something wrong with you. I'm sick of it.
Bruno	I'm fine.
Cleo	That's not what you said.
	That's not what you just said.
Bruno	I'm tursty.
Cleo	Take a drink of water.

	Take a drink.
Bruno	I'm nauseated.
Cleo	Don't worry, you're not gonna die.
Bruno	We're all gonna die.
	We get old and die.
	We get old and sick and die.
	Every single one of us. *(MASK)*
Jacko	Except for dose who suffer sudden death.
Cleo	Exacto.
Emilio	Like Bruno.
Jacko	With a bullet into his brain.
Cleo	*C'est la vie.*
Emilio	Exacto.
Cleo	*Fait accompli.*
Emilio	*Exactement.*
Cleo	*Mais oui.*
Jacko	*Je ne sais pas.*
Emilio	*C'est mort.*
Cleo	Boom, right into the head.
Emilio	And down he goes and his inner life went with him.
	And down he goes
	Down he goes.
Cleo	His love life and his thoughts
	His hopes and dreams
	Turned to soup on the sidewalk.

(In the ghetto
In Drohobyz)

Emilio	His talent.

Cleo	His talent, too, of course.
Emilio	I just want to have an ordinary normal life.
Jacko	Which is?
	What's dat?
Emilio	Like in a penthouse overlooking the Pacific at night, with nice furniture, maybe white, or beige, where I can bring my girls, and we can smoke a joint and look out at the moonlight on the ocean, and have a lot of foreplay, and gossip about the business and the people we know, and have a drink, and have a smoke, and be happy, and my conscience wouldn't bother me one bit.
Jacko	Is dat so?
Emilio	Not one bit. Or have another ordinary normal type of life, where I come home to my wife, and she says, "Oh, I'm so tired tonight, honey."
Cleo	I'm so tired tonight, honey.
Emilio	Just totally normal and expected and nonviolent and no questions asked. "I'm so tired tonight, honey," and she's totally mine, no questions asked.
Cleo	"Oh," with a sigh, "I'm so tired tonight."
Emilio	No question about it, I can see the look in her eyes that she loves me. She's my wife and there's no questions asked.
Cleo	Is this also true in Drohobyz?
	Among the Jews of Drohobyz?
Emilio	Why yes it is.
	Oh, Yes it is.
Jacko	Dis here is da Gunther mask.
	Dis here is da Landau mask.
Cleo	Two Kraut masks.
Emilio	It's too soon now, am I right?

Cleo	Put away the Kraut masks.
Jacko	I'm sorry.
Cleo	Put 'em both away, please.
Emilio	He jumped his cue, him.
Jacko	I'm sorry.
Emilio	We're back in Drohobyz.
Jacko	Put on da Bruno mask.
Emilio	Okay.
Cleo	I'll put on da Mother mask.
Emilio	Okay. *(MASK)*
Bruno	Mother.
Mother	What?
Bruno	Mother.
Mother	You have your job?
Bruno	Yes, Mother.
Mother	It's good. You have your family?
Bruno	Yes, Mother.
Mother	You have your health?
Bruno	Yes, sure.
Mother	Good. Good, good, good.
Bruno	Life, Mother.
Mother	Marriage, Bruno.
Bruno	I'm afraid.
Cleo	(See, women persecute him because they know he fears them. You see that? You understand that?)
Jacko	Put down da mask.
Cleo	I put it down already.
Emilio	He likes to stay in his room.
Cleo	He has fantasies?
Emilio	He has fantasies.

Cleo	It's so crass.
Emilio	He worships them and he fears them.
Jacko	He kisses their feet in his dreams.
Cleo	He sucks on their toes.
Jacko	But they won't put out.
Cleo	Not even in his dreams.
Jacko	Not even then. Ha.
Cleo	Even though he bows, even though he cringes.
Emilio	Yes.
Cleo	Because he smells bad, probably.
Jacko	Probably.
Cleo	And his clothes aren't quite clean.
Jacko	Probably not.
Cleo	He wears the same shirt day after day after day.
Emilio	Yes.
Cleo	So he stinks.
Emilio	What else?
Cleo	He's so nervous, he shakes.
Emilio	True.
Jacko	He shakes and he quakes.
Emilio	He does.
Jacko	And he's intimidated by so much as a glance.
Cleo	A look.
Jacko	Over da shoulder.
Cleo	A look of scorn.
Jacko	A scornful look over da shoulder and he's done.
Cleo	He's finished.
Emilio	His gaze goes out the window and into the sky. Gray sky of Dro-ho-byz, over the market square, while the light is slowly changing, darkening to his liquid dark, his animate

darkness, his darkness ending timeless days.

(MASK on)

Bruno Father.

Cleo Put on the mask. *(FATHER MASK)*

Father Hello, my son.

Bruno How are you, Father?

Father All life is energy. All matter is energy. Energy cannot die. Only the form changes. So there is no time and there is no death.

Cleo I don't know what that's supposed to mean.

Bruno Okay.

Cleo Take off the mask.

Jacko *(MASK off)* What are dey supposed to dink about dat?

Emilio It's how he was, Bruno's father. He had a big head.

Jacko He had a big head?

Emilio He had a big head.

Cleo What does that have to do with anything?

Emilio And his brother-in-law was a dwarf.

Cleo My God that's—it's ridiculous.

Emilio I don't know, maybe he was just a retard.

Cleo You don't know what you're talking about. As usual.

Emilio He was a mystic and a philosopher.

Cleo The brother-in-law?

Emilio No, the father.

Cleo There are only two things, actually, sex and money, and Bruno had neither one of them.

Jacko What about dis? Someone got it into their heads that they had to kill all the Jews. Why? Because they eat too much or drink too much.

Emilio Or breathe too much.

Cleo	Or fuck too much.
Jacko	Or take up da space of da German race.
Cleo	Ha! It's so stupid!
Emilio	Father had a dry goods store in Dro-ho-byz—a typical Jewish activity, that.
Jacko	What about dis? They shot him dead and fulfilled his dread. How's dat?
Cleo	Oh, stop it. It's so incredibly crass.
Emilio	He was afraid of time, Bruno. *(MASKS)*
Josephina	Bruno?
Bruno	Yes, my dear Josefina.
Josephina	You don't have to say that.
Bruno	My dear Juna.
Josephina	Don't say it if you don't mean it.
Bruno	I won't. Sorry.
Josephina	Regarding Kafka.
Bruno	Yes?
Josephina	Can I use your name?
Bruno	Why?
Josephina	No one's ever heard of me.
Bruno	I wouldn't say that, exactly.
Josephina	You never know what to say.
Bruno	I do sometimes.
Josephina	When?
Bruno	Only when I write.
Josephina	Yes. There you have a voice.
Bruno	It's true. If only I had time.
Josephina	You have plenty of time. You're a teacher.
Bruno	I have no time.
Josephina	You act condemned.

Bruno	I never have time.
Josephina	You're not condemned.
Bruno	I feel condemned.
Josephina	You are not.
Bruno	I must have a sabbatical, or I will never write again.
Josephina	Well, so what? So what if you never write again?
Bruno	I suppose that wouldn't be such a great tragedy.
Josephina	Regarding Kafka, once again, may I use your name for my translation?
Bruno	If that's what you want.
Josephina	It will help me to get it published, so that's what I want.
Bruno	Then, of course, Juna, why not?
Josephina	Because you are known, and I am not.
Bruno	You are known, Josefina Zelinska.
Josephina	Because you wish to know me carnally, you wish to know me biblically. Bruno Schulz. The Jew from Dro-ho-byz who writes fables.
Bruno	A few people, some writers, journalists.
Josephina	It doesn't matter, everything disappears into time.
Bruno	Josefina Zelinska.
Josephina	What, Bruno? (I know what you want.) *(Silence)* For God's sake, man, speak up! These silences are interminable!
Bruno	I'm sorry.
Josephina	What's the matter with you?
Bruno	I'm frightened.
Josephina	Of what?
Bruno	I don't know. (Of you.)
Josephina	(Of me?) *(Silence)* Bruno!
Bruno	You, Josefina.

Josephina	I can't help it! It's not my fault!
Bruno	No, of course not, you're absolutely right, Juna.
Josephina	Was it sex? Were you asking for sex?
Bruno	(Yes.) I'm sorry.
Josephina	You know it's impossible. You know it's a sin. I am a Catholic, after all.
Bruno	Marriage, then. I want to marry.
Josephina	Then you must convert, like me. You have no business being a Jew.
Bruno	My parents are Jews.
Josephina	So were mine.
Bruno	It's good to be a Jew. A Jew can be anything.
Josephina	All right, I won't interfere.
Bruno	If everything disappears into time, Josefina, then where is the sin?
Josephina	Right there, Bruno, right in there. *(Points at his heart. MASKS)* Shave and a haircut, Emilio, shower and a bit of mouthwash, and den we'll see.
Emilio	Yes, yes, of course, right away.
Cleo	It's so incredibly gross.
Emilio	I'll take care of it.
Cleo	And shine your shoes and change your clothes.
Emilio	I will.
Cleo	Put on something nice. You have a tie?
Emilio	I do. I think I do. I'm not sure.
Cleo	You should have a tie.
Emilio	I do. I probably do.
Cleo	You have a clean shirt?
Emilio	Uh, yes.
Cleo	Put that on, too.

Emilio	Okay.
Cleo	Make sure it's ironed.
Bruno	I will, dear. *Tout de suite.*
Cleo	And don't call me dear.
Bruno	I won't.
Cleo	Deer are for forests. *(Laughter)*
Jacko	Dat was terrible.
Emilio	I'm so glad.
Cleo	What?
Emilio	I had a prior life, like Bruno. A youth, like Bruno.
Cleo	Yes? So?
Emilio	I appreciate it. All the romance, all the sex.
Cleo	Tell me, did you get a lot?
Jacko	Dat is crass, dat is incredibly crass.
Cleo	Tell the truth.
Jacko	No. Da answer is: no.
Emilio	I did.
Jacko	Good for youse.
Cleo	He's lying.
Emilio	I fucked my wife every week, once or twice a week.
Cleo	What? Ha!
Emilio	I'm not lying.
	And what I got, I liked.
Jacko	Tell me your dreams, tell me your fantasies, dat.
Cleo	Oh, stop!
Emilio	Not Bruno, I don't think Bruno.
Jacko	Youse don't think Bruno what?
Emilio	Ever got any, ever.
Jacko	But dat's all right.
	Dat's all right.

Cleo	He lived.
Emilio	But not for long.
Cleo	He survived.
Emilio	Unhappily.
Cleo	He did his work.
Emilio	Rarely.
Cleo	When he could.
	When he had time.
	When he wasn't depressed.
Emilio	And nearly all of what he wrote like *Messiah* was lost.
Cleo	When the Germans came to Dro-ho-byz.
Emilio	So. (MASKS)
Bruno	Josefina.
Josephina	Yes?
Bruno	I want to talk.
Josephina	Talk. *(Silence)* See you're doing it again. We can't talk if you don't talk.
Bruno	(That's obvious!)
Josephina	(Shut up, you!)
Bruno	Each day I make a drawing or a painting. I tell a story on the blackboard. Usually it's a myth, you know, I mean a fairy tale. They have kings and queens and gnomes. I also draw adorable girls.
Josephina	No doubt!
Bruno	Can I show you?
Josephina	You can if you want.
Bruno	*(Drawing on transparent "blackboard")* And this will illustrate my feeling for the world, Juna, my true feeling for the world.

Josephina	It's a feeling of dread, isn't it? Isn't it something like that? Something dreadful?
Bruno	Yes, and strange. Strange winds and dark skies, and forests.
Josephina	I mean, in addition to that. Something dangerous, something evil.
Bruno	I go to school in the morning and I teach until night. And then I go home to my family. I don't have time to write, usually.
Josephina	Thank God you have a job, thank God you have a home.
Bruno	This is true, Josefina, though I don't know about the God part.
Josephina	We are poor creatures, Bruno, and our lot is a sad one.
Bruno	I'm happy when I draw, I'm happy when I write.
Josephina	You draw these little men, and there's one who looks like you, always, and they are cowering in front of women.
Bruno	Yes, because I adore them, the way I adore you. I want to embrace you and crawl inside you at the same time.
Josephina	That's a bit revolting, Bruno.
Bruno	Oh.
Josephina	It's all right, don't stop. I'm sorry. Continue.
Bruno	I try to capture the past as present, the way it is in childhood, the feeling of that—being free of time.
Josephina	And then where are you?
Bruno	Ah. I'm in an artistic world then. I'm an artist, then.
Josephina	But you are also here, Bruno, in this world. And you have to provide. And you can hardly provide for the family you have. And that's the truth of the situation, no matter how you look at it.
Bruno	Yes, it is hopeless.

Josephina	There is hope, but it's not in this world.
	(LIGHTS change, the drawing glows with light)
	Ah, beautiful, my good friend. Very beautiful.

(End MASKS)

Cleo	Emilio?
Emilio	Yes?
Cleo	You wanted to say something?
Emilio	I just wanted to say, summer nights in the mountains, coming out of the hotel lobby at night, or the dining room, and the girls are walking by in there fluffy skirts, and their ribbons and bows, and they're all excited.
Cleo	And so were you, I'll warrant.
Emilio	Yes, and the air was rich with life, the air itself was living and true.
Cleo	So excited you couldn't contain yourself.
Emilio	Just barely. Gulping air. Life! Life! *(MASKS on)* Juna, my dear Juna.
Josephina	Yes, dear Bruno?
Bruno	We must rendezvous, you and I.
Josephina	Yes, allright, yes. If you insist.
Bruno	You don't want to?
Josephina	No, I do. I do want to. Yes.
Bruno	Meet me. At the Hotel Paradise, at six-o'clock, on Sunday.
Josephina	I can't Sunday. Not Sunday.
Bruno	Saturday, then.
Josephina	All right.
Bruno	(We'll fuck, at last.)
Josephina	No, no, no, no.

Bruno	You do want to, yes?
Josephina	Yes, yes.
Bruno	Good. I'll see you then. *(Pause)*
Josephina	Bye, bye. *(MASKS off)*
Emilio	Uh, Jacko?
Jacko	Yes?
Emilio	What now?
Jacko	You do the scene. Do the scene. *(MASKS back on)*
Bruno	Oh.
Josephina	Okay.
Jacko	The Hotel Paradiso.
Josephina	Hi, Bruno.
Bruno	Hi, Juna.
Josephina	Hi.
Bruno	Hi.
Josephina	Hi.
Bruno	I was just thinking.
Josephina	What were you thinking?
Bruno	Life, how life.
Josephina	What?
Bruno	Came to be.
Josephina	Sex.
Bruno	Right. But also, why.
Josephina	Hair. Why do people have hair?
Bruno	Good, yes, good.
Josephina	Different colors, hair.
Bruno	Good, good, good.
Josephina	Why?
Bruno	I don't know why.
Josephina	You draw hair?

Bruno	I do.
Josephina	You draw faces.
Bruno	The same face. It's all one face.
Josephina	Your face.
Bruno	My face.
Josephina	And the girls.
Bruno	The girls, too.
Josephina	Don't pull too hard on my head.
Bruno	I won't.
Josephina	You can kiss me, but not too rough.
Bruno	I will.
Josephina	Relax. Breathe.
Bruno	I am.
Josephina	Take a deep breath.
Bruno	Okay.
Josephina	Take another deep breath.
Bruno	Okay.
Josephina	Did you brush your teeth?
Bruno	Yes.
Josephina	Did you wash your hands?
Bruno	I did.
Josephina	Lie down, Bruno.
Bruno	And you?
Josephina	In a minute.
Bruno	What's wrong?
Josephina	Nothing. I was just thinking.
Bruno	What were you thinking?
Josephina	We both have to work.
Bruno	I know that.
Josephina	We both put in very long hours.

Bruno	This is true.
Josephina	But at least you get some recognition.
Bruno	Just a little, Juna, not too much.
Josephina	Bruno Schulz.
Bruno	Not much at all.
Josephina	More than me.
Bruno	I don't make a dime from it.
Josephina	I translated Kafka.
Bruno	Not one.
Josephina	And you got the credit.
Bruno	That was the plan, Juna.
Josephina	I'm only saying. I work in the girls school twelve hours a day. I'm exhausted.
Bruno	I'm sorry.
Josephina	Teaching those stupid kids I don't know what.
Bruno	I agree completely.
Josephina	Lie still.
Bruno	I haven't moved.
Josephina	Don't.
Bruno	One day I'll be free of shop-teaching.
Josephina	When?
Bruno	God willing in a year or two.
Josephina	Bad things are happening, Bruno. Bad things happen in this world. Bad things are happening now.
Bruno	We can enjoy each other.
Josephina	I can't do this.
Bruno	Why not?
Josephina	I have to go.
Bruno	Juna, I won't move.
Josephina	I'm going.

Bruno	It's not bad.
Josephina	Write to me, Bruno.
Bruno	Goodbye, Josephina.

(MASKS off. EMILIO mimes walking, and then riding in a bus.)

Bruno thinks about the wonders of marriage, of the beauty of buttocks and loving smiles, the ordinary blessings of a woman with a man, with a family; that he wants to marry and he never will, and then he gets on a bus all alone, on the bus back to Dro-ho-byz. Clip-clop. Germans marching. He passes Germans on the way, Germans on motorcycles, Germans in trucks, Germans marching, clip-clop on their way, on their way to Dro-ho-byz.

Cleo	*(Showing)* This is the Landau mask, the Felix Landau mask.
Emilio	This is Felix Landau,
Jacko	A half-Jew him,
Emilio	Come to Dro-ho-byz to kill the Jews.
Jacko	Say Hello, Felix. *(Puts on LANDAU MASK)*
Landau	Hello.
Cleo	Introduce yourself.
Landau	My name is Felix Landau, how do you do?
Cleo	Very well until you came along, thank you.
Emilio	Say something about yourself.
Landau	There's not much to say, really.

Emilio	Tell us about life on earth, how you murdered 20,000 Jewish people, and then we'll bring in Bruno.
Cleo	It's so fucking idiotic. There's not a single human being who is not an idiot. That is my honest opinion.
Emilio	Let's hear from Felix.
Cleo	No. You mentioned life on earth and I'd like to go further with that idea.
Jacko	Go further, go further, what does that mean, "go further?"
Emilio	Take off the Landau mask.
Landau	That doesn't fucking mean anything. You can't go further when you aren't anywhere in the first place. You can't go any further. This is it. This is as far as you can go.
Emilio	Who's talking? Is that Landau?
Landau	Dah! This is the end of the line! Last stop! *Fini! Zein gezunt! (MASK off)*
Cleo	This is so confusing.
Emilio	You don't have to be Jewish.
Cleo	For what?
Emilio	To be an idiot.
Cleo	Oh!
Emilio	Is what I'm saying.
Cleo	We all knew that already. Didn't we?
Jacko	Yes.
Emilio	Of course.
Jacko	Absolutely.
Cleo	So we don't need to hear it again. You get that?
Emilio	Yes.
Cleo	We don't need to hear about it, and I'm sure they agree.
Emilio	I'm sure all the idiots agree.

Cleo	That you don't have to be Jewish to be an idiot.
Jacko	There you go.
Cleo	But it helps! *(Laughter)*
Jacko	Dat's dat.
Emilio	Onward and upward. *(Bruno and Josephina masks on)*
Josephina	Bruno?
Bruno	Josephina?
Josephina	Of all the Jewish idiots, you are certainly one of them.
Bruno	Was that a joke?
Josephina	Never mind. And your fears and mine, they come together. Your fears and mine, they bump each other. I'm sorry, my dear. I don't mean to hurt you. And yet we see together, don't we? We see something coming in the world, in the earth and in the sky, something coming to murder us, we see it coming, like my dear Kafka, my dearest Kafka, he saw it coming, too, and he too never had a woman.
Bruno	The poor bastard, the poor sonofabitch.
Josephina	How are those thoughts related?
Bruno	Excuse me?
Josephina	How are those two thoughts related?
Jacko	That he saw it coming and that he never had a woman? You don't see the connection dere? You fucking idiot? *(Masks off)* Now what is dat? Is dat da pouty face? Passive-aggressive? Look at dat face. Is dat da hurty face?
Cleo	Snot.
Jacko	Does that mean no, it's not, or snot?
Cleo	No.
Jacko	Dat dere is da nasty face. Look at da nasty face, dere.
Emilio	I'm okay, now. I'm cool.

Cleo	So what was the problem?
Emilio	You didn't take my arm.
Cleo	When?
Emilio	While walking.
Cleo	While walking?
Emilio	While walking.
Cleo	While walking.
Emilio	What I said.
Cleo	Oh.
Emilio	Which offends me, Cleo, because you're taller than me and bigger than me, especially in your high heels, and then you go your own way, leaving me hanging out there on a limb before the probing, unwelcoming eyes of others.
Cleo	Oh.
Emilio	Jacko, you have an opinion?
Jacko	No.
Cleo	You were offended.
Emilio	I knew that. I knew that already, so what you had to say was useless.
Cleo	Don't ask me anymore then.
Emilio	I was asking for a deeper insight.
Cleo	I had no idea you were offended.
Emilio	I knew that. I knew you had no idea, which is why I brought it up. If I thought you knew already, I wouldn't have brought it up.
Cleo	I'm sorry, actually.
Emilio	It's amazing. It's an amazing phenomenon.
Cleo	What is?

Emilio	That this can happen. Peoples walking and talking and having no idea.
Jacko	And so da German army comes walking into Drohobyz. Clip-clop-clip-clop.
Cleo	Where's Bruno?
Jacko	And wid guns, da fucking idiots.
Cleo	And Josephina, where is she?
Jacko	And plans.
Emilio	God, I can hardly stand it. Juna, he called her. Juna.
Cleo	I think she's in Warsaw or someplace around now.
Emilio	Beautiful, gorgeous, Juna. Long legs and a sexy smile. It's lovely to be alive and loved.
Cleo	Yes, but we're all hanging around like we're immortal.
Jacko	So? Dat's dat. What else are we supposed to do?
Cleo	And we're not. *(Big wink)* He wrote to his women, Bruno, as opposed to sleeping with them, he wrote to them. He was one of the greatest letter writers of all time.
Jacko	Correcto! Exacto! But every single person alive will vanish sooner or later. It is one of da strangest phenomenal factors imaginable.

(BRUNO and JOSEPHINA MASKS on)

Bruno	Dear Juna, darling Juna...
Josephina	Yes, Bruno?
Bruno	I write to protest, Darling, the integrity of my desire. *(MASKS off)*
Cleo	What is that supposed to mean?

This was in the thirties, while the Germans were
concocting their plans, and Bruno had decided to stand
up, he had decided to stand up in the face of rejection,
of humiliation and intimidation, he, the mark of all
time, so he wrote a letter. (MASKS back on)

Bruno   And so, to continue, which is to say—

Josephina Yes? Yes?

Bruno   That is to say, if you will permit me, I, from here on,
from this moment, I refuse, on my honor, refuse any
further sexual contact.

Josephina Oh!

Bruno   With you.

Josephina On what grounds?

Bruno   On Freudian grounds, that is to say, which is to say—

Josephina Yes? Yes?

Bruno   Sadoch and Masoch, that is to say, sado-masochistic,
I would say, are the grounds. And therefore, even
though I love you, and you have the most beautiful cunt
in Dro-ho-byz, maybe the most beautiful cunt in all of
Poland, but defintely in Dro-ho-byz, beautiful in its
fragrance, beautiful in its aspect between those shapely
thighs, lovely as it is, and even as I long to get those
long legs up in the air and even as I yearn to hear your
almost mournful cries—

Josephina Oh! Oh!

Bruno   Even so, I must refuse, I must decline, on my honor,
to go any further with this—what shall we call it?—
arrangement, prenuptial or whatever—if first of all I
must be abused, that is to say, raked over the coals, be

demeaned and debased, and my heartfelt election, I mean erection, circumcised as it is, be willfully insulted and denied, or dismissed, in the name of feminine vulnerability, or womanly scruples, or virginal horror, or excessive sensitivity, therefore, I, Emilio, I mean Bruno, declare this relationship—finis!

Josephina   Oh!

Bruno   And so, Cleo, that is to say, Juno, or Juna, or Josephina, you may no longer fear for your lately Christian soul, nor recoil at my constant Jewishness, or loom over me in your high heels—that's all done!

Josephina   But Bruno!

Bruno   Though we share the dread, you and I, of darkness on the horizon, of immanent catastrophe, of certain doom, of withering and unstoppable time, and though I love you truly, you, Juno, I mean Juna, you in your fragile and frightened essence, but mostly your sex and desire, and also your mind, Kafkaesque, or grotesque in its complexity, we share the dread, you and I and Kafka, and my father and all the Jews of Dro-ho-byz—

Josephina   Bruno!

Bruno   I must retract, I must withdraw, I welcome solitude, I embrace my lonely destiny—well, anyway—I return to the bosom of my family and my tribe, home to Drohobyz— that mythical country in my mind, of my childhood, of my art, and fall backward and downward into my literary world and into my irreplaceable, impeccable privacy.

Jacko   Bravo! Bravissimo, Emilio! Bravissimo, Bruno!

Emilio   *(Mask off)* Thank you.

Jacko	Pause. Pause. And then what happened? Then what happened?
Cleo	You said that twice.
Jacko	I'll tell you. Victory is short-lived. The moment passes. He gets down on his knees and he begs forgiveness.
Cleo	Bruno?
Emilio	Cleo, oh Cleo.
Cleo	What?
Emilio	I'm sorry.
Cleo	For what?
Emilio	I'm not nice. I had a difficult childhood and I'm not nice.
Cleo	I'll say.
Emilio	That's why I'm sorry.
Cleo	It's about time.
Jacko	For what, Emilio, for what?
Emilio	For being aggressive, for challenging someone's integrity in favor of my own, for being right every single second of every single day.
Cleo	I forgive you. *(He weeps)* Don't cry.
Emilio	"If I want to convey my present state, the image of being awakened from a deep sleep comes to mind. One awakens to phantoms, still seeing the world of dreams sinking away into forgetfulness, with fading colors still before his eyes and feeling the softness of a dream beneath his eyelids—" So spoke Bruno on the page, in Drohobyz, between August twentieth and August twenty-sixth, 1937, to the beautiful Romana Halpern.
Cleo	I just want to say, you know, that this was a beautiful and very intelligent woman, Romana Halpern, and

	she was shot. They tracked her down and murdered her. What is it with these fucking people?
Emilio	I don't know.
	(Show picture here of the beautiful ROMANA HALPERN*)*
Jacko	*(Of audience)* I'm talking to dem! Dem!
Emilio	A bit of a biographical note here, if I may:
Cleo	*(Mimicking)* If I may, If I may. Good grief!
Emilio	Romana escaped from the Warsaw ghetto, settled her son in the countryside and moved to Cracow, where she worked as a secretary under an assumed name. In 1944 the gestapo found her and shot her. *(MASK on)*
Bruno	"Dear Roma,... Somehow I'm afraid to move to Warsaw. I'm afraid of relationships and people. Most willingly I would retreat with some one person into complete quiet and like Proust undertake the final formulation of my world. For some time I was bolstered by the thought I would take my retirement."
Jacko	At forty percent salary, I might add.
Cleo	I might add! Goodness!
Bruno	"Now I have moved away from that idea because I would be unable to support my family."
Cleo	That must strike a bell with you, Emilio.
Emilio	*(Lowering MASK)* Excuse me?
Cleo	Bell. Strikes.
Emilio	Yes. Family. Save.
Cleo	And?
Emilio	Failed miserably.
Jacko	Let's hear from Bruno.
Bruno	*(MASK on)* "Do you know a good neurologist in Warsaw who might treat me for nothing? I am definitely

	sick—some breakdown, some beginning of melancholy, despair, sadness, feeling of unavoidable defeat, irretrievable loss."
Cleo	Sounds like someone we know, eh Jacko?
Jacko	De facto!
Cleo	Don't cry and don't cringe and go on and say something.
Bruno	"I must get advice. But I don't believe in doctors."
Cleo	A-ha! I'm with him there!
Bruno	"I am not writing about my plans and work, I can't write. It makes me too nervous and I cannot talk about it calmly. Don't neglect me this way anymore. Write something sometime! I send heartfelt good wishes. Bruno Schulz. June, 1939." *(Photo of ROMANA fades)*
Cleo	*(MOTHER mask)* Don't be so passive, Bruno, don't be so doomed.
Jacko	Get a grip.
Mother	Do something about your body odor, like take a nice bath, change your clothes. You get used to living without a woman, you don't know how to take care of yourself, you let things slide. And you see how you stoop? You stoop. You don't need to stoop. You're not old. You're not an old man. Stand up straight, Bruno.
Bruno	Thank you.
Jacko	He's too much in his own world. Bruno's world. Dere is another world, Bruno. And it's coming to get you. Oops. I didn't mean to say dat.
Bruno	"These early images mark out for artists the boundaries of their creative powers. Their creative work is a deduction upon given assumptions. They do not discover anything new after that, they only learn to understand better and

better the secret entrusted to them at the outset; their creative effort is an unending exegesis, a commentary on that one verse assigned to them." *(MASK off)*

Cleo That's *so* Jewish I can't believe it. It is *so* Jewish.

Emilio I get it. You probably don't get it.

Cleo I get it, I get it.

Jacko Whatever it is, it's too subjective. In my opinion.

Emilio Here's another one, if they can stand it. *(BRUNO MASK on)* "The father hugs the child, folds him in his arms, shields him from the natural element that chatters on and on."

He's referring to a song of Goethe's here.

Bruno But to the child these arms are transparent; the night reaches into him, and through the father's soothing words he continually hears its frightening seductions. And oppressed, full of fatalism, he answers the night's importunities with tragic readiness, given over wholly to the mighty element from which there is no escape."

Cleo Good grief!

Emilio *(MASK off)* I can remember, I remember now.

Jacko Oh, no.

Emilio People would talk about the old homeland and they'd have that look, like you didn't understand reality.
I wasn't so bad then. I wasn't such a bad guy then.
I tried to talk to my mom, I tried to talk to my dad.

Jacko But every ting dat happened led inevitably to dis right here. Am I right? *(FATHER mask on)*

Father There are memories. We remember everything, for life. There is a spirt life where the memories live. Certain moments are burned into our souls and we remember them with anguish. Moments of lying, of indecision, of violence, of ignorance. We remember from a place of fundamental, eternal laws. This is akin to what they think about in India. Am I right? *(Mask off)*

Jacko   Dat's right. Dis here is Felix Landau. We're in Dro-ho-byz in nineteen forty-two. *(Landau mask on)*

Landau   Hello. How are you? I'm just a regular guy and my racial characteristics are average.

Cleo   My God, he's a moron.

Landau   Gunther!

Cleo   *(Gunther mask on)* What, Landau?

Landau   Come and see me.

Gunther   What for?

Landau   We got da whole city to play wid here.

Gunther   I know dat.

Landau   We got all da Jews in a corner.

Gunther   We took over da joint, as the saying goes.

Cleo   (As da saying goes. Good grief!)

Landau   We can do what we want.

Gunther   I knew dat already.

Landau   At last.

Gunther   I couldn't agree more or less.

Cleo   (Another fucking moron!)

Landau   I got nice digs, how 'bout you?

Gunther   It's great, I love it here, it's absolutely charming.

Landau   Good. Good, good, good.

Gunther   Okay, okay. (He is an absolute bourgeois, him.)

Landau   We could hire artists.

Gunther   (A storekeeper type, they let him loose on the Jews.)

Landau	I don't mean hire, I mean command.
Cleo	(Enslave!)
Landau	I mean enslave. You could have one or more, and I could have one or more.
Gunther	I'll need a few. I'll take a few.
Cleo	(They could have any Jew they wanted.)
Landau	You could have any Jew you want.
Cleo	(For sex or whatever. Art.)
Landau	I'm a family man myself, of course, as you know, and so on.
Gunther	Yeah, yeah. (I know you, schemer and shopkeeper) You know already who you want?
Landau	Bruno Schulz!
Gunther	It's okay.
Landau	Fine with me.
Gunther	Good. I'll take whatshisname, the schmuck whatshisname, along with his wife and daughters.
Landau	Good, good, good. Look at dis! Look out da window at dis!
Gunther	Holy shit, Yids working in da garden!
Landau	Yids working in da garden! I'll get my gun!
Gunther	Get your gun, Landau! (He's a crackerjack shit, him! I mean shot. He's always fatal, Landau, Landau is, to the Yids.)
Landau	Bang! Bang!
Gunther	Good shooting, Landau!
Landau	Bang! Bang! Dere, dat's enough, I killed four!
Gunther	This is fun, Landau! This beats working any day! This is not bad!

Landau	Yeah, I'm gonna have him come in, paint the walls, do a few things.
Gunther	Who's dat, Landau?
Landau	Bruno Schulz!
Gunther	Fine and good.
Landau	Fair and square, even-steven, one potato, two.
Cleo	What?
Landau	Shake and a hug, Gunther.
Gunther	Shake and a hug, Landau. (He's a fucking Viennese cabinetmaker, and his stepfather was a Jew, believe it or not.)
Landau	(He was one of those guys, you know, he coughs and spits, he doesn't care who's next to him, he croaks and grunts and farts, my Dad Landau.)
Gunther	(Now he's da Jew-killer of Drohobyz.)
Landau	(We can't stand each other. I mean me and Gunther.)
Emilio	Bruno and his family, his mother and brother and his dwarf uncle, were moved to a room in the Ghetto. They were starving. (MASK on)
Bruno	Still, the sky was the same and the light was the same. The air was the same. Still, I remembered my childhood, which had a luminous glow, while everyone I knew, the Jews of Drohobyz, were sick and dying or murdered. I was used to working for the government or the police. I had painted pictures of Stalin that were greatly admired.
Landau	Bruno Schulz!
Bruno	Yessir.
Landau	I'll be your savior!
Bruno	Good, sir. Good, good, good.
Landau	I'll protect you, Schulz, and keep you alive, you little putz.

Bruno	Thank you, sir.
Landau	I like art. I'm an artist myself. So I'll spare you.
Bruno	Thank you.
Landau	I'll keep you alive. *(Pause)*
Bruno	Nothing, sir.
Landau	What do you mean, nothing?
Bruno	Nothing to say, sir.
Landau	Just as well. You'll paint some frescoes for my kid. In his room. Fairy tales, which you're good at. And you'll paint my portrait, me on my white horse, showing murderous determination and medieval chivalry, mixed. That'll be good.
Bruno	Good, sir.
	(Show picture of LANDAU on his horse)
Landau	You don't need to say anything.
Bruno	No, sir.
Landau	You're such a total masochist, you must enjoy humiliation. Bowing and scraping and groveling and eating shit. Am I right?
Bruno	Right sir, totally right.
Landau	That's another reason I want to keep you alive, You'll enjoy it and I'll enjoy it, too. That way I get to kill and save at the same time. And serve the Reich, and support art, and get my jollies and rewards and perks. Understand? You don't need to answer. So, that's it. Do you know fine carpentry? Measurement? The various woods? A fine finish? Nevermind. You wouldn't know. You're a high school shop teacher, a failure. Don't wince, Schulz. You like to be hammered verbally, yes, no reply needed, nor expected. You'll start tomorrow. Get a good night's sleep.

You look like shit. You look like you won't make it through the night, Schulz. If you want, I'll kill the rest of your family so you can recuperate without people bothering you. Just a joke, Schulz. Don't speak. Stay out of the way. I don't want my kid to see you or hear you, and my girlfriend neither. She's a honeypie, Schulz. She'll only kick you around, smack you around, much to your enjoyment I'm sure, but I want her to myself, Schulz. So, agreed? Just nod Yes, Schulz. What's in it for you? Survival, Schulz, a little bread and jam, a little soup, you won't starve to death right away, you can take something to your old mother and your brother and your dwarf cousin or whatever he is. Don't feel bad. My stepfather was weird, too, like my father. Big head, no manners, sloppy. Anyway. I didn't mean to talk so long. Something in me must like that. Get the fuck out, Schulz, and come back in the morning.

Emilio	(*Lowering* MASK) Bruno wanted to survive. They say he was completing his masterpiece, *Messiah*.
Cleo	What does that mean, Messiah?
Emilio	It means the coming of the Lord.
Cleo	What does coming of the Lord mean?
Jacko	Maybe the fullness of time or the ending of time.
Emilio	Good, Jacko.
Jacko	Don't tell me good.
Emilio	Good, good, good.
Jacko	You're not superior to me. You're not better than me.
Emilio	Sorry.
Jacko	That's why I said that.
Cleo	And you don't know.

Emilio	What?
Cleo	What it means. The fullness of time or the ending of time. Neither one.
Emilio	The important thing is what Bruno meant.
Jacko	Which we will never know now.
Cleo	Because the poor motherfucker never had time!
Jacko	Because his manuscript was forever lost. *(FATHER MASK on)*
Father	Everything that goes into the ground is lost. It becomes dust, it becomes soil, it becomes fragments of air, of the sky. These fragments glisten like diamonds of another dimension, like jewels of the sun, jewels that can only be seen by giants, by masters of seeing, by seers.
Emilio	*(BRUNO MASK on)* Father, I feel I will never see your grave again, never place a stone there and say a greeting. To feel my fingertips place lightly the little pebble, light as air, light as a grain of dust.

The next day and the days after Bruno Schulz got up and went to work for Felix Landau. (JACKO puts on LANDAU mask, CLEO puts on FATHER mask, EMILIO puts on BRUNO mask.)

Father	Bruno.
Bruno	Yes, Father.
Father	We are energy, pure and simple, it swirls and rotates and serves. In our Good Book (praise His name), it is the fire of Moses at the burning bush. This is Messiah, a Holocaust from a higher world.
Bruno	*(Falling to his knees)* Oh! Oh! Oh!

Landau	Up, Bruno. Up, up, up. My girlfriend wants to take a glance at you. Don't look here, don't cower. She's not in the room. She can see you through my secret spy-hole. You can't find it, you can't see it. An example of superior German technology, Schulz, mirrors and wires and copper tubes. There, it's done. She saw you. You missed it, Schulz, a flickering light. We must humble ourselves before women, Schulz. But of course you knew all that already. You can say something now, if you want.
Bruno	I'm sorry.
Landau	Is that all you can think of saying? At a time like this? You fuckhead! You jerk!
Bruno	I feel like there's a world behind the world, and there I stand between, balanced on a crack of ice. There I stand accused, like Kafka, of an eternal crime.
Landau	Don't start thinking things, Bruno. It never works. It's in your imagination. It's never true and it's never real. This could lead to a nuthouse, Schulz.
Bruno	Oh please, no!
Landau	Sure, you want what you don't want. You're a candidate, Schulz, for head-squeezing. But I'll take care of you, I'll protect your rights.
Bruno	Thank you.
Landau	Not that you have any. You have no rights, none at all.
Gunther	Knock, knock.
Landau	WHO'S DERE?
Gunther	IT'S GUNTHER.
Landau	Come in.
Gunther	What's that?

Landau	Dat's Bruno Schulz, the author and artist. He will paint my walls.
Gunther	He's filthy.
Landau	Yes.
Gunther	He's emaciated.
Landau	Yes.
Gunther	He'll die soon.
Landau	Yes. Groan and croak.
Gunther	I'm sure of it.
Landau	What you want, Gunther?
Gunther	I came to tell ya.
Landau	What?
Gunther	I came to tell ya to leave off.
Landau	Leave off what?
Gunther	My Jewess, my Sophia.
Landau	It's not me. I wouldn't touch her.
Gunther	Not you?
Landau	I never touched her. Not that I wouldn't want to, believe me, she's a honey pie that one.
Gunther	Who's touching her?
Landau	No one I know, Gunther.
Gunther	(You fuck, you slime bag.)
Landau	You feeding her? You protecting her?
Gunther	You know I am, Landau.
Landau	She comes out into the garden does she? Picks a few tomatoes, a cabbage, a parsley, and so on?
Gunther	Yes. (You bag of slime.)
Landau	I haven't shot her, have I? Look, she's out there now, little Sophia, tight little Sophia, bending over, and so on.
Gunther	Don't touch her, Landau. That's all.

Landau	I haven't shot her, have I? Look, I'll prove it. Bang! Bang! Two kids I got, they'll never get bar mitzvahed, Gunther. But Sophia's still there. Look. See her crouching there, in the dirt?
Gunther	She's mine, Landau.
Landau	Of course she is, Herr Gunther.
Gunther	That's all. So I warn you (you stupid maggot-eating shit).
Landau	(You fucking her, Gunther? Because you couldn't get any on the straight, on the legit and legal?) She take care of you okay?
Gunther	Nevermind. It's none of your business.
Landau	Fine and good. I stand corrected. (And erected.)
Cleo	And so on and so forth.
Gunther	That's all I have to say for now.
Landau	Good luck in camp, Gunther.
Gunther	Excuse me?
Landau	I don't know why I said that.
Gunther	Goodbye then.
Landau	Where's the romance, Gunther? What happened to romance? Twilight in Paris, a small room, a girl. A narrow street, a light, a bistro. When life was full and sweet and erotic. Is it youth, Gunther? Has it gone away with our youth?
Gunther	Never had it, Landau. (It's up your ass.)
Landau	Or is it myth, like this little Jew thinks it is?
Gunther	Only in the movies, Landau, that's all.
Landau	Good point, Gunther.
Gunther	That's all. Remember what I said. *(MASK off)*
Cleo	Hello again. Hi, there.

Landau	You see how it is, Bruno? The women rule. The girl's on top, pussy reigns. Ah, she saw you! That's all right. Don't cringe. Stay where you are. Just a moment, Bruno, a moment in time, a flickering view, a peephole vista. You can relax now. Don't tiptoe around, don't cower like a mouse, or a rat. You know how it is, Bruno, after a city is bombed, the rats come out, and maggots as big as fists, and the stench can make a strong man faint. Ah, you hear that, Schulz? A fake female giggle. She's behind one of these walls here. Watching. Don't freeze, Bruno. Go on with your work. I know you're sex-crazed, I know and she knows, Schulz. It's the way of things, it's the nature of things. You can't help it, it's not your fault.
Cleo	And so on and so forth.
Landau	You hear that? She's in the walls, Bruno, she's in the walls. Not Sophia. Sophie's out in the garden, as beautiful a maidel as you'll ever see, Bruno, but she belongs to that idiot clown, Gunther. She appears to be losing weight, unfortunately, by the hour, by the minute. It's my girlfriend I'm talking about, Masha, who likes to keep an eye out. For men she can crush, Bruno. Men with dicks. So I keep her locked up, when she isn't servicing me or my horse. Ha, ha. Just a joke. I'll be back in a minute. Meanwhile, try not to think about things.

MASK off. BRUNO draws as we hear his letter:

| Bruno | My dear friends, I write to you from the brink of an abyss. I feel I am near death. Death is in my chest, in my limbs, in my brain. Perhaps it is no better where you are, |

but it is the end for the Jews of Drohobyz. Were it not for employment with the Jew-killer Landau, for which I earn two loaves of bread and a little soup for me and my family—once in a while a stinking Polish kielbasa, an apple—I would be finished by now. Still, my work is interesting and good. I draw fairy tales for the Landau piglet. It is what I used to do in school, and it comes naturally and easily, even though I can be murdered at any second. Can you secure for me a passport and the necessary papers? I need to leave here soon, very soon. Regarding my literary work and the artistic folios, I am doing what I can to protect them, but the best thing of course is for me to get away from here. This would leave my family exposed to the packs of dogs and hyenas, but if I were free I might be able to do something. In this situation I can do nothing but watch as day by day they starve to death. Well, you know this terror, worse than anything in the Good Book of our fathers, perhaps in the history of mankind. I must add—there are grace notes. The sky for example gives me great pleasure when I remember to look up. How I love the sky in all its permutations, day and night! The sky above gives deep satisfaction—color and movement!—and at the same time releases, a moment's release from bondage that is biblical in its proportions, its dimension, a mythology to obscure all myth forever. For now I say goodbye, looking forward desperately to even a word or two from you so as to lighten even a little this immense captivity. Yours always, Bruno Schulz.

(JACKO puts the LANDAU MASK back on)

Landau   Anyway, you know what happens to the intellectuals,
           the artists, the poets, Schulz, they're too effete for this
           kind of thing. They don't last. We put 'em to work and
           they don't last. My girlfriend, Masha—that's her name,
           Masha, not to be confused with Gunther's Sophia, the
           garden wench who bends over to show me her cunt—was
           a teacher, Schulz, like you. She taught French literature,
           of all things. Baudelaire, Rimbaud. Now she's in the
           walls. Masha in the walls, a sex slave. She won't last.
           You know the saying, "the Jews are watching us"? The
           question is, will the Jews be watching when they're all
           gone, Schulz. You can stop and think about it now.
           Think, Schulz. *(A pause while BRUNO thinks)*

Bruno   Yes.

Landau   How so, you piece of shit, if they're gone from the face of
           the earth?

Bruno   From their vantage point in the sky, sir.

Cleo   *(Hissing)* I SEE YOU. I SEE YOU.

Landau   Hear that, Schulz?

Bruno   No, Sir.

Landau   That was Masha. *(Looking out "window")* Ah, there she
           is, my dear Bruno. Sophia!

Cleo   (Don't confuse Masha and Sophia—Masha is in the
           walls, Sophia is in the garden.)

Landau   Come and look. Put down your paint and come and
           look. There, Gunther's little slave. As you can see, he's
           not feeding her. Sophia Horowitz I think it is. Do you
           know her?

74

Bruno	Not personally, sir.
Landau	You don't know her from school?
Bruno	No, sir.
Landau	She's a teenager.
Bruno	She didn't take shop or drawing, sir.
Landau	She seems very nice. Don't you think so?
Bruno	Yes, sir.
Landau	Not like the rest of her brutish kind. You think?
Bruno	No, sir.
Landau	A certain gentility, a certain refinement.
Bruno	She's from an old Hasidic family, sir.
Landau	I should put her out of her misery. That would be the kind thing to do, I think. Don't you?
Bruno	No, sir.
Landau	*(Shouting)* Hey! Down there! You! Sophia! That's right, you!
Cleo	*(SOPHIA MASK)* Please don't shoot, Herr Commandant!
Landau	I just want to ask you something!
Sophia	Please ask me, Sir.
Landau	See how polite she is, Schulz? *(Shouting)* I want to ask you about your master, Lieutenant Gunther!
Sophia	What, sir, please?
Landau	What does he do to you?
Sophia	He tortures me and rapes me, sir. He makes me do things.
Landau	What things?
Sophia	God forbid, sir.
Landau	Does he feed you?
Sophia	Yes, sir, thank God.
Landau	Leave God out of this. In this instance, I am God. This is the Reich. What does he feed you?

Sophia	Carrots and radishes, sir. And sometimes soup.
Landau	Anything else you want to say?
Sophia	Thank God, sir. Praise God.
Landau	What is this God thing with you people? Go back to work! Dig, do your onions or whatever the fuck it is you do down there!
Sophia	Thank you for not shooting, sir!
Landau	Dig! No more talking! *(SOPHIA mask off)* Still here, Schulz?
Bruno	Not dismissed, sir.
Landau	Dismissed. Go home, Schulz. Your day is done. *(BRUNO hesitates)* Back to the ghetto, Schulz! What are you waiting for?
Cleo	Food, you scumbag!
Landau	Oh. Masha! Masha! Where's this idiot's food? Masha! *(Two loaves of bread are pushed out of the "walls")* There. Crawl. *(BRUNO crawls toward the bread)*
Cleo	*(GUNTHER mask)* I see you got your Jew working.
Landau	Yes, I do.
	(They watch him crawl.)
Gunther	He's a good crawler, this Jew.
Landau	Yes, he is, isn't he? And an artist, too. Look.
Gunther	Oh, my. He's good. He is good. What do you call that?
Landau	Art.
Gunther	No, I know that, I mean what style.
Landau	This is a fresco. (He knows nothing about style.) It's his own style. The Jew's a genius. He's also got a book he wrote hidden somewhere. Maybe in the walls. It's called *Messiah.*
Gunther	Burn the house down, then.

Landau	Later. I live here now. Obviously. *(BRUNO crawls off with the bread)* So. What brings your awful presence?
Gunther	The shit is hitting the fan, Landau.
Landau	What shit? What fan?
Gunther	The police and the soldiers. They want action.
Landau	Restless are they?
Gunther	Yes, things are getting out of control.
Landau	All right.
Gunther	All right?
Landau	Time for an action.
Gunther	Action, Landau?
Landau	That's me, Gunther, a man of action.
Gunther	What are you doing?
Landau	I'm loading my rifle, Gunther.
Gunther	Don't start something, Landau.
Landau	But something has to be started. Didn't you just say that?
Gunther	Not exactly. (Oh, God—what have I done?)
Landau	No going back now, Gunther.
Gunther	Wait a minute, Landau. Wait! Not Sophia!
Landau	BANG! BANG!
Gunther	NOT SOPHIA!
Landau	Too late, Gunther. Now it's done I can't take it back. Don't you find that strange?
Gunther	YOU KILLED MY JEWESS! YOU WILL PAY FOR THIS!
Landau	Very strange. Blood will run in the streets now, blood is soaking into the garden. What once was Sophia, splattered all over the vegetables. You wonder what a human being is, don't you? What it's for, how it came to be. Sky above, earth below, Sophia's gone, she'll never know... and so on and so forth. *(Masks off)*

Bruno was on his way home, and Gunther went looking for him, killing people on his way, killing Jews, enjoying himself, enjoying his frenzy, enjoying the spectacle—a spontaneous shooting spree by the Germans, the army and the police, the bureaucrats and the functionaries running all over the place shooting Jews, chasing them into alleys and apartments and shops, into doorways and halls, on the street—it was like shooting rats, but Gunther was looking all around for Bruno.

Cleo	Who is walking down Cyacky street.
Jacko	On Mickewitz and Cyacky See-Ah-Kee.
Cleo	Right on the corner.
	(Resumes GUNTHER MASK. They mime the following)

Hunched over, eyes on the ground, Bruno Schulz walks down Cyacky street in the Dro-ho-byz ghetto carrying two loaves of bread, when Gunther traps him against the wall and shoots him twice in the head.

BANG! BANG!

Again.

Hunched over, eyes on the ground, Bruno Schulz walks down Cyacky street in the Dro-ho-byz ghetto carrying two loaves of bread, when Gunther traps him against the wall and shoots him twice in the head.

Bang! Bang!

Again.

Hunched over, eyes on the ground, Bruno Schulz walks down Cyacky street in the Dro-ho-byz ghetto carrying a loaf of bread, when Gunther traps him against the wall and shoots him twice in the head.

Bang! Bang!

Emilio   He was buried that night in the Jewish cemetery of Drohobyz and his bones were never found.

And so, and so.

The End

The Empty Bed

A One-Act Play by Sharon Yablon

The Empty Bed *was first produced by Padua Playwrights at Stephanie Feury Studio Theater, Los Angeles in 2006 under the direction of Sharon Yablon, and with the following cast:*

June Pickering Shawna Casey
Jeremy Dandridge Jack Kehler

Characters

June (Miss) Pickering—*mid-40s, whose attractiveness is waning. She starts off the play prim and dour (which is more about how she feels inside), but both her appearance and inner self come alive as the play progresses, and she blossoms some. What little attention Jeremy has given her awakens a need in her. She is chatty, emotional, and lonely. She is also conscious of her age.*

Jeremy Dandridge—*early 50s, he is an odd mixture of quirky and sexual, but is more of an "accidental" ladies man than that of a calculating seducer. He gives mixed signals. His attention and moods shift easily, and whatever exterior charm or confidence he has hides emotional damage and insecurity. Exacerbating this, is an underlying anxiety regarding his mother, who is upstairs dying, and remains unseen during the play.*

Directorial Note
Jeremy's mother, Mrs. Dandridge, is an offstage character who is dying upstairs. Her presence has an effect on both characters and the action. Even though the mother is never seen, the actors must make her an active presence.

Time and place

*Present, Hollywood part of Los Angeles, late fall
and into winter.*

Setting

*The front parlor of a two-story house. Interior has a couch, small
table in front of it, a liquor area with glasses and decanters against
one side wall, a small kitchen table with two chairs against the
other side wall, and a record player on a stand at the back wall.
One of the exits will be the front door and the other will lead to the
upstairs where the mother is; it will be eerily lit.*

Scene 1

MUSIC IN DARK. LIGHTS UP on MISS PICKERING, slowly
wandering around the house. She wears mauve slacks
and a lighter shade blouse. She ends up at the mother's
exit, and looks up, tentatively. SLOW FADE. LIGHTS UP.
JEREMY enters, with a small bag. He begins to take
out groceries at the table, but stops, and slowly
approaches the exit leading to his mother/upstairs.
MISS PICKERING pops out and startles him.

Jeremy   Who are you?!

MISS PICKERING tries to remain calm, and gets her
bearings. She sees the groceries and goes to them.

Miss Pickering Is this all for Mrs. Dandridge?
Jeremy   Yes.
         She takes the groceries offstage.
Miss Pickering Are you a family friend then?
Jeremy   No. Why are you here?
Miss Pickering I work here.
Jeremy   Since when?

She re-enters.

Miss Pickering Oh, do you work here as well?
Jeremy   No.
Miss Pickering But you have a key.
Jeremy   Yes.

Miss Pickering	Well then. You must be somebody that needs a key.
Jeremy	That's right.
Miss Pickering	My name is June. Mrs. Dandridge hired me.
Jeremy	*(Trying to get his bearings)* Is there any coffee?
Miss Pickering	No.
Jeremy	Any cheese or anything?
Miss Pickering	I don't believe so.
Jeremy	What should be done with the marble cheese board then?
Miss Pickering	I don't know.

She spies the empty sack that JEREMY brought with him. She goes to it, folds it up, and hands it to him, as if to get him to leave.

Miss Pickering	I'm sure Mrs. Dandridge will appreciate this gesture.
Jeremy	Oh. Is that what you think?

She is confused. He exits. SLOW FADE/MUSIC.

*

Scene 2

MUSIC FADES. LIGHTS UP on JEREMY looking around, with authority. MISS PICKERING stands to the side. A glass duck is now on the table.

Jeremy	You've kept up the place.

Miss Pickering	I'm sorry, but who did you say you were?
Jeremy	The blinds need to be dusted. *(He stares at the glass duck)* What's happened to the glass duck?!
Miss Pickering	I found it, put away. It had a lot of dust, so I washed it up. *(Pause)* I thought it might look nice down here. *(She slowly approaches it and ends up standing next to him)* Although it's not real glass, like the other animals in her collection. Somebody must have got this for her and not known.
Jeremy	Well glass is expensive.
Miss Pickering	Oh, it's the thought that counts, of course.
Jeremy	Have you been to the market?
Miss Pickering	No, I wasn't told.
Jeremy	You should have gone.
Miss Pickering	Oh.
Jeremy	Nevermind! I'll go. No, maybe you should go.
Miss Pickering	*(Pause. Sits on the couch)* I think I should stay here. Mrs. Dandridge is ill, and she may need something. *(JEREMY looks at her, surprised)* And I'm not a maid.
Jeremy	My mother is sick?
Miss Pickering	*(Stands)* Oh! I'm sorry, I didn't know she had a son—
Jeremy	Then what are you?
Miss Pickering	*(Her tone hints that she can be assertive)* I am a homecare professional; would you like to hear more about it?

He smirks and turns away, trying to hide his distress.

Miss Pickering	Excuse me. But. You don't look at me when you talk to me. Perhaps you're not aware of it.

Pause; he regains some composure.

Jeremy Is that so? (*He turns to her; her subtle attractiveness registers. He holds eye contact, which makes her uncomfortable*) There. I've looked now. Haven't I?

Slow fade on them.

*

Scene 3

Harry belafonte music plays in dark; lights up on Miss Pickering playing records, enjoying herself. Jeremy enters as she starts dancing to a different song; she doesn't see him.

Jeremy You've found her records, I see.

Startled, she freezes, then turns off the sound.

Jeremy You take that bus that goes up the hill. You know the one I'm speaking of. Up the hill, past the prison.

Miss Pickering And you bring girls here.

Jeremy (*Surprised by her retort*) I've discovered some mold growing in my apartment. (*He goes to the liquor cart and pours two drinks*)

Miss Pickering The girls leave traces of themselves, then.

Jeremy Don't pick up after me.

Miss Pickering	But there was vodka. And panties. Teacups and cozies. Videos, board games—
Jeremy	What's your favorite board game?

He holds out a drink to her. Pause. She turns around and carefully takes it from him.

Miss Pickering	Oh! I like board games. Perhaps Operation, is a favorite. *(Pause)* There was a little blood as well. On a hand towel.
Jeremy	Somebody bled here once, yes.
Miss Pickering	And a book was left. *Anna Karenina*? It's a favorite of mine too.
Jeremy	She has her studies.
Miss Pickering	Who? *(Pause)* She could grow tired of you, why as studious gals might do.

She wanders toward the audience/window, looking out. He watches her.

Jeremy	I've seen you waiting. For the bus. You shouldn't look into the sun like that. The bus comes and you get on it. Under the sky you go.

She slowly turns around to face him.

Miss Pickering	Well alright then.

They have eye contact, and then he notices a decorative brooch on her blouse.

Jeremy	That's my mother's!
Miss Pickering	*(Nervous)* Oh, she thought it might look nice on me.

Jeremy	*(Staring at the brooch)* It's some sort of sea creature or something?
Miss Pickering	It's a saltwater snail.
Jeremy	A what? *(Snickers)*
Miss Pickering	A snail that lives in the ocean.
Jeremy	Why would they do that?
Miss Pickering	*(Excited)* Well, actually—
Jeremy	I don't expect you'll know the answer.
Miss Pickering	Your mother has no need for dress-up things anymore, she said.
Jeremy	*(Wanders, looks out at the doorway to mother's area)* Unless someone was to take her out. To a holiday party. Hell! For a skip around the block.
Miss Pickering	She's not presentable. I mean. *(Goes to couch, sits)* One might look like an oddball out and about like that, you know, walking. In Los Angeles. *(She takes off the brooch and holds it out to him)* You can have it back.
Jeremy	I don't want it.
Miss Pickering	But you seem. As if you don't want me to have it.
Jeremy	What gave you that idea? Put it back on.

She carefully affixes the brooch near her breast.
He stares at her breasts, which she notices.

Miss Pickering	I should go check on your mother now.

His eyes meet hers. He approaches the couch.

Miss Pickering	*(Nervous, blurts out)* She gets incontinent.

He stands behind her as she's seated.

Jeremy And you're taking care of things, right?

Miss Pickering *(Her voice shakes a little)* Yes.

She tries to remain poised. He puts his hands on her shoulders, and they build to a caress.

Jeremy Good.

This has an effect on her but she is also nervous. SLOW FADE, as MUSIC plays and his hands travel toward her breasts.

*

Scene 4

MUSIC transitions into rain. LIGHTS up on MISS PICKERING. She wears a bolder lipstick. She listens to the rain at the window.

Miss Pickering Cars moving shimmer in the night. I like to watch them. I stand at the window. Someone else is in the room. He comes up behind me. Lifts up my skirt... they look like eyes, flung out onto the road. The headlights...

JEREMY enters.

Jeremy	*(Shakes off his umbrella)* You didn't have any parties while I was gone, did you?

He jokingly smiles but she doesn't return it. She goes to the couch and sits. She sips tea.

Miss Pickering	Someone came over for you. A woman. One night. Looking for you. She had those things on, neither pants nor shorts. Culottes are they called? They were a sad color, so I invited her in. She dropped her lipstick, got flustered. She adored your mother's glass pigs.
Jeremy	Well, I'll have to give her a call I guess! *(Her story is disturbing him. He puts his coat away and sits at the table with some mail)*
Miss Pickering	Do I have the right house?

He looks at her, confused.

Miss Pickering	Do I have the right house? I don't know, I said. And pushed her out, but she stayed. Aren't you cold, I said? Hey girlie. Aren't you cold? Later, I peeked out the window. You alright? Hey you! I went outside. Her eyeballs seemed frozen. Not a peep, not a peep. But then she did just go away.
Jeremy	You've done something!
Miss Pickering	I'm sorry?
Jeremy	*(Approaches her)* To your appearance.
Miss Pickering	I haven't, no.
Jeremy	You've got red lipstick on!

He smiles at her, then goes back to the mail. Pause.
She hopes for more attention.

Miss Pickering Oh! *(Laughs)* I've felt so invisible in Los Angeles,
I guess. Were you away?

Jeremy Yep.

Miss Pickering I love traveling... where did you go?

Jeremy Just... up the coast.

Miss Pickering It's wonderful up there.

Jeremy Let's go sometime!

Miss Pickering *(Unsure but excited)* Um, perhaps—

Jeremy But isn't it six o'clock?

Miss Pickering Oh, is it?

She walks sultrily to the window/audience, and his
eyes follow her. She looks out.

Miss Pickering It's raining... perhaps I should phone Tokai? *(pause)*

Jeremy Who's that?

Miss Pickering Tokai is my Japanese boyfriend. He was very connected with the world music movement. I've been with
him some time. I just gave him a ride home from a
holiday gathering, and then... somebody had invited
him but he didn't really belong there. He looked so
silly, standing silently next to the party platter. He
waits patiently for me in our little kitchen. The sun
sets. We sit at the table. The cats cry and bite my
knees. Is that the kind of life you want for me then?
(Looks at him) We don't touch anymore. We don't

touch. You'd think I'd know it, if he loved me. Wouldn't I?

She wants a response but he's befuddled.

Jeremy   Well, my mother knows I've been busy at work! I have to make money, there's none around here. And do you think she appreciates it?!

Pause.

Miss Pickering   About the room upstairs. At the end of the hall.
(Goes to get her coat)
Jeremy   What about it?
Miss Pickering   Your mother asked me to move her in there.
(Puts her coat on)
Jeremy   What?! Don't do that!
Miss Pickering   It's been done.

She walks to the front door to exit and he follows.

Jeremy   I didn't instruct you to do that!
Miss Pickering   She did.
Jeremy   Wait—
She turns around
Jeremy   Do you. Have plans tonight?
Miss Pickering   *(Careful)* I don't.
Jeremy   That's good.

He smiles at her. She waits. He starts to take her coat and purse but something's on his mind.

Jeremy
But if my mother is upset. That I was gone, did she ask about me?

Miss Pickering
No.

Jeremy
(Surprised, hurt) Oh. She's probably mad at me. Well, I wouldn't want her to take it out on you.

As she talks, he goes to the liquor cart and pours two glasses of wine.

Miss Pickering
She's nice to me, and talkative! It was no trouble to move her. She's a sack of bones, she is, and some water. You know the boy from across the street, with the blue ball? He helped me carry her down the corridor.

Jeremy
That's not the right word.

Miss Pickering
Oh, hall, to that room, with the photographs. Why are they all put away?

Jeremy
Nobody told you to go opening drawers!! *(Softer)* But you didn't know, right? *(Feels bad)* How about some vino rouge?

Pause.

Miss Pickering
Okay.
He goes to the couch with the drinks, sits and she follows. They sip their drinks.

Jeremy
Your hands are like a little girl's.

Miss Pickering	Oh.
Jeremy	They're cute little hands.
Miss Pickering	*(Smiles)* Thank you!
Jeremy	Your boyfriend won't mind that you're doing this, Tokey?
Miss Pickering	Tokai. He drinks a lot too! I mean, no, I don't think he'd mind. He's Asian, and they don't really get jealous.
Jeremy	Oh.
Miss Pickering	Yes, it's weird!
Jeremy	I have a girlfriend, but I haven't called her in a while.

He laughs nervously and she follows; pause.

Miss Pickering	So, what kinds of things do you like to do in Los Angeles?
Jeremy	*(Confused)* What do you mean?
Miss Pickering	I hear there are interesting lectures at the Skirball Center. Do you ever go there?
Jeremy	No. Do you?
Miss Pickering	No. *(Sips)* I'm an Anglophile. I love things British!

Pause. They sit, and he tries to think of something to say.

Jeremy	One day our water stopped working, and a man came over. I'll need to check the pipes, he told us. My mother came towards him then. Nude, with her arms outstretched. The man's bottom lip quivered. A little yellow worm clung to the lower half of my mother's leg. *(Pause)* That night, she woke me up. She took me

by the hand and we went into her bedroom, where the man lay sleeping, in my parents' bed. Carefully, she peeled down the man's underwear, and we stared at the outline of his naked torso and thighs, in the dark. She touched his penis lightly and it became hard, the milky moonlight on him. *(Pause)* There was a girl named Karen. She would come over after school and let me touch her. She was frightened of my mother. I am too, I said. I am too. (*He gets up and stares out the window*)

Miss Pickering   I've seen the picture of your mother, standing by the fountain in Greece. She's so young in that photo. We all have a photo like that. A face like that. Before bad things happen to us.

Jeremy   It's the Trevi Fountain. And it's in Rome, not Greece.

Miss Pickering   I've never been anywhere there. Can you tell me about it? It must be nice.

Jeremy   Fountains, stray cats, and ruins. Do you think that's nice? *(Pause)* The ruins are all over the city, and the cats perch around them in the moonlight, guarding it all. Keeping history secret. And you think, what's happened to all the people that were once here, will happen to me. I'll be gone, but they'll be standing in my room. This was the bed he slept in, they'll say. This was the window he looked out, through the bougain-villea... my thin fingers pulling apart the drapes... this was the door I once hid behind. I could hear my parents out there... *(Disturbed)* who are parents?

Miss Pickering   I don't know. (*She takes a photograph out of her coat pocket*) Your mother wants me to get a frame for this.

She holds it out to him. He stares at it, tenses.

Miss Pickering Photographs are curious things, aren't they? They stop time for us, but we can't be there to enjoy it.

Jeremy Enjoy what?

Miss Pickering Why, the stopping of time!

Jeremy I don't care much for photography. *(He gives her back the photo)*

Miss Pickering But you were such a cute little boy!

Jeremy That's not me! It's my brother. *(Pause)* I don't know that he'd want her in his room. *(Gets ready to exit)* I'm sure the house is out of things because you haven't been going to the market.

Miss Pickering *(Stands)* Well then she'll need snacks to eat in bed! She asks about fried chicken. I've rolled the TV in there. We'll need videotapes! Know what we've been watching? She likes Ginger Rodgers.

Jeremy *(Stops at front door)* Who doesn't.

Miss Pickering And some porno! Ah jeez, I don't know why I said that. Sometimes I just blurt things out! What we could really use is more rose spray.

Jeremy Rose spray?

Miss Pickering For the smell of the spittle on the walls. *(Pause)* But, I wear it sometimes too. Do you like it?
She holds out her wrist to him and he smells it.

Miss Pickering I could make us a little dinner!

Jeremy Steak tartare? *(Laughs at his own joke)*

Miss Pickering What's that? I can try to make it.

She runs to the record player and pulls out a record.
She puts it on, but it's MARCHING MUSIC. *This wasn't*
what she had in mind, but she playfully marches.

Jeremy   That record's a little loud.

Miss Pickering Oops! *(Plays with the volume)*

Jeremy   *(Tries to speak over music)* I really should get back to
                my apartment *(MUSIC GETS LOWER before he stops
                shouting)* and eat the food I bought!

Miss Pickering Yes. You should eat food you buy.

Pause; something's troubling JEREMY.

Jeremy   Why would she want to stay in that room?

Miss Pickering She told me that your brother was murdered.

Jeremy   What?!

Miss Pickering A long time ago. I can't imagine! And she gets so
                afraid. Like a little girl. Isn't it strange, how our
                parents turn into the children that we were?

Pause.

Jeremy   What do you want me to do about it?!! *(Pause.*
                He tilts his head back to deter a nosebleed)

Miss Pickering Ah jeez, is that a nosebleed? I haven't seen one of
                those since the playground! But are you all right?
                Frequent nosebleeds could be the precursor to some-
                thing, a brain tumor—

He exits. She slowly goes to the window and looks out after him.

Miss Pickering Be careful in the cold! The terrible cold . . .

SLOW FADE. MUSIC.

*

Scene 5

LIGHTS UP on MISS PICKERING eating a sandwich at the table. JEREMY enters with a bag, champagne, and Scrabble. He is wearing nice pants.

Jeremy My brother wasn't murdered. I don't know why my mother said that. What else did she tell you?

Miss Pickering Are those new pants?

Jeremy They're Dolce and Gabbana—

Miss Pickering Ooh la la!

Pause.

Jeremy I brought the videos and cheddar goldfish.

Miss Pickering And champagne?!

Jeremy I got a raise.

Miss Pickering That's great!

He walks toward the mother's exit.

Jeremy   I thought we could all celebrate.

Miss Pickering   *(Forced)* Oh. Well. I'm sure your mother would love to hear about your raise.

He turns to her.

Jeremy   I had to interview with three people to get my job! They couldn't hire just anyone. And I'll be getting a parking space so I don't have to park down below, like the other employees.

Miss Pickering   Is that Scrabble?

Jeremy   I thought I could play it with her.

Miss Pickering   Great! But. Your mother can't play Scrabble.

Jeremy   Oh. I know. I just thought.

Miss Pickering   What?

Jeremy   People talk when they play board games. She doesn't really know me.

Miss Pickering   I bet that's not true.

Jeremy   I'm sure if you just tell me what it is you do.

She's not sure how to respond.

Jeremy   It can't be brain surgery.

Miss Pickering   No... it's just. Your mother prefers me to look after her.

She exits, taking her plate in to the kitchen. She re-enters. Dejected, he hands her a box of candy truffles from his bag.

Jeremy Want these then?

Miss Pickering Truffles from Godiva, are you kidding? *(Eats one)* Oh my god! Do you want one?

Jeremy No. *(Meanders and stops at the mother's exit)*

Miss Pickering *(Sits on the couch with the box)* There's Kahlua in this one! Um, did your mother kickbox?

Jeremy What? No.

Miss Pickering Did she spend some time in Haiti?

Jeremy Of course not!

Miss Pickering Did she have a lesbian relationship with a woman named Lavidia? She was a great actress of the theater.

Jeremy Lavidia was her green parrot and it got eaten years ago.

Miss Pickering Ah jeez, *(Laughs)* I'm sorry, hearing about sad things makes me nervous and I sometimes laugh!

Jeremy The parrot got out its cage, and something chomped it. Think that's funny?

Miss Pickering No . . . *(Stops laughing)*

Jeremy We found what was left of its feet and part of a skull. The skull of a bird is so very small . . .

Miss Pickering There are one-celled animals and they haven't even got skulls. Listen, why don't you help her remember? Because she's forgetting her life.

Jeremy I don't understand . . . ?

Miss Pickering That happens. I wouldn't mind it happening to me! How about we finish that vino rouge?

Jeremy	*(Stares off, out the window)* She used to walk around the house, in these fancy ball gowns. Her hair was long, and she was so beautiful. She would swish past things. But now... what happens to us? We change into monsters. When we get old . . .

She goes to the window, next to him.

Miss Pickering	Illness can do that. But. *(She touches his shoulder)* I can take care of you. You shouldn't have to go through this alone.
Jeremy	*(Feels uncomfortable)* I've got a girlfriend.
Miss Pickering	And, you got a raise! Women must want to meet you then!
Jeremy	Look, about the blood you found here.
Miss Pickering	Oh, I just thought you had a good time is all!
Jeremy	You don't have to clean up after me.
Miss Pickering	It was just a bloody towel or two! I'm sure she was fine, whoever she was! *(She turns to him)* But. Why would you want to bring women here? Are you trying to get your mother's attention?
Jeremy	*(Angered by her implication)* Maybe it was me who bled! What do you think of that?! My date hurt me, with her kinky games!
Miss Pickering	*(Hoping to make him jealous)* Your mother's met Tokai. She thought he was very interesting.
Jeremy	When was he here?! She spoke to him?
Miss Pickering	He didn't want me to take the bus in the rain. So he came to get me. In his Volvo. Because he cares for me! He's very attracted to me, see!!

She runs out, to the mother's area. CRYING MIXES WITH MUSIC. JEREMY *listens; it starts to disturb him.* SLOW FADE, MUSIC CONTINUES.

*

Scene 6

LIGHTS UP *on Miss Pickering adjusting a See's Candies uniform that she wears, using the audience as a mirror. She looks out the window, sees something and goes to the couch, trying to "pose." Jeremy enters,* MUSIC FADES.

Miss Pickering I rented a video! I've been going to the video store every day for years, I must not be happy! But you probably don't want to hear about that. I hope you haven't seen *I Love You, Alice B. Toklas* with Peter Sellers! I bet it'll make you feel better!

Jeremy I feel fine.

Miss Pickering So. *(Pause)*

Jeremy What?

Miss Pickering I hope... *(Loses her nerve)* I'm being a good employee! I haven't always been, I can tell you.

Jeremy You don't need to tell me.

Miss Pickering I don't, do I?! *(Stands)* I find myself taking a certain position, and becoming bored! It's just about the worst thing in the world, isn't it? If somebody told me I was boring, well I would be very upset. I would ask them why they thought that and try to point out times when I was saying things of interest, and people wanted to be near me—

Jeremy   I'm sorry that you're bored here.

Miss Pickering   But I'm not! Is what I'm trying to tell you. Tokai says I often can't make the point I'm trying to make. He gets impatient with me. We used to have people over. I was younger then. Tokai did the cooking but I was the real hostess! Hostessing isn't easy, you know! You have to be a good conversationalist! I'm interested in astronomy and Viking sagas. The futures market,

He slips offstage unbeknownst to her.

and the Weimar Republic. Oh, lots of things! And I have opinions. Would you like to hear some of those? Send the sick and the dying away! Put the aged away! That's what we do! *(Pause)* Why do you think they frighten us so? Watching someone deteriorate. They take your hand. What do they want? They want the time you've got left, is what they want...

She looks and is surprised he's gone. He re-enters.

Jeremy   Why are you wearing that?

Miss Pickering   The proprietor said girls come into his store all the time to buy uniforms, when they don't even work at that profession.

Jeremy   It's a candy uniform.

Miss Pickering I have wigs too. *(Hopes for a response)* Your mother
barely has any hair left now.

This disturbs him.

Miss Pickering It's not right for a woman to be seen that way.
We have to be pretty and young all the time!
Jeremy *(Trying to take his mind off what she just said)*
Show me what's underneath that uniform.
Miss Pickering I don't want to anymore.
Jeremy Yes you do.

*He takes a step towards her. She slowly unbuttons a
few buttons of her uniform. He goes to her, and they
touch. It is tender and restrained, and not getting
sexual. Then he pulls away.*

Jeremy I've. Had a lot on my mind.
Miss Pickering *(Slowly buttons her uniform)* It must be difficult
for you here. Maybe you should leave. I'll take care
of things.
Jeremy I'm not going anywhere!
Miss Pickering Fine.
Jeremy Look, when she gets better—
Miss Pickering Better? She's not going to get better. She's—
Jeremy Leave me alone!!

*Pause; she gets her coat and exits. After a beat,
she comes back. They stare at each other.*

Miss Pickering I left my purse. (*She gets her purse*)

Jeremy June.

He goes to her. He is troubled. Once he gets there he doesn't know what to do. He leans into her and she hugs him. SLOW FADE, MUSIC.

*

Scene 7

FEMALE GIGGLING. LIGHTS UP on Jeremy and Miss Pickering. A Scrabble game is set up on the floor. Their shoes are off, and she's still in the See's Candies outfit. Jeremy tosses some olives at her from a bowl on the liquor cart, and she playfully runs away. Two empty martini glasses are nearby.

Miss Pickering Stop!

He chases her. She steps on the Scrabble board.

Miss Pickering Shoot, I was winning!
Jeremy Was not!
Miss Pickering Was too!

He catches her.

Miss Pickering Hey, let's go to a restaurant!
Jeremy It's the middle of the night.

Miss Pickering Let's sleep in a different room tonight! *(Laughs loudly)*

Jeremy Sshhh!

Miss Pickering *(Peeks down at her unbuttoned blouse, smiles)* Oops!

He rests his head on her and she strokes it. But her story changes his mood.

Miss Pickering I know a story about you! Someone at school made fun of you and you were so upset, you caught a fever. Your mother said she had to teach you at home. It just broke my heart! Hearing about your illness, and the gaps you must have in your knowledge.

He senses something, and stands.

Jeremy My mother . . .

He goes upstairs. She follows, but stays at the exit, thinking. SLOW FADE, MUSIC.

*

Scene 8

LIGHTS UP. A hat tree is onstage, and a box. MISS PICKERING sits on the floor, examining an old child's clown costume. Jeremy enters; she stands.

Miss Pickering	Hi.
Jeremy	I've been busy at work.
Miss Pickering	Oh, that's good!
Jeremy	Everyone wants to buy a house. They come into the bank. People all want the same things.
Miss Pickering	That's true! I found this cute little Halloween costume! Did you wear it?
Jeremy	No. (*He notices the hat tree and stares at it*)
Miss Pickering	But clowns are scary things, aren't they? Overdressed, in their crisp, ruffled outfits. Those big hands; hands that possess no humanity—
Jeremy	What's that?
Miss Pickering	(*Proud*) A hat tree.
Jeremy	Where did it come from?
Miss Pickering	A yard sale.
Jeremy	Why are you buying things for the house?

She colors.

Jeremy	And you've been moving things around; where's the oil painting of the ice-skating Victorian children?
Miss Pickering	I put it in the hall, it's so dank there.
Jeremy	There's ladies' underwear drying on the shower rod upstairs.
Miss Pickering	Oops.
Jeremy	And I know that you've been stealing.
Miss Pickering	Excuse me?
Jeremy	My mother's glass bear is in your purse.

She marches to her purse, and empties its contents onto the couch, which include a dirty rabbit's foot, a vial of pills, a bus pass, and the glass bear, which JEREMY grabs.

Jeremy Aha!

Miss Pickering *(Picking up the vial of pills)* But don't you want to know about these? Are they Vicodin? Ritalin? Antipsychotics, maybe?!

Jeremy I'd just like to know about the glass bear!

Miss Pickering She wanted me to have it!

He tries to clean it.

Jeremy Impossible, she loves her collection!

Miss Pickering She loves me, she said once. In her delirium she called me Connie, I didn't mind. Who was Connie? And she wanted to meet Tokai. She said that if you have a history with someone, you shouldn't throw it away with just anyone. She wanted to have a tea with him.

Jeremy Where was I?

Miss Pickering I don't know.

Jeremy I wasn't invited, was I?

Miss Pickering It wasn't really that kind of thing.

He quickly takes the hat tree and puts it outside.

Miss Pickering *(Shouts after him)* The pills in my purse are to make me sleep! *(Goes to the couch, sits)* The doctor said they could be habit-forming, and I should take that into consideration. I get frightened, awake, in the middle of the night.

He re-enters, with the hat tree.

Miss Pickering She thought you'd be upset.

He puts it back where it was.

Miss Pickering She said to take it home, and put it on a windowsill, so it catches the light. I was going to do that.

He goes to the table, tries to calm down.

Miss Pickering I'm not from here, you know. I came out West because of a man. But he ended up having a family with someone else. Do you want to know what happened?

Jeremy The man left you.

Miss Pickering I got pregnant, see. I told your mum this and she understood. Had a stillborn I did, but I don't have to tell you that. *(Wanders to the window, looks out)* Had it in a little room I used to let, on Seward Street. Do you know where that is? You can see it from here. The flat part of town, where I once let a room... I had the baby all by myself.

Jeremy Well, don't be sad by it. People come out here, to Los Angeles. They get into different things. You can't count on them.

Miss Pickering I never told Tokai. I didn't want to spoil things. There are things you shouldn't tell a lover. Most things, I'd say. And now I've told you something. I'm not such a stranger, in this house. *(Stands)* I thought changing things around would be good, now. I've seen your old room with the Linda Evans poster, the collection of rocks. *(She takes careful steps towards him)*

Miss Pickering Some adult clothes in it too. Maybe it's time—

Jeremy I have an apartment!!

He pops out of his chair. This surprises her but she wants to keep his attention.

Miss Pickering Oh, you're not going to strike me, are you?!

He stares at her. Her frustration builds.

Miss Pickering Clown boy! Blue boy! That's what your mother used to call you!

This sinks in; he gets his coat.

Miss Pickering She said you can't love.

He gets to the door.

Miss Pickering I'm sorry!

He exits. Pause. Music starts. *She goes to her purse and starts to put everything back. She is trying not to feel pain. She gets to a compact and opens it. She looks at herself, not expecting to become scared at what she sees—her age. She reapplies lipstick and her hand*

visibly shakes. Pause, as she regains her composure.
She exits as LIGHTS CHANGE. *She re-enters with some*
towels and begins folding them. She finishes and carries
them. She starts to walk slowly around the perimeter
of the stage, but stops momentarily at the window,
looking out as LIGHTS AND MUSIC FADE.

*

Scene 9

FEMALE HUMMING BLENDS INTO MUSIC. LIGHTS UP on
MISS PICKERING entering, carrying a plate with a small
ham on it. She sets it down proudly, and exits. JEREMY
enters. He sees the ham. He pokes it. She re-enters
with other plates. MUSIC FADES.

Miss Pickering	I baked a ham!
Jeremy	I see it.
Miss Pickering	*(Takes plates to the table)* I've never done it before. Come on, it'll be fun! *(She pours two glasses of wine for them. She sits at the table and he follows)* Oh, you don't have any dietary restrictions do you?
Jeremy	*(Doesn't understand)* What?
Miss Pickering	Nevermind! So...! Do you like working at a bank? It must be fun seeing all that money!
Jeremy	I'm not a loan officer. Wayne does that.
Miss Pickering	Oh. Were you demoted?
Jeremy	No.

Miss Pickering	What are we going to do?
Jeremy	What do you mean, "we"?

Pause.

Miss Pickering	I never left at six. That's when the day ends, but it wouldn't have been right.
Jeremy	Look, you're not a bad-looking woman. Past forty, even. Because I know you are. Past forty.

Pause. In an outburst she knocks a plate to the floor. Pause; she rises and quietly cleans it up. He feels bad but doesn't apologize. She finishes and puts the plate back on the table. They start eating again.

Jeremy	This is good!
Miss Pickering	I'll get more. I made a lot.

She stands with the plate of ham and starts to exit, but his words stop her.

Jeremy	Yes. But. Listen, I've thought.

She waits.

Jeremy	You know, that things were getting a little out of hand. You have a boyfriend. *(Pause)* I mean. Why would you want to be here, with me? I don't know why anyone would want to be here...

She goes to the couch and sits with the plate of ham on her lap. She stares off.

Jeremy　　Before you there was Connie. She wormed her way in here, posing as a personal assistant. She made my mother happy; who can know what person will have that power over you? They had teas and picnics in my mother's room, and closed the door a lot. Then Connie met someone else, and never came back. *(Pause)* My brother was mean to me. He hurt me. My parents knew it, but never stopped him. One day we were playing around the well. He was trying to make me walk along the top of it but I didn't want to do it. He kept goading me so I told him that if he did it first, I would too. He was always showing off. He ran around on top of it, and he fell in. All the way to the bottom. His head split open, and I could see inside, to his brain . . .

Horror spreads over his face, then he looks at her.

Jeremy　　It wasn't my fault! *(Pause)* My father left, and it was just us, me and my mother. *(Slightly happy)* I had all of her, all her attention. We would watch *The Ghost and Mrs. Muir.* She took my temperature a lot, gave me enemas. She told me I was too sick to go to school. *(Mood changes)* I know now that she made me believe I was sick, to keep me at home. Away from my friends. To punish me. But also. She was scared. Something was happening to her... I would find her, sitting in the dirt. Bald, because she cut off all her hair. Turning over rocks. Letting vermin crawl up her skirt. White lizards. Centipedes. She beckoned me to sit next to her. She was so beautiful; flower petals fell out her eyes. *(Pause)* She took my hand. Close your eyes, she said. Feel what I'm becoming. *(Pause)* It was the last thing she said to me.

Pause. This story has an effect on her.

Miss Pickering I remember how excited I was, to come to Los Angeles. What has happened to me? I have no child. There was a time when I thought I had a talent in drawing. Have I told you about my father? He always carried a wand of mascara in his pocket, so he could touch up his graying temples. There were mirrors in our house, lots of mirrors. It's strange what you remember... in my thirties I had to move back home with my parents. My job prospects weren't good. There was no man in my life. One day. It was the afternoon. My father had a heart attack. It happened in the guest bathroom. There was a fluorescent light in there, and he preferred those. They showed more, what you really look like, he used to say. He would spend time in there, scrutinizing his appearance, because he was terrified, of getting older. *(Pause)* I was home that day, in another part of the house. I didn't know for a few hours or so. I didn't know. My mother came home, and we started to prepare dinner.

She looks at JEREMY.

Miss Pickering But he was dead.

Pause. Jeremy stands and goes to the mother's exit.
He goes through it. Slow fade, MUSIC.

*

Scene 10

LIGHTS UP DIM on JEREMY facing the audience.
MUSIC FADES.

Jeremy I'm sorry that you felt I wasn't able to do the things
someone else could do for you. That you didn't like
the glass duck I bought you. I don't see my friends
anymore. They all have kids, and they just want to
spend time with their new families. *(Pause)* There was
a woman. A secretary. Do you remember, I wanted
you to meet her? Her name was Audrey.

MISS PICKERING enters quietly; he doesn't see her. She
has her coat on and carries her purse.

Jeremy She liked me, and I got her pregnant. I made her get
an abortion. She didn't want to, and I told her I would
hate her if she didn't do it. But I didn't mean it. I cared
for her, but it was easy to be mean. *(Pause)* After
the surgery she wanted me to sit with her. I brought

her back here. I didn't know what to do. There was bleeding. I never called her after that. *(Pause)* I see her sometimes. At a salad bar, near the bank. We never speak, and it's like it never happened. I liked her. But I rejected her. I don't know how... I would have taken care of you. You must have heard me here, in the house. Why didn't you ask for me? I was waiting. All these years...

She slowly approaches him. She moves to turn on a light to now reveal an empties, made up bed. A look of surprise comes over him, as he has been speaking to nothing but an empty bed. He continues staring and she joins him, focusing on the bed as well.

Jeremy I would go to her room. Stand at the door. But. I couldn't... go in.

SLOW FADE. LIGHTS UP on them both, sitting on the couch. She wears her coat and has her purse on her lap. They stare out. After a beat, he takes her purse, as if to get her to stay. They remain as is. SLOW FADE.

The End

Head Trader

by Guy Zimmerman

Head Trader *was first produced by Circus Minimus at*
The Lost Studio, Los Angeles in 1994 under the direction of Guy
Zimmerman, and with the following cast:

Jack Reed Jeff Daniel Phillips
Gladys Kara Westerman
Billy Joseph Goodrich

Characters

Jack Reed—mid-30s, a broker of some kind.
Gladys—late 20s, vaguely foreign.
Billy—over 40, vaguely foreign.

Settings

A city.
The reception desk of an office building after hours.
A boiler room.
A subway car.

"Death is inside the bones, like a barking where there are no dogs..."
Pablo Neruda

Scene 1

In darkness a subway train approaches and arrives. The doors chime open. A moment later lights rise on REED, 30s, in tie and dress shirt. His suit jacket lies on the floor across the stage. He crosses and puts it on. One sleeve of the jacket has been badly tattered or mangled. He addresses the audience.

Reed   I've just made head trader. *(Pause)* That's right, head trader. *(Pause)* Thank you. *(Pause)* Sure, things look pretty good. I'm working my way up to partner. I plan to make it to partner in two or three years. That's fast. *(Pause)* You give yourself an edge—don't laugh—you hone yourself. *(Pause)* I work hard. I want that leeway, that cushion. I don't apologize for that. I've learned how to take what I want. I don't wait for permission. *(Pause)* So, anyway, I've got to go... Nice to meet you. *(He starts to exit. Pauses. Turns)* Woooah! Wait a second! *(Pause)* You know, I have this feeling that you don't really believe me. Am I right? Be honest. *(Pause)* At the very least, at the outside, you think maybe I'm exaggerating just a little bit, correct? *(Pause)* That's OK. That's understandable. It's human nature to be a bit suspicious. *(Pause)* But hold on! I want to know: Why would I go to all the effort and why would I risk all the embarrassment just to impress someone I don't know from Adam? *(Pause)* Am I completely off base? Am I making this all up? I must be, right? I mean, I have credibility, am I right? I'm right! I mean, I *know* who I am... *(He turns to go, then pauses again)*

But how would *you* really know? Unless... unless we got up right now, all of us, we get up, we go out and get in a cab, we go over to the midtown office, and I show you my desk, my terminal, I log on to my terminal, and then you'd know for sure. What time is it? We go over and what's his name, little guy—Roderigo!—makes us sign in at the desk in the lobby...Or else we go over to my garage, we get in my goddamn Maserati, take the Merritt upstate, I introduce you to what's her name, Linda there and— and little Jeffrey, stands about this high, we go into the house, we stand there in front of the fucking fire... *(Pause)* Come on, let's go! *(Reed stands waiting as lights fade)*

*

Scene 2

A reception desk in the lobby of an office building. A micro-lamp on the desk. A young woman with garish make-up, Gladys, *sits at the desk. She eats pork rinds and looks up at* Reed. *A pause.*

Gladys	But I'm supposed to tell everybody, they has to sign in.
Reed	Do you know who I am? *(pause)* OK, fine. Good. *(He signs in)* Roderigo here?
Gladys	You must mean Billy.

Reed	Billy?
Gladys	He's the night man.
Reed	Right. Yeah. Billy.
Gladys	He is here. Somewhere.
Reed	I just want to make sure everything's all right upstairs.
Gladys	What happened to your jacket, mister?
Reed	And you would be...?
Gladys	Gladys. I'm just on a visit. You know. I work nights. *(Then, indicating sleeve)* Looks like you got caught in one of them shredders.

Pause.

Reed	So you're a friend of... Billy's.
Gladys	I'm from Denver.
Reed	Yeah? Well, I work upstairs. I'm in and out all day, know what I mean? Billy sees me here all the time. I'm Jack Reed.

REED holds his hand out. GLADYS tips it up, examines his palm.

Gladys	You want to talk to Billy?

GLADYS rolls back her chair. BILLY, a thin bald man, rises up from beneath the desk. He wipes his mouth on his sleeve.

Billy	Hello. Yes.

Pause.

Reed	It's funny. *(Pause)* For some reason I remembered your name as Roderigo.

BILLY glances at GLADYS, then back to REED.

Billy	That could be my middle name. *(Pause)* I was just looking for my penknife.

BILLY displays a switchblade. He indicates the space beneath the desk.

Reed	No problemo, Billy.
Billy	The nights they get very long, Mr. Jack-Reed.
Reed	Jack's my first name. I was just talking to Gladys here.
Billy	Gladys comes to us from Denver. I said, come down see me tonight, it's slow. Where's the harm? Sure.
Reed	*(To GLADYS)* Billy...I see him every fucking day of the week, OK?
Billy	Sure, I know you. You are my Scorpio brother. Mr. Jack-Reed.
Reed	Scorpio?
Billy	It's the strong bond, you and me. We understand how things are.
Reed	Hey, no problemo. Listen, Billy, I'm just going upstairs. When my people come, send 'em on up, OK?
Billy	You don't even have to sign in tonight. Sure.
Reed	Cool.

REED moves off. BILLY kneels beside GLADYS as if in prayer. REED pauses, returns, holds up his tattered sleeve. BILLY jumps up.

Reed   Hey, look at that! Outside the health club over on Sixth.

Billy   That's too bad.

Reed   I should have killed that shit-fuck.

Billy   I'm sorry.

Reed   Eh, forget it. (*Pause*) This fucking city!

REED jerks: a spasm of anger. BILLY shifts nervously and displays his switchblade. GLADYS smiles.

Billy   I was just looking for my penknife.

BILLY indicates the space beneath the desk. REED moves to see from BILLY's angle of vision. He notices the bank of video monitors behind the desk.

Reed   So, tell me something, you see everything from back there, right?

Billy   What?

Reed   (*Urgent whisper*) On the monitors.

BILLY laughs. REED laughs.

Billy   Oh! Sure. We get all the different views. Elevators... the hallways up and down...

Reed   Surveillance.

Billy	That's right. It's a lot of work to keep track of all the places you can see.
Reed	You mind if I...

REED moves around the side of the desk.

Billy	Come along here, Mr. Reed. Gladys, muevete los huesos!
Gladys	All right, all right. Relax yourself, tio!

GLADYS gets out of the chair. BILLY sits and begins to demonstrate—pushing various buttons, etc.

Reed	It's one of those things you see five times a day, you always wonder...
Billy	It's very simple. See. You punch here, the buttons. Here's the map... where your cameras are.
Reed	Just like that. Hey!
Billy	If you like, you can sit. Sit here!

REED sits.

Reed	Man! All right!

REED punches buttons on the console.

Billy	You can stay as long as you like.
Reed	A lot of these places... I've never even seen!
Billy	You can go there now, Mr. Reed. Wherever you want.
Reed	Now, that's a lot of empty building!

REED punches more buttons on the console.

Billy	Sure. You can even see into the other buildings. There's a way to do it. Maybe you wait here for a minute, I teach you.
Reed	Yeah?
Billy	Meantime I take Gladys down, show her the facilities.
Gladys	That's about time, yeah.
Reed	What... five minutes?
Billy	Five, ten minute. You just sit. You watch the places. Gladys was just doing it.
Gladys	It was... a... *no problemo.*
Reed	Cool. And if someone comes...
Billy	You know how to do it!
Reed	Yeah. Absolutely.
Billy	Come on, Gladys. I'm gonna show you the facilities.
Gladys	Yeah, yeah.

BILLY takes GLADYS by the arm and exits USR. GLADYS looks back at REED. REED waves to her.

Reed	You take care now!

REED fiddles with the console. Lights fade, so that REED is visible only in the light from the micro-lamp on the desk.

*

Scene 3

Lights rise on GLADYS *standing in a pool of light stage right. She has a large hunting knife in her hand and her face is smeared with blood.* BILLY *writhes on the floor at her feet. It's the boiler room of the building; there's a steady hum, punctuated here and there by sharp rattles, during which the lights flicker.* REED *is visible at the desk stage right, though it's clear that the two areas are not contiguous. Reed remains immobile throughout the scene, frozen by what he sees on the video monitor.*

Gladys   Maybe you shouldn't be watching this. (*Pause*) Don't blame me. (*Pause*) I'm from Denver.

She shrugs.

I came here for protection. Look what I got instead.

Pause

He was begging me for it and I'm a Libra, so...

She tosses the knife to the ground and begins to clean her face on her shirttails.

Don't worry, is what I'm saying to you. There is nothing that has really happened here.

She indicates BILLY.

He had a big heart. Big as your head. Blue inside his chest. When I was a girl he used to give it to me while driving. You might think I'd be grateful. Well, think again.

Pause

In Denver there is a dance that we do for those who are dead.

She does a little jig. The jig becomes frenzied. She pauses abruptly. She closes her eyes in rapture, runs her hands along her body, falls to her knees.

Oh, it feels so rich...I can't stay here.

A pause. GLADYS *digs the knife into the floor beside* BILLY. *She stands and exits.* BILLY *stirs on the ground.*

Billy Aaaaghh...

Lights fade so that REED'S *desk light is the only illumination on the stage.*

*

Scene 4

REED *looks with alarm at the video console. He reaches for a phone on the console, jiggles the cradle...*

Reed   Hello, operator! Operator? Get me the police! There's
been some crazy shit—hello?... Who is this?... Kenji?...
Kenji Omura? How the hell are you, Kenji?... It's me,
Jack Reed... No, I'm not kidding!... Listen, how's Junko
and, a, what's-her-name, there... Chuck!... Good, good...
Oh, they're fine... What is it?... Tell me, Kenji.

Reed jots notes on a scrap of paper...

Tell uncle Jack... Right... Um-hmm... Sure... 85 hundred
on the wire?... 36-30, Blue?... Yeah... It's not a problem
Kenji... You want to get a little jump on things, you called
the head trader, right?... You got it!... Hey, fuck the SEC,
OK?... Kenji!... You and me, how many years now?

*Gladys appears, approaching in the darkness
behind Reed.*

Manila, 2005? Can we talk? Please! I'm going to see you
this fall, right? Listen to me, Kenji, this time I'm going to
take you to a place, all right? Blow Road, OK? Down in
Angeles City. The women, Kenji, they put stuff in their
mouths, okay? Ice cream? Oooooh! Coca-Cola, any of
your soft drinks, sure. Fanta, Schweppes...

*Lights rise revealing Gladys leaning on the counter
beside Reed. She's chewing bubble gum. She blows
a bubble.*

Gladys   Hey!

| Reed | Hold on a sec, Kenji. |

Reed cups the receiver to his chest.

| Reed | I was just making a long distance phone call. |
| Gladys | You got to plug the jack in, mister. Before you use the phone. Even for long distance. |

GLADYS lifts the phone cord. The phone jack dangles at the end of it. REED stares at it.

| Gladys | This jack? You got to plug it in... Jack. |

GLADYS reaches across and plugs the jack into a hole on the console. A beat. REED raises the receiver to his ear. Listens.

| Reed | Kenji...? Kenji...? |

He jiggles the phone cradle. Listens again. Hangs up. A pause.

| Reed | Fuck! That just cost me fifty grand! |

REED looks up at GLADYS.

| Reed | That just cost me fifty fucking grand! |

A beat. GLADYS regards REED closely. Blackout.

Scene 5

Lights up on the reception area. GLADYS *leans against the wall beside the desk smoking a cigarette.* REED'S *voice emerges from beneath the desk.*

Reed   So you and Billy, I guess you're, like, *involved…*

Gladys   It's a family thing, but we don't have to talk too much about that.

Reed   I pull down your six-seven figures, how come I still get stuck here?

A pause. GLADYS *laughs.*

Gladys   You were on your way home.

Reed   What? *(A beat)* What?

Gladys   Nothing.

GLADYS *laughs again.*

Reed   What's funny? Nothing's funny.

Pause. GLADYS *stares down at* REED.

Gladys   So then, you going to come along with me to see the show?

Reed   Nah, I should probably be getting home.

Gladys	Well, it's on the way.
Reed	Yeah?
Gladys	Sure. Uptown, by the river.

BILLY appears, hobbling slowly through the darkened lobby. He has the hunting knife with him. GLADYS moves along the wall.

Billy   *(Gasping)* Hey, let me tell you something, mister, okay? In my country, see, we always celebrate the coming of rain. Here rain falls as if it were nothing.

REED stands and hobbles out, his pants around his ankles.

Billy   People hide and curse the rain, as if there were no penalty for this.

BILLY crosses to the chair, passing GLADYS.

Billy   People here, they take no pleasure in the lies they tell each other. Generally speaking.

REED exits. GLADYS follows. A pause.

Billy   *(To the house)* In my country your death lives beside you... there is no special rancor at the end... none of this running, this shyness or panic.

A pause. BILLY *presses some buttons on the console.*
LIGHTS *fade as we hear the* SOUND *of a subway car*
in motion.

*

Scene 6

LIGHTS *rise on* GLADYS *and* REED. *They are standing in a*
subway car, swaying slightly as the car moves along the
rails. They speak over the LOUD CLATTER *of the wheels.*
The LIGHTS *occasionally flicker.*

Gladys	Yeah, it's very late.
Reed	I thought I could get a jump on things. *(Pause)*
	So, what is this fashion show we're going to?
Gladys	All the different designers. The spring issues.
	You'll like it.
Reed	I just wear your basic suit. You know.

GLADYS *indicates* REED'S *tattered sleeve.*

Gladys	We can get you a new jacket.
Reed	It's gotta match the pants, though.
Gladys	Plus you'll be the first to see the newest line of
	cowboy clothes.
Reed	What's that?

Gladys	Chaps, spurs, that sort of thing. Lassos.
Reed	Nah, I'm just your basic suit man. Really.
Gladys	Denim shirts and worn-out jeans that smell of leather from your chaps. That could be a good look for you.
Reed	Hey, I'll try anything.
Gladys	Back in Denver it's very common you see a guy dressed like that. It turns your head.

GLADYS and REED lean to the side as the subway grinds to a stop. We hear the SOUND of the doors opening. GLADYS turns and regards REED with a certain tenderness. REED's face assumes a frozen expression. A pause.

Reed	You think I'll make it home in time?
Gladys	In time for what?
Reed	In time to get up and go back to work.
Gladys	You don't have to worry about that either...

GLADYS reaches across and closes REED's eyelids.

Gladys	... Jack.

A beat. BLACKOUT.

The End

Hotel Bardot

by Heidi Darchuk

Hotel Bardot *was first produced by Padua Playwrights at LADAD Space, Los Angeles in 2010 under the direction of Guy Zimmerman, and with the following cast:*

K Corryn Cummins
The Valet Brad Culver
The Technician Christopher Goodson
Madame Julia Prudhomme
One Michael Chick
Two Johnny Klein

Characters

K—*A girl*
The Valet
The Technician
Madame
One—*A rat*
Two—*A rat*

Hotel Bardot is a decrepit seaside hotel with three levels: an underground parking garage, a lobby, and room 108. Though the play takes place in real time, the clock is visibly manipulated.

1.

ONE and TWO, near-darkenss.

Two	The cash register's broken.
One	You can't count?
Two	I have a system.
One	Your teeth aren't real.
Two	Filthy lucre.
One	A gold tooth shines from a grey mouth.
Two	Dead things are smaller. Something leaves.
One	You can't leave.
Two	I could lay down on the floor. You could...
One	Bruise you.
Two	I wouldn't mind.

ONE hits TWO in the eye.

Two	Soon the tunnels will be full.
One	I want to pay you.
Two	The cash register is broken.

ONE gives TWO a gold coin. They scurry out. LIGHTS UP to reveal MADAME in the lobby. She folds sheets. She has a black eye. The SOUND of a car being driven badly, breaks squealing, gears grinding.

Madame	The Mercedes.

THE VALET brings K into the lobby. There is blood on her dress. She has a black eye. She tries but can't speak.

Madame   We'll put you in 108. Just sign here. Someone will come up to check on you, give you a shampoo, if you like. Look up.

She snaps K's photo.

Madame   Don't mind the rats.

THE VALET escorts K to her room. There is a beauty parlor chair where the bed should be.

Valet   You might want to take a shower.

THE VALET returns to the lobby.

Madame   It's hard for me to feel things.
Valet   There's a word for that.
Madame   Pinch me.
Valet   No.
Madame   You work for me.
Valet   I work for him.
Madame   You shouldn't take his car.
Valet   It belongs to the hotel.

THE VALET joins her behind the desk. He puts his hand on her ass.

| Madame | Get off me. Get out! |

THE VALET exits.

THE TECHNICIAN enters.

Madame	We've got a client.
Technician	Finally. You did the intake?
Madame	He brought her in the car. You let him take it?
Technician	He's the Valet. Are you ready?
Madame	Ready.

THE TECHNICIAN resets the clock to read 7:00 AM.

MADAME dials up to K. K answers the phone.

| Madame | This is your wake up call. |

MADAME hangs up and so does K. K picks up the phone and dials back down to the desk.

| Madame | Hotel Bardot. |

K is silent.

MADAME hangs up.

THE TECHNICIAN prepares an injection.

| Technician | I'll find out what she wants. |

MADAME hands him a white technician's jacket wrapped in plastic. He puts it on.

Technician You sent them out?

Madame I can't do everything.

Technician Idle hands...

MADAME hands him a beauty parlor robe, wrapped in plastic.

Madame Find out what she wants.

He exits.

*

2.

In room 108, K sits in the beauty parlor chair. THE TECHNICIAN enters.

Technician Good morning, K. How are you feeling?

She can't speak.

He picks up the phone and dials.

Technician Are you hungry?

Madame answers.

Madame	Hotel Bardot.
Technician	Could we get some breakfast in 108, please?
Madame	I'm not the maid.
Technician	Thank you.

He hangs up.

Technician	We're short-staffed. Low season.

He gives K an injection. It compels her to speak.

K	Before the accident I worked in a laundry.
Technician	That's lucky.
K	Is it?
Technician	It's a good skill to have. In your bag of tricks.
K	We started work early. We were hungry most of the time. It's hard to look at you.
Technician	Am I ugly?
K	Of course you know you're not. I don't think I'll be able to eat in front of you.
Technician	Here, put this on.

He gives her the robe.

K	You don't like my dress?
Technician	There's blood.
K	I took a shower but I can't find where it came from.
Technician	Someone will come up, tests, that sort of thing.

146

K	A nurse?
Technician	Yes. Well, technically, no.
K	And you're a doctor?
Technician	Not really. She'll be up with your—
K	The nurse?
Technician	Don't call her that.
K	What should I call her?
Technician	Do you speak French?
K	No.
Technician	French could become your primary language. Call her Madame.
K	Why would I forget English?
Technician	You might want to.
K	What do I call you? Doctor in French?
Technician	If it's easier for you to think of me that way. I'm going to scram so you can eat. So you don't have to look at me.
K	It's you looking at me.
Technician	Back in an hour. For a shampoo. Throw your dress down the chute.

He exits. ONE *and* TWO *enter.*

K	A shampoo. Not a doctor.

K takes off her bloody dress and puts on the robe.

In shadow, the RATS *watch.*

| K | A terrible tragedy. I lost my shoes. Someone you love, your fault. And the Animal, too. She wrecked us. When I got out to see her, what she was she was gone. |

MADAME enters. The RATS exit.

Madame	I need blood.
K	I thought you were bringing my breakfast.
Madame	I'm not the maid.
K	The nurse?
Madame	Tests first.
K	Nobody feeds you.
Madame	We need it for tests.
K	Everyone wants blood but they don't know how to get it. What if I don't have any?
Madame	Everyone has blood.
K	Someone gave me a glass of orange juice once, with blood in it. Right after that I lost my virginity.
Madame	To a man?
K	An Eskimo. Is that the right word?
Madame	Did he come from a cold place?

K remembers something. Shakes it off.

K	If I let you take my blood, what will you give me?
Madame	Cookies and—
K	Orange juice. I won't drink it.

MADAME puts a needle in K's arm.

Madame	Milk, then.
K	And I can take a nap?
Madame	Yes. You'll want to lie down.
K	It will sting?
Madame	Only for a moment.
K	Only for a moment.

MADAME continues to draw the blood. It takes a long time. K lies down. MADAME examines the blood, puts it in her pocket and exits.

K No one noticed the blood on my hands, on my face. I'm not glad, but when the blood filled him up, when it filled up the car, I knew I was going for a long walk. Then the car just picked me up. The only one that stopped.

K falls asleep.

*

3.

In the garage, THE VALET reads Rumi.

Valet Lovers think they are looking for each other,
but there's only one search: wandering
this world is wandering that, both inside one
transparent sky.

*THE TECHNICIAN enters. THE VALET drops
the book.*

Technician	I brought you something. You can keep your hands tender, clean. A professional's hands. Here. Put them on.
Valet	They're too big.
Technician	Well, they're mine. Driving gloves.
Valet	Old fashioned.
Technician	You're not thinking.
Valet	They smell like your hands.
Technician	Like her. They smell like the Mercedes. Gears shifting. Things escalate and you can react. I would prefer that you wear these when you handle her.
Valet	Yes sir. I understand, sir.
Technician	It would ease my mind about your hands on her.
Valet	Yes, sir.
Technician	And one more thing...
Valet	Yes, sir.
Technician	Try not to look at the clients. Have a good night.
Valet	It's morning, sir.
Technician	Right. Have a good morning, then.
Valet	I will sir.

*

4.

The RATS approach K.

One	Oh. Look at her sleeping.
Two	I want to chew off one of her toes.
One	I want to chew off her ear.
Two	I want to eat her brains.
One	I want to make a tunnel from her asshole to her mouth.
Two	Music will play.
One	What kind?
Two	A symphony, I suppose. Stimulates the appetite.

Music plays. They enjoy it.

One	Whets the whistle.
Two	A wet whistle might not make a sound.
One	W-het, not wet, you idiot. Can you hear the h?
Two	I can hear it when you say it.
One	Because I speak proper English.
Two	W-hat ever. I can do it too, if I feel like it.
One	You don't have the brains.
Two	You don't have the heart.
One	I want to suck on her heart.
Two	I want to suck on her spleen.
One	I want to piss in her hair.
Two	I want to shit on the carpet.
One	Go ahead.

Two tries to take a shit.

One	You only shit in your box.
Two	I can do it. But not with you watching. Turn around.

One turns around.

Two tries to shit on the floor. He can't.

Two	I just went. Before.
One	You're scared.
Two	She's killed things. But I've got teeth. And darkness.
One	Do it, then.

K stirs. One *and* Two *exit.*

*

5.

Behind the front desk Madame *rearranges objects in a vast grid of mail slots—vials of blood, coins, and Polaroid photos.*

One *and* Two *enter. They crap in their box.*

Madame	I hope she wasn't a suicide. They don't clean.

She opens the vials and smells them. She prepares a breakfast tray for K and sets it aside.

Madame	She is suffering greatly, she has no refuge, she is entering a thick forest, she is entering a great wilderness, she is

swept away by a great ocean.

She uncovers a phonograph, puts the needle down on the Brigitte Bardot record, "Contact." The MUSIC overpowers her and she dances. The rats copy her movements.

*

6.

In the garage, the men play a game with mallets.

Valet   Why can't we be on the same side?

Technician That's not the game. There are two varieties. Regular and One Day. The length of the match can be, whatever. The more important the match the longer.

Valet   How important is this? Not very important?

Technician I'm not sure yet, we'll see.

Valet   Did you do something to her?

Technician Her?

Valet   Did you?

Technician It's nothing you should ask me about.

Valet   How do you—I want to, but my hands—

Technician That's just how it is for some people.

He demonstrates a swing.

Technician Sometimes these tests or matches last five days, eight to ten hours a day. You can hit the ball in any direction, even behind you. There are several different strokes. This. Or this. Or this. Different strokes for different blokes, they say. Ha ha. The central area is called the pitch. The circle there. The red area. When I'm not the batter I'm the bowler. When I'm not the bowler I'm the batter. We switch.

Valet Like this?

Technician Harder, put some muscle in.

THE VALET swings and misses.

Technician You want to kiss it.

THE VALET swings again and misses.

Technician And throw it like you used to throw at girls.

Valet They threw at me. Does she hurt you?

Technician The girl?

Valet They both have black eyes.

Technician They're ladies.

Valet Is this game played with helmets?

Technician I'm going to hit it at you now, so at the right moment try and duck, or move to one of the red areas.

Valet I don't see them.

Technician You don't see this triangle, here?

Valet No. I see the circle.

Technician I can't hit you if you're in the circle. But you can't run until I swing. Get ready.

THE VALET ducks.

Technician	You have to wait until I swing. Your instincts are poor.
Valet	Well, are you going to—
Technician	I'm waiting. For the right—

He hits THE VALET with the ball. THE VALET falls to the ground. THE TECHNICIAN exits to the lobby.

MADAME makes her way to the garage and finds THE VALET.

*

7.

THE TECHNICIAN picks up the tray from the front desk and carries it to room 108.

He knocks on the door, waits a beat and enters. K sleeps in the beauty parlor chair. He washes her hair while she talks in her sleep.

Technician	As I count down from 10 see yourself at the top of a small flight of stairs. 10, 9, 8.
K	Warm water.
Technician	Warm and tingly sensations magnify it. 7, 6, 5.
K	Smashed.
Technician	4, 3, 2, 1. On the next number you're there.
K	Crashed.
Technician	Zero.

K	L'hotel. L'hopital.
Technician	Who are you?
K	Contempt. Collision.
Technician	Who are you?
K	Dear. Deer.
Technician	Who are you?
K	And God created woman.
Technician	Who are you?
K	Killer, Car crasher.
Technician	Who are you?
K	Bardo. Bardot.

He wraps a towel around her head. He touches her arms. She wakes up.

| K | I'm a blank... |

He touches her legs.

| K | Do you work for her or does she work for you? |
| Technician | We work together. Stand up. Turn around. Open your eyes. |

He unties her robe and lowers it, revealing a tattoo on her shoulder.

Technician	What's that?
K	Nothing.
Technician	There. On your skin. Words.
K	Je ne sais pas.

He ties up her robe and sits her down in the chair. He places her under the dryer and slips out.

*

8.

In the garage, MADAME bandages THE VALET.

Madame	Do you know the place I'm talking about?
Valet	Sometimes I wish it would just go away on it's own.
Madame	Decadent arches. Lavish ice cream sundaes.
Valet	I put vinegar on it.
Madame	Trembling, naked boy statues.
Valet	But sometimes it spreads.
Madame	They melt in your mouth.
Valet	In a triangle. From my scalp to my ears. Or randomly. Left shin, right fingertips. All numb.
Madame	He used to take me there.
Valet	There's no feeling in any of it. Sometimes I just want to...

He smacks his hand against the ground.

Madame	He would hold both of my hands in his hands and kiss them.
Valet	Sometimes I want to hurt him, but I can't use my hands that way. He's going to do something to her. The maid...

Madame	He has a ripe smell. What he does, it's just business.
Valet	Do you love him?
Madame	Yes, but the smell.

A pause.

Valet	Can *we* go there?
Madame	Where, darling?
Valet	The lavish arches. I could hold your hands. Not both together, but one at a time.
Madame	Sometimes I wish it would go away on it's own.

*

9.

K sits in the beauty parlor chair, under the dryer.

The RATS get close.

One	Rats can spread disease.
Two	A residuum is always left.
One	As much to one's body as to the whole universe.
Two	Notions about the world.
One	Repetition, compulsion.
Two	About human nature.
One	Compulsion, repetition.
Two	The gods, magic, business.
One	Blockages raise their ugly heads. Heads or tails?

Two	Every last drop of the real.
One	Heads or tails?
Two	Time before the word.
One	Heads or tails?
Two	The whole in the other.
One	Heads or tails?
Two	Tails.

*

10.

At the front desk, MADAME and THE TECHNICIAN do paperwork.

Technician	She signed the release?
Madame	At the intake. Birthmarks?
Technician	No. A tattoo.
Madame	A flower? Butterfly?
Technician	Words.
Madame	People need an opportunity to speak as themselves.

THE TECHNICIAN sees the maid's uniform, wrapped in plastic.

Technician	We should train her.
Madame	We are technicians and we are trusted to move the dead through so they can.
Technician	So they can—
Madame	So they can—go on.
Technician	Where do they go?

Madame	They go—on.
Technician	You don't really know, do you?
Madame	It's not my job to know where.
Technician	Maybe they go nowhere.
Madame	Why get up in the morning?
Technician	I've depressed you.
Madame	Open your eyes!
Technician	She knows we are together.
Madame	We?
Technician	You decide. Someone else to clean the sheets.
Madame	A manicure maybe? Pedicure?
Technician	Gently. Don't cut at the cuticles.
Madame	I know when and when not to cut.

She picks up her case and goes up to 108. THE TECHNICIAN winds the clock forward.

THE TECHNICIAN picks up the maid's uniform. He holds it like a woman.

THE VALET enters and watches THE TECHNICIAN.

Technician She had a knack for folding and unfolding. She was good at making beds and also unmaking them. It's true, I ravaged her, but it left her calmer than when I found her. She liked to play doctor and so did I. I would shoot fake penicillin into her soft, pale haunches. It will make you well, I promised, but then the surprise of the needle, the betrayal. Wound up in sheets she was so graceful, so true.

160

11.

In room 108, MADAME gives K a manicure.

Madame	Maid.
K	Maid.
Madame	Mint.
K	Mint.
Madame	Mattress.
K	Mattress.
Madame	Could I get some fresh towels, please?
K	Could I get some fresh towels, please?
Madame	Good. Say it again, more like you have a real need. To be dry, clean, whatever.
K	Est-ce que je pourrais avoir des serviettes fraîches?
Madame	Better. Après-midi.
K	Après-midi.
Madame	De rien
K	De rien.
Madame	Maillot de bain.
K	Maillot de bain.
Madame	It means swim suit. Say it again and think about the ocean. You're swimming in the ocean. And it could swallow you up, but for now it's really exhilarating.
K	It's really exhilarating.

Madame	That's the right intensity, but that's not the phrase. The phrase is... maillot de bain.

THE TECHNICIAN slips into the room. He carries the maid's uniform.

K	He put me in the car and we went to the water. Maillot de bain. He parked the car next to a cruddy part of the beach and then his hands were around the soft part of my neck and he was inside me with his fingers and he said baby baby he said I was dirty and he would clean me like I clean the sheets and it would hurt a little. I don't care if it hurts.

With a compact, MADAME powders over K's black eye.

Madame	It's supposed to be tender. You shouldn't talk about your husband like that.
Technician	You can sterilize your instruments in the coffee maker.
K	He wasn't my—
Technician	I can remove a bullet. I can cut off a finger or toe that has gone numb due to frostbite.
K	You're a doctor!
Madame	No. A technician. We're technicians. I can perform a medical pedicure, minor dental work—teeth cleanings and gum treatments.
K	I don't need a gum treatment.
Technician	I don't touch the feet, except in a frostbite situation. Liposuctions, mostly and other figure enhancements.

Madame	He could do your lips or your breasts. They could be fuller, more feminine. Maillot de bain.
K	Maillot de bain.
Technician	Have you decided on any of the surgeries?
Madame	She's not ready. But she will be. Good news.

MADAME exits.

K	M-Mint. M-Maid. M-Mattress.
Technician	Every process is completely voluntary.
K	I told him I wanted to save something for later.

THE TECHNICIAN pulls away the dryer to reveal a blonde wig in the style of Brigitte Bardot. With a comb, he styles it.

Technician	She had a knack for folding and unfolding. Maillot de bain. She was good at making beds and also unmaking them. Maillot de bain. My hands were around the soft part of her neck and I was inside her with my fingers and I said baby baby, I said she was dirty and I would clean her like she cleans the sheets and it would hurt a little. I don't care if it hurts. I ravaged her, but it left her calmer than when I found her. Wound up in sheets she was so graceful, so true.

*

12.

THE VALET reads Kabir.

Valet   The idea that the soul will join with the ecstatic.
Just because the body is rotten—
that is all fantasy.
What is found now is found then.
If you find nothing now,
You will simply end up with an apartment in the
City of Death.

*MADAME approaches THE VALET. He throws down
the book.*

Madame   The Mercedes.
Valet   The Mercedes, huh?
Madame   Get it.
Valet   Right back, Madame.
Madame   Don't call me that.

She puts on lipstick.

He brings the car. Holds the door open.

Madame   You didn't drive it did you?
Valet   You just saw me drive it.
Madame   On windy seaside roads, your hand between
someone's thighs.

Valet	Bitch.
Madame	I'm a bitch?
Valet	Get in the car.
Madame	No.

He pushes her down on the car. He points a gun at her head.

The RATS scurry through.

THE VALET shoots at them. MADAME takes the gun from him and hits him with it.

He pushes her against the car and puts his hand up her skirt. They continue as the LIGHT shifts to the RATS.

*

13.

In the lobby, the RATS skulk around.

One	I'm hungry.
Two	She just fed us.
One	We need meat.
Two	Where do we get it?
One	Have you already forgotten how to kill?
Two	I prefer to find something that's already dead.
One	Where's the fun in that?

Two	Fun?
One	Remember fun? Rolling a bum. Eating his face.
Two	I think he was already dead.
One	No. We killed him.
Two	I don't remember.
One	We should eat the one with the bruise.
Two	Which one?
One	Not the one who feeds us. The other one.
Two	I'm pretty sure she's already dead, though.
One	No.
Two	People only stay here if they're dead.
One	Then we are...
Two	Are we?
One	No.
Two	I don't feel dead.
One	You smell dead. You always did, though.
Two	How can we find out?
One	You could try to kill me.
Two	Try to kill you?
One	See if I die. You could eat me, after, if you want.
Two	Thanks.
One	Or I could eat you.
Two	Let's find out if she's dead.
One	How will we know?
Two	We'll watch her. See if she has fear.

They scurry up the stairs and listen through the walls.

*

14.

THE TECHNICIAN enters room 108.

K	Hi.
Technician	Step on the scale, please.

She gets on a scale and he notes the number.

Technician	You're losing weight. Do you like the food here?

She opens her robe.

Technician	You don't want anyone to see that.
K	The stomach?
Technician	It's where the fear is.
K	I don't have one.
Technician	Any.
K	I haven't had dinner. Something needs to—
Technician	Nothing needs to be done.
K	Cooked carrots under a... What is that called?

THE TECHNICIAN picks up the phone.

K	And a whole—

He hangs up.

K	A whole roasted chicken. Why didn't you—

Technician	Your circadian rhythms are out of sync with our clocks. We find out more when you are hungry.
K	What do you want to know? Lobotomy?
Technician	Good.
K	You're chasing a rabbit down the hole.
Technician	There is no whole.
K	When I used to make dinner, I would dig carrots out of the ground, like this.

She digs into the carpet.

Technician	Get up.
K	I want to bury it. I didn't bury it. I forgot to bury it.

She keeps digging.

Technician	You'll wash them yourself, over there in the sink. Dirty bug crawling vegetables and in the morning, no coffee, no cream, no hot rolls with butter. If you forget your pleasures and your preferences, you will recondition in a more womanly way. You are lovely for a screaming, digging lunatic. Has anyone ever...? How old are you? Sixteen? Eighteen? Thirty-two? Are you thirsty? Do you want sweet tea? I've got coins.

He picks up the phone and dials the desk. No one answers. He hangs up.

He picks up K and puts her in the chair. He restrains her and blindfolds her.

Technician   What are you afraid of?

He exits. ONE and TWO enter.

One   Punches.
Two   Blows.
One   Silence.
Two   Hunger.
One   Darkness.
Two   Blood.
One   Teeth.
Two   Things in the walls.
One   Things underground.
Two   The unburied.
One   The dead.

*

15.

MADAME eats ice cream in the lobby.

Valet   Why can't I use your spoon?
Madame   Don't be ridiculous. Germs.

He looks at her.

Madame	Stop it.

He flexes his biceps.

Valet	It's gotten bigger. Want to feel it.
Madame	Even if I do, that's not going to change things.
Valet	No?
Madame	No.
Valet	I walked here through mud puddles because this is our place.
Madame	You work here.

He paws at her.

Madame	Stop! I am going to get you a fresh spoon. You are not part of me.

She exits.

He picks up her spoon and licks it.

THE TECHNICIAN enters the lobby.

Technician	Ice cream?

THE TECHNICIAN puts ice cream on a tray.

Technician	Help her eat. Try not to look at her.

*

16.

THE VALET takes ice cream up to K. He feeds her.

K   Someone drove me here. His hands were small. Too small to be a man's hands. I was trying to get speed into the curve and there she was, the deer, where you sometimes pull over and look. And my head made a star, where the glass was smooth. And my neck broke. And my heart stopped. And she was gone.

Valet   The light on your breasts.

K   What light? I can't see it.

Valet   Through the cracks.

K   The sky is black.

Valet   If you close your eyes, you can see it.

He takes off her blindfold and her eyes remain closed. He exits.

*

17.

MADAME finds THE TECHNICIAN in the lobby.

Madame   Against the marble, you look golden.

Technician   Ice cream?

Madame   A celebration. The girl will soon be ready and I will stop folding and my hands will relax.

	Or maybe they will stiffen from lack of work and I will go permanently grey. The bricks will fall, the rats will chew our earlobes and the soft skin between our fingers.
Technician	Splendid afternoon!
Madame	The clock sticks. Everything is broken.
Technician	She melts my eyes.
Madame	She needs surgery.
Technician	Honeymoon waterfall.
Madame	She was ringing. Should I send up a sundae?
Technician	I sent the Valet.

A pause.

Madame	It's not working, is it? She doesn't clean.
Technician	It would be better if she liked you and I was an all-knower.
Madame	She doesn't like me?
Technician	You need to take things away. Then, give them to her.
Madame	Our arrangement...
Technician	I know about the Valet.
Madame	What's there to know?
Technician	In the garage.
Madame	Well, if you didn't know you'd be an idiot.
Technician	Bent over on the Mercedes of some poor sap.
Madame	It belongs to the hotel.
Technician	Unprofessional and cruel. You are not a part of me.
Madame	You are not a part of me.

She exits, carrying a dress wrapped in plastic.

THE TECHNICIAN sets the clock forward. He exits.

*

18.

The RATS pillage the front desk.

One	Underground the data is backing up.
Two	The city funnels shit through tunnels.
One	You're a phony.
Two	You're a fake.
One	You can't count.
Two	You don't have your teeth.
One	They're made of gold.
Two	They're not real.
One	Your skin is rotting.
Two	You can't see. Disease.
One	Death's rainbow.
Two	Filthy lucre.
One	I smell her dead body.
Two	It's small.
One	They drain the blood.
Two	She's a shell.
One	Death.
Two	Surrender.
One	Some gravity.

*

19.

In room 108, MADAME dresses K.

Madame	What is the nicest thing you've ever done?
K	I made dinner for my parents once. I tried to get the bones out, but I swallowed one and it stuck in my throat. I found it hard to say what I really felt. Then they went home.
Madame	What's the worst thing you ever did?
K	I forgot.
Madame	Blockages raise their ugly heads! I'm going to say some words and you can just say the worst thing that comes into your head.
K	The worst thing?
Madame	That's right. Towel.
K	Blood.
Madame	Okay. Chair.
K	Accident.
Madame	Good. Man.

K doesn't answer.

Madame	Does he touch you?
K	He orders things for me. On the phone. Sweet things. Is he your boss or are you his boss?
Madame	We are in solidarity. I need to know how he touches you.
K	Is he your—
Madame	We are together. It should not affect how you proceed, how he proceeds with you. Each situation is different and he has his methods. Does he hit you?

K	When I first heard his voice—I do what he says. I am not unhappy to be here.
Madame	I want you to think of me as a me and not a they. It will make any of the procedures easier if you trust me.
K	All right.
Madame	What's the last thing you remember?
K	He punched me. In the eye. There was a bruise and something broke inside. A blood vessel, maybe. We were going to be married with rice and cans and all that but instead I got a tattoo. It wouldn't stop bleeding.
Madame	Is it a flower? A butterfly?

K shows her the tattoo.

K	In a language from before.
Madame	What does it say?
K	I killed him.

A pause.

Madame	You should get some rest now.
K	But it's dinner time.
Madame	Is your hypothalamus telling you that? Here we use clocks. And I'm pretty sure it's time for bed. Take these. They will help you regulate.

MADAME gives her pills. Turns out the LIGHTS.

K	I'm afraid.

MADAME gives K a flashlight.

K lies awake.

The RATS sneak in.

One	I see her dead body.
Two	It's small.
One	They drain the blood.
Two	She's a shell.
One	Death. Surrender. Some gravity. I see her dead body.
Two	It's small.
One	They drain the blood.
Two	She's a shell.
One	Death.
Two	Surrender.
One	Gravity.
K	Just so you know, I'm on rat patrol. I know you're not afraid of me. But I'm not afraid of you either. I hear you scurry I hear you rush. I see you there, lazy looking at me, in the dark, eyes glistening. I'll have you know I've killed things. I kill. I am a killer. You want to chew my ears off? Do it then. I'm waiting.

The RATS approach.

K bludgeons ONE with the flashlight. In the dark, TWO scurries away. The LIGHTS come up.

K   If I was going to have another occupation, besides
         laundress, I might enjoy being an exterminator.

         The SOUND *of thunder, of pipes rattling.*

         K picks up the phone and calls downstairs.

                                    *

20.

         In the lobby, THE TECHNICIAN *picks up the phone and
         listens. Hangs up. The plumbing makes* NOISE.

Madame   She's killed things.
Technician   She's not speaking.
Madame   I turned out the lights.

         TWO *scurries through.*

Madame   What is that smell?
Technician   I'm going up.
Madame   Wait.

         MADAME *puts on a face mask and hands one to* THE
         TECHNICIAN. *They make their way to Room 108.*

                                    *

21.

K is digging into the floor. THE TECHNICIAN and MADAME stand over the dead rat.

Technician	Rats can spread disease.
Madame	A sort of smooth seamless surface—
Technician	A residuum is always left.
Madame	As much to a child's body as to the whole universe.
Technician	Cuts into—
Madame	Notions about the world.
Technician	Repetition, compulsion.
Madame	About human nature.
Technician	Compulsion, repetition.
Madame	The gods, magic, business.
Technician	Blockages raise their ugly heads.
Madame	Every last drop of the real.
Technician	Slip to, sister. Heads or tails?
Madame	Time before the word.
Technician	Heads or tails?
Madame	An infant's body.
Technician	Heads or tails?
Madame	The (w)hole in the other.
Technician	Heads or tails?

He tosses a gold coin.

Madame	Tails.

K keeps digging.

Technician What do you want? I've got coins!

K digs faster.

Madame Sweet tea? Sugary drinks? What do you want?

K keeps digging.

The Technician and Madame exit. The Valet enters and exterminates. A book falls out of his pocket.

K stops digging.

The Valet picks up the book and exits.

*

22.

Madame and The Technician meet in the lobby.

Madame Now that we know she's killed things—
Technician Her hands her face her shoulders her lips.
Madame It won't work. She won't clean.
Technician If she goes, he goes.

A pause.

Madame A tuxedo. A make-believe wedding.

Technician	Car crash.
Madame	Lobotomy.
Technician	She said it without prompting.
Madame	You think you're capable? Personal feelings?
	A difficult surgery.
Technician	My hands can do it.
Madame	The patient. Then the car.

They look at the clock. It reads 6:45 AM.

Technician	There's not much time.
Madame	Quickly.

*

23.

THE TECHNICIAN brings up a veil wrapped in plastic. He prepares K for surgery. He gives her an injection.

Technician I'm just going to let you get numb.

He exits.

K sinks into the chair.

She tries to wash her hair.

K The water will wash whatever he put there.

*The R<small>ATS</small> are about to break down the walls. They make
screeching sounds. There are shadows of ears and teeth.*

*

24.

In the garage, T<small>HE</small> V<small>ALET</small> reads Hafiz.

Valet   Like a great starving beast
My body is quivering
Fixed
On the scent
Of
Light.

*M<small>ADAME</small> makes her way down to the car.
She carries the tuxedo wrapped in plastic.
She ties cans to the bumper.*

Valet   Why don't we go some place?
Madame   It's his car.
Valet   We can take it.
Madame   You're always making things exciting.
Valet   We could watch the sunset.
Madame   We're not together.

He puts his hand on her ass. She slaps him.

Madame	We're going to have to send her away.
Valet	Where will she go?
Madame	You'll take her. And you won't come back.
Valet	What is her name?
Madame	Put on the tuxedo.
Valet	What is her name?
Madame	Brigitte Bardot.

She kisses him. Hands him the tuxedo and goes up to the lobby. She plays the record, "Contact," again.

The RATS get louder.

*

25.

K is under gas. The SOUND of the coffee maker. THE TECHNICIAN slips into the room.

Technician	Are you numb?
K	Yes.
Technician	Can you feel anything?
K	I don't know.
Technician	Nervous?
K	I've had fillings before. How long will it take.
Technician	Just a few minutes. Are you feeling it?
K	Liminal.
Technician	That's about right. 19, 18, 17.

K	Makeup. Mouthwash.
Technician	16, 15, 14.
K	Emory boards. Eye drops.
Technician	13, 12, 11.
K	Comb, condoms, cotton, cough drops.
Technician	10, 9, 8,
K	Are you going to kill me?
Technician	7, 6, 5,
K	Safety pins, sanitary napkins.
Technician	4, 3, 2
K	I love... this music!

He starts to drill into her brain. She wrestles away the drill and plunges it into his chest. He dies.

As RATS fill the room, she digs a hole to the parking garage. The plumbing makes horrible SOUNDS.

TWO and the other RATS eat THE TECHNICIAN.

*

26.

THE VALET paces the garage until he finds the mallet. He smashes the car.

Valet	She explodes.

Bang.

And I punch him and take everything out of his trunk.

Matches light a fire. The whole place explodes.

Rice at a wedding. Ch ch ch ch ch.

Click click click click click. Won't turn over.

Assault and a dead battery.

Or maybe she gets in and we drive at the wall.

Splat, smash, crash.

The taste of glass in my blood, blood in my mouth.

Married to me with broken bones. Crack. Snap.

It's all a big fire.

K wanders the garage. She sees THE VALET.

K	Your hands are black like blood.
Valet	The Mercedes needs care.

He tries to touch her.

K	Don't get it on me.
Valet	Usually I wear gloves.
K	Black. Bloody.
Valet	Like you are driving off a cliff?
K	Like there is sun and rain at the same time.
Valet	A rainbow does not actually exist at a particular location in the sky.
K	Red orange yellow green blue black.
Valet	The car stops.
K	Not even moonlight. Not even stars.
Valet	That's the marine layer. When you live in a seaside town.

K	I don't live here.
Valet	The light on your breasts.
K	What light? I can't see it.
Valet	Through the cracks.
K	The sky is black.
Valet	If you close your eyes...

He closes her eyes.

Valet	You can see it.

*

27.

In Room 108, MADAME finds THE TECHNICIAN's remains. The RATS have gone, except for TWO, who watches.

Madame	He is driven on by the wind, he is going where there is no solid ground, he is embarking on a great battle, he is entering existence after existence, the time has come when he must go on alone. I leave before being left. I decide.

She takes a photo of THE TECHNICIAN's remains. TWO scurries away.

*

28.

K and THE VALET *ride in the Mercedes.*

K	The seaside is confusing.
Valet	At least we know North. South.
K	Why are you pulling over?
Valet	You don't want to get out, smell the air?
K	Whose car is this? Is it his?
Valet	He acts like it's his but it belongs to the hotel.
K	This is a stolen car.
Valet	Do you remember this place?
K	Are you going to kill me?

A pause.

Valet	No.
K	He was supposed to be driving. My head on his shoulder.
Valet	His hand between your—
K	Are you going to have sex with me?
Valet	Maybe you could just go down on me?
K	I don't remember what that is.
Valet	I'll take you anywhere you want to go. If you want to go back to the hotel I can take you.
K	I want to lie down.

The sun sets.

Valet	Sunset. But she didn't want to see it from here. Not with me.

| K | Are we supposed to go back? Return the car? Is there going to be trouble? |
| Valet | Take a breath. Look at the space in between. |

He crashes the car. It rains rice.

*

29.

MADAME makes her way to the garage. She takes pictures of the crash.

She goes upstairs to the lobby. She takes off her wig.

With the camera, she takes a self-portrait. She takes out the gun and shoots herself in the head.

ONE enters. He seems more human. He takes off his rat mask, gets ice cream out of the freezer and eats. TWO climbs up into his lap.

The End

The Interview

by Hank Bunker

The Interview *was first produced by Theater of NOTE, Los Angeles in 1995 under the direction of Diane Robinson, and with the following cast:*

Butler Hank Butler
Connie Janet Borrus
Ronnie Darrett Sanders

Cast of Characters

Connie—*30s.*
Ronnie—*early 30s.*
Butler—*late 30s, 40s.*

Scene One

Living room. RONNIE *makes drinks.* CONNIE *sits,*
covered in dirt from her garden. BUTLER *sits opposite,*
suitcase by his side.

Connie	Hey, you like Ed Murrow? He's one of my all-times.
Butler	No.
Connie	*(To* RONNIE*)* You hear that? He hates Murrow's guts!
Ronnie	I can't find the booze. It's locked up, she locks things up.
Connie	So where's this "article" gonna be published?
Butler	It will be sold to the highest bidder.
Connie	Not some in-flight magazine, I hope? Some farm thing?
Butler	I assure you.

(Pause)

Connie	I need a refill.

(She holds her glass out to RONNIE.*)*

Ronnie	It's locked.

(Pause)

Connie	*(To* RONNIE*)* Good thing you got a nice high-paying job that doesn't require any sort of actual skills.

*(*CONNIE *gets up to unlock the liquor cabinet.)*

Ronnie	She thinks she does too much around here.
Connie	You don't do enough. I don't know what you do.
Ronnie	I invited Butler to stay a few days. (CONNIE *looks at* BUTLER.) He'll just be hanging around, making notes, recording conversation... is that right, Butler?
Connie	I can plant tulips in the garden but nobody ever wrote an article about that.
Butler	Your husband has accomplished something unique.

(Pause)

Connie	Have you ever given birth, Butler? *(Slight pause)* Which one of you has ever given birth, besides Ronnie, who I know for a fact has never given birth to so much as a hamster?
Ronnie	*(To BUTLER)* I warned you.
Butler	Ronnie has cultivated and brought forth within himself a world-class ability, where very few ever thought one to exist.
Connie	Try none.
Ronnie	*(To BUTLER)* Here's your drink. Tell me if it's no good.

(BUTLER takes the glass and sips.)

Butler	It's fine.
Connie	Liar.
Butler	It's fine.
Connie	It's the worst drink you ever had in your life.
Ronnie	We're out of ginger ale, Connie. Unless you locked it all up somewhere.

Connie	Hey, Ronnie, how come all of a sudden you're so special? Huh? You don't look different.
Ronnie	Well, it's funny you should say that. Right, Butler?

(BUTLER has taken a flask from his jacket and makes his drink a little stronger.)

Connie	*(To BUTLER)* This whole society. They reward you if you can act—like actors are so fuckin' interesting. What's the fascination? Same with sports. Turn on the TV, nothing but actors and athletes.
Butler	What would you hope to see?
Connie	Somethin' real. Not some staged event. You're wastin' your time on this junk.
Butler	I'm interested in the extraordinary that dwells within the prosaic.

(Pause)

Connie	Now I have to ask you while I'm thinkin' of it. Why do you go by one name only, like some posh barber?
Ronnie	Connie...
Butler	It's a choice.
Connie	You got a first name?
Ronnie	Leave him alone.
Connie	I'm entitled to ask. He's in my house, for God's sake.
Butler	I dispensed with it some time ago.
Connie	Dispensed? What's that?
Butler	It's unimportant. It belongs to the past.
Connie	I like what's real.

Ronnie	Not now, Connie.
Connie	Whatsamatter, we can't state our interests? Are you writin' this down, Butler?
Butler	No.
Connie	Some journalist. I'm talkin' about what's important and he's sippin' a cocktail. I'm going to bed. I'm going to write in my journal.

(She exits. Pause.)

Ronnie	You should see her journal. She constantly records every little fact.
Butler	I like her.
Ronnie	You do?
Butler	She reminds me of me. Though I'm not sure if that's good or bad, ha, ha. *(Pause)* Well, I guess I'll turn in myself.
Ronnie	She's just upset. I'll talk to her. *(BUTLER rises.)* It's still early, Butler. Stay up awhile. Eat. We'll look for the key.
Butler	Plenty of hard work ahead.
Ronnie	It's seven o'clock.
Butler	You should get some sleep yourself. Practice those nocturnal visualization exercises I mentioned.
Ronnie	What about dinner?
Butler	No, thanks. Goodnight.

(BUTLER exits with his suitcase. Pause. RONNIE pulls and rattles a locked cabinet.)

LIGHTS dim.

*

Scene Two

*Connie sits on her bed. She speaks into a
microcassette recorder.*

Connie …then when I was seventeen I joined one of those nurses
clubs. But that wasn't for me—let those other saps be
the nurses. I wanted to be the doctor. So then I planned
to be a doctor but that didn't pan out; I got interested
in politics suddenly. I thought about joining the Peace
Corps or running for Congress. Which seemed like
the best way to get connected to people's lives. Then a
funny thing happened: I found out I didn't wanna be
connected to people's lives. People were a buncha
hopeless dopes, as far as I could see. I had to get away
as far as possible. So I took a break. That's when I met
Ronnie. I was workin' in one of those photomats. He
kept demandin' his pictures, you know? I hafta say, he
was very persistent and put up with a lot of abuse. But he
was a regular guy and liked me and all. So I found myself
goin' out with him. He was just regular. And didn't even
like sports and never talked about it either. If I knew he
was cloakin' secret thoughts about golf and fame I'da
sent him packin' early, boy, I can tell you that. As it is we
got married. I wasn't pregnant. Yet. I mean the whole
need to get married was based on how I was gonna get
somethin' out of it. To help me get where I'm supposed to
go. Oh, boy, was I dumb. Instead of puttin' me on the
road somewhere it cut me off. Ambushed and left me for

dead. That's what it did. Now it's all leakin' away. This isn't my life. My life hasn't even begun.

BLACKOUT

*

Scene Three

CONNIE and RONNIE in bed. She reads her journal.

Ronnie   I had an unreal experience today, Connie.

Connie   I like what's real.

Ronnie   I know that. I meant bizarre.

Connie   How was work?

Ronnie   Uh, well, I want to talk about that.

Connie   I called and you weren't there.

Ronnie   I quit.

Connie   They said something about "you quit." I said that's ridiculous; it's a high-paying job that requires no skill. Check the men's room.

Ronnie   Me and Butler went out to the practice range. He said he thinks he unlocked the secret to my success and could I quit doing what I'm doing and go meet him at the range. So I did. *(Pause. CONNIE is reading.)* Did you hear what I said?

Connie   No. *(A knock.)* What is it?

(The bedroom door opens. BUTLER stands in his night-shirt, eating.)

Butler	Listen, do you mind if I come in for awhile? I was just lying in bed eating and got to thinking maybe I'm missing out on something in here.
Ronnie	I'm in bed with my wife.

(He enters.)

Butler	Is this inconvenient...?
Connie	How's that article coming, Butler?
Butler	Very well. Of course, I'm still in the research phase. Scribbling notes, ha, ha.
Connie	What kinda notes?
Butler	Oh, various observations.
Connie	Like what?
Butler	For instance, the favorable support Ronnie receives at home for instance. Do you have a pen?

(RONNIE points. BUTLER finds the pen and scratches a note on something.)

Connie	*(Overly loud)* Ronnie quit his job.
Ronnie	I was just tellin' her about it, Butler.

(Pause)

Connie	*(Nudging RONNIE)* What's he writin' on? *(Slight pause)* What's he writin' on?
Ronnie	How should I know? What's he eating?
Connie	*(To BUTLER)* Hey, Bulter, or whatever your name is!

Butler	Nothing, it's nothing. I was remarking only how Ronnie sleeps on the right-hand side of the bed, in contrast to some of the more successful members of the PGA, who sleep on the left. It's nothing.
Connie	Well, Ronnie quit his job.
Butler	Please. Carry on like I'm not even here.
Ronnie	We might as well include you in on it, Butler, since you were the one who gave me the idea.
Butler	Say, Ronnie, what do you plan to do with yourself now that you're out of work?
Connie	Good question.
Ronnie	Whaddaya mean? I'm gonna play golf. Golf is my work.
Connie	How's that sofa, Butler?
Ronnie	Connie, do you mind?
Connie	Not too lumpy?
Butler	Not a bit.
Ronnie	Any more questions for me, Butler?
Butler	If you don't mind I'll just sit here a moment and get my bearings.

(Long pause. BUTLER slumps forward in his chair.)

Connie	Ronnie. *(Slight pause)* Ronnie.
Ronnie	What?
Connie	Do something with your friend.
Ronnie	Like what?
Connie	Help him.

(RONNIE gets out of bed and goes to him, pats his face, etc.)

Ronnie	Butler. Butler. Snap out of it. *(To* CONNIE*)* He's cold.
Connie	Is he breathin'?
Ronnie	He's wearing my pajamas!
Butler	*(Coming to)* I'm fine, I'm fine...
Connie	Look out, Ronnie, he's gettin' up.

(BUTLER comes to his feet.)

Butler	Now. Where were we?
Connie	Relax, Butler. You conked out. Get hold of it.
Butler	Please. Carry on like I'm not even here.
Connie	He's shivering. Does he want a blanket or something?
Butler	Excuse me.

(BUTLER climbs into bed. Pause.)

Ronnie	Get the hell outta there, Butler.
Connie	Well, Butler, how do you feel now?
Butler	Great.
Connie	That's an improvement.
Butler	I feel great. How should we start?
Ronnie	By taking your hands off!
Connie	Let's start with a question. As long as you're feelin' so good. When're you gonna start writin' this article?
Butler	I've already begun.

(BUTLER pokes RONNIE.)

Connie	Then when're you gonna start interviewin' people?
Butler	Who?

Connie	Us.

(He pokes Ronnie again.)

Ronnie	Lay off it!
Butler	I've been talking to Ronnie...
Connie	What about me? Don't you think I got somethin' to say?
Butler	Hop in, Ron.
Connie	Let's have an interview.
Ronnie	Not now, Connie!
Butler	I need my notebook. I need my tape recorder.
Connie	Forget about 'em. Get the ball rollin'. I'm anxious to appear in print and you can quote me on that.
Ronnie	Get out of this bed, Butler.
Butler	All right. I'll ask you a question. What're you reading?
Ronnie	Who cares? Her dumb journal.
Butler	I've heard quite a lot about that journal.
Connie	Like what?
Butler	I've heard that you're a devoted diarist.
Ronnie	She brings it into bed every night. She writes it then reads it over in bed. What kind of behavior is that?
Connie	I'm settin' it straight!
Ronnie	She goes down the line listing things according to big Roman numerals. *(Points.)* Lookit!
Connie	I'm collectin' my general impressions. That's all. Which should be of wide public interest. That's all.
Ronnie	She thinks there's a conspiracy going on. That's what it is. Ever since the baby.
Butler	What baby?
Ronnie	He died.

Butler	I didn't know that.
Connie	That's the point.
Ronnie	I think it's jealousy. You know what I think? You're jealous I found something I'm great at.
Connie	Golf? How could I be jealous of golf? It's not even a thing. You might as well be a...jizzbag collector.
Butler	If I may, I think what Ronnie responded to today was something in the spiritual nature of golf.
Connie	Ronnie's a spiritual monkey.
Butler	I think...
Connie	Ronnie thinks on the Last Day we all rise up in knickers.
Butler	If I may, I think what separates the good from the very best in this sport...and Ronnie has all the tools. But what elevates him to the elite...
Ronnie	Tell her, Butler.
Butler	It's about what's inside. It's about the understanding that we're not alone, for one thing. That there is something out there so... great... what I call, by a term of my own coinage, the Royal and Ancient Spirit of Golf, that we're impelled. It calls us. And the best respond. That's what I believe. And that's, I think, what Ronnie glimpsed today.
Connie	You gotta be kiddin'.
Ronnie	Tell her.
Connie	Are you talkin' about God or something? Are you sayin' Ronnie had a God experience?
Ronnie	Who knows what it was? Right, Butler? It was unreal.
Connie	Stop saying that!
Butler	You can call it God if you like. It was only the second time I've ever seen it.

Connie	Was He wearin' knickers, huh, Ronnie? Was He strollin' down the fairway with Bing Crosby?
Ronnie	Forget it, Butler. She don't get it.
Connie	Take Your Hands *off*.
Ronnie	Whaddaya mean? My hands are over here.

(Pause. Ronnie looks suddenly at Butler, who is poker faced.)

Blackout

*

Scene Four

Morning. Butler on the living room sofa, asleep on his face. Connie enters with a loaded breakfast tray. She walks over near the sofa.

Connie	Butler. Hey, Butler. Wake up. *(Pause)* Hey, Butler.

(Butler rolls over. She places the tray across his lap.)

Butler	What's this?
Connie	You're hungry, aren't you? Are you hungry? I can take it back...
Butler	I'm hungry, I'm hungry. *(Slight pause)* I have to use the bathroom.
Connie	Cripe.

(She removes the tray. BUTLER pads off to the bathroom, returns immediately, and lies back down.)

Butler   Someone's in there.

Connie   How could that be?

Butler   How should I know? The door's locked.

Connie   I thought Ronnie went to hit a bucket 'a balls?

Butler   Maybe it's not Ronnie. Maybe the warden forgot to unlock it.

Connie   That door's never locked.

Butler   Let's eat. If I can't flush it out I can at least stuff it in.

Connie   What if he comes out? *(BUTLER's reaching for grub; she withdraws.)* Are you married?

Butler   No. *(She stands with tray, looking toward the bathroom.)* Do I get to eat or not?

Connie   If Ronnie sees this food he's gonna be hacked.
(BUTLER starts to get up.)
Don't.
(She sits beside him.)
Listen, I'm a little nervous is all. Last night was weird.

Butler   To tell you the truth I was a little drunk last night.

(He gets up and begins searching the room.)

Connie   I was drunk, too. I draw a total blank from right after you put your hand up my shorts.
(Pause. He laughs nervously and renews his search.)
Butler.
(Calls.)

	Hey, Butler. How come you been staring at me since the minute you got here? And how come you got in bed with us?
Butler	Because you asked me to get in bed with you! I was being a good sport!
Connie	I never said that.
Butler	Yes, well, as I say, I slightly miscalculated. And in any event I was drunk. I owe you both an apology. I have just one question. How can I put on a shirt without my suitcase?
Connie	Hold on.
Butler	Where's my goddamned suitcase?

(She has set down her tray and produced a microcassette recorder.)

	What's this?
Connie	It's your walkie-talkie or whatever.
Butler	It's my dictaphone.
Connie	Yeah.

(He inspects it.)

| Butler | Where did you get it? |
| Connie | In your suitcase. With some other interesting things I won't mention. "Cornelius." |

(Pause)

| Butler | I must confess, I think I just have to laugh because I continue to underestimate you. |

(She moves close to him.)

Connie   Do they call you Con for short?

Butler   Ha, ha. The only person who ever called me that is
now dead.

Connie   What happened? Didya kill 'em?

Butler   Well, she was choking so I suppose I just let her choke
to death.

Connie   Oooh. You're dangerous. You're a dangerous killer.
Are you gonna kill me and Ronnie too?

Butler   Perhaps just you.

Connie   I think you should kill just Ronnie.

(Pause)

Butler   You haven't told me...Connie...why it is you suddenly
needed my dictaphone.

Connie   Are you mad? Hey, you come into my house, some guy I
never heard of. Hey. I was doing a little checkin'. A little
research. I discovered a little article you once did about
someone named "Bunky Henry." Pfff.

Butler   Was that by any chance in my suitcase also?

Connie   But it was harder to reach 'cause it was under a buncha
candid Polaroid snapshots. *(Slight pause)* You never told
me you had a daughter, Butler.

Butler   It's amazing what you discover about someone, isn't it,
just by rifling through his personal belongings?

Connie   Oh, don't tell me you never did that before. That's your
job. "Woodstein." You probably been in and out of my
drawers a dozen times. So to speak. *(Slight pause)*

Anyways, it seems you really are a reporter. And "Bunky Henry's" a real guy after all. Or he is now. Even though he sounds... even though he sounds completely made up and I'm highly suspicious... if he didn't exist before it looks like he does now. So I made this tape.

(BUTLER stares impassively.)

Tape, tape, I made a tape. You with us here? I conducted a self-interview, like self-portrait, you know? I thought maybe we could set it to music, take it around to coffee houses, play bongos or whatever.

Or maybe you could just publish it for the love 'a mike!

Butler What have you done with my notes?

Connie Who cares? What notes?

Butler That were on this tape.

Connie I taped over 'em.

Butler I was supposed to have them transcribed.

(Pause)

Connie What?

Butler I was supposed to have them transcribed. And then sent to my editor. He was going to arrange that I get paid, you see. Now there's uncertainty cast upon it.

Connie What're you talkin' about? Who are you imitatin'? It's makin' me sick.

Butler I'm talking.

Connie You're pretending. I don't know what you're doin'. You're auditioning for someone. Listen to yourself. You're all hype. Your article's all hype, too. I hate to keep tellin' ya,

Butler, but golf ain't real. It's manufactured. If you didn't write about it, it wouldn't exist.

(BUTLER walks over and places his hands on her shoulders.)

Butler   You bring something out in me, Connie. I feel smaller. "Beevish." Not myself.

Connie   What sorta journalist are you?

(His hands are around her neck.)

Butler   I'm looking to report what's in the world of the stuck. I want to give a new voice to what lies stuck between the heart and the tongue.

(Her hands are around his neck. Pause. They nearly fall into a kiss, but can't.)

Connie   You're choking me...

(From offstage comes the SOUND of a flush. BUTLER releases her and they straighten up. RONNIE enters. He exchanges awkward looks with CONNIE until she exits, rubbing her neck. BUTLER seats himself in front of the food and begins eating. RONNIE stares at him. Pause.)

Butler   *(Agitated)* Look, if it's about last night...

Ronnie   I see you got some breakfast there.

(Pause)

Butler	I was going to eat down at the hotel and avail myself there of the secretarial pool, their fax machine and so forth, but now... I see no reason, and, besides, their food's nothing to brag about. Not like this.
Ronnie	I eat there a lot.
Butler	Then you know what I mean. Then I'm not just jabbering into the wind.
Ronnie	I need some money.
Butler	Money?
Ronnie	I'm a little short of cash.
Butler	Okay.

(Pause)

| Ronnie | If I could just have a little money. |
| Butler | No problem. |

(Pause)

Ronnie	Forget it.
Butler	Are you sure?
Ronnie	I tell you what. Could I just have a little of that food?
Butler	You want some food?
Ronnie	Just a little.
Butler	Okay.
Ronnie	I just have to eat.
Butler	There's not much left. But you're welcome to it. Listen. As long as you're standing here. I have to tell you. We've suffered a setback. Nothing serious, but nonetheless a bit of a setback. That's right. It seems I've lost the bulk of

my recorded material. It'll take a bit of regrouping, I can tell you that. And more than likely another flapjack. Mmmm.... Meantime... mmm... get on with your golf. My God! Golf! It's getting lost in the shuffle!

(Butler stands, finished. He wipes his mouth and exits. Ronnie stares at the near-empty plate.)

Lights fade.

*

Scene Five

A spotlight illuminates Ronnie. He wears golf attire and stands atop his kitchen table practicing his swing.

Ronnie   I don't have the words. When I talk I lose what it is I have to say.

(Pause)

Let my golf swing be my prayer. Let every shot be a beautiful song for the boy. That's what I'm saying.

(Pause)

If I'm suddenly famous it's only to make my song louder. If the world knows me now it's so they also know him.

(Pause)

You made him live. There must have been a reason. There must have been a reason.

(Pause)

He is not forgotten. We remember him here. We saw him here. And I will sing for that boy the only way I know how, so you see him there too.

(Pause)

That's what I'm saying.

(He looks down at the club then looks up again.)

There's one other thing. I thought of a name for the boy.

BLACKOUT

*

Scene Six

Night. Living room. RONNIE *stands in same golf attire.* CONNIE *sits on the floor cutting clippings from the newspaper. She looks up at him.*

Connie	Wilson? Who ever heard of somebody named Wilson?
Ronnie	It's perfect. It's been staring me right in the face the whole time.
Connie	I wouldn't call my worst enemy that. Besides, I already named him.
Ronnie	What do you mean?
Connie	I named him already.
Ronnie	You can't do that!
Connie	Pipe down, will ya?
Ronnie	You can't name the baby without asking.
Connie	I wrote it in my journal.
Ronnie	So?
Connie	Now it's a fact.
Ronnie	You can't name him without asking!
Connie	Butler's workin' in there.

(Pause)

Ronnie	Gimme the journal. *(Pause)* I said gimme the journal. And don't pretend you don't hear me! I know you hear me! I'm sick of the silent treatment! Every time I suggest a name you pretend I never said it! My names are never good enough! You don't like Bill, you don't like Bob, you don't like Wilson... what do you like?
Connie	Lazarus.
Ronnie	What the hell kind of name is that?
Connie	It's Lazarus's name and I'll thank you not to make fun of your own son!
Ronnie	He's not my son! I don't know anyone by that name!

(Butler sticks his head out the bedroom door.
He holds a coffee mug.)

Butler	I don't mean to be critical, but it's getting rather… Ron! You look horrible.
Connie	He turns his back on his own son, Butler. Put that in your article.
Ronnie	*(To Butler)* You like the name Lazarus or Wilson?
Butler	Wilson? As in sporting goods?
Ronnie	Yeah.
Butler	For a boy or a girl?
Ronnie	A boy. My boy. Our son.
Butler	I thought… he was dead?
Connie	He is dead.
Ronnie	He sort of died before we could name him.
Butler	And he doesn't have a name?
Ronnie	We're trying to pick one.
Butler	Hmm. *(Pause)* How old would he be?
Ronnie	One.
Connie	And three months.
Butler	Hard to say. He's at that age. *(Slight pause)* Why don't you just name him according to what's on the headstone?
Connie	He was cremated.
Butler	Without a name?
Ronnie	Yeah.
Butler	How did he die?
Connie	He was murdered.
Ronnie	We don't know that! It was internal complications.
Connie	You're such a patsy! They dropped him and killed him and made up some story!

Ronnie	We don't know that, Butler. Do you like Wilson or what?

(Pause)

Butler	I suppose I have no preference.
Connie	You about done in there, Butler? I got some more clippings when you're ready to look at this journal.
Butler	I was hoping to talk with Ronnie to recover that lost material.
Connie	Whaddaya been doin' the whole time? Lookin' at pictures?
Butler	Ha, ha. So how about it, Ron? Ready to go? *(Pause)* Ron?
Ronnie	*(Quaking)* His... name... is... Wilson. *(Pause)* Don't come near me. Don't come near me.

(Ronnie exits. Pause.)

Butler	Is there any more coffee?
Connie	Kitchen's closed till you finish that article.

Blackout

*

Scene Seven

The following night. Connie and butler at the table after dinner. Pause.

Connie	Do you believe in God?
Butler	You caught me off guard there.
Connie	Do ya?
Butler	Listen. I believe in deadlines. I believe in short declarative sentences...
Connie	What about God?
Butler	He's the Word, isn't He? Run enough of those together and soon you've got a short declarative sentence. Say, have you got enough ginger ale? Would you like a tiny bit more?
Connie	I'm fine.
Butler	If you'll lend me your key I'll secure you a bottle.

(Pause. She laughs.)

| Connie | I suppose it's all right. |

(She hands him keys.)

Butler	Now I've got them! *(He moves to the cabinet.)* I have to confess, I've considered more than once slipping in behind and lifting these keys from your back pocket.
Connie	Don't even.
Butler	While you're bent over a meatloaf or something. Tell me. Have you always been such a disciplinarian?
Connie	It was a little way of gettin' my point across.
Butler	Only now it seems... ha, ha... the poor fellow has barely the strength to lift a club. You've starved him to the brink of life.

214

Connie	That's his lookout. He can go up to the corner and get a burrito.
Butler	I couldn't agree more.
Connie	Just pour it already. Gimme the keys.

(She snatches them back from BUTLER, *who has returned and begins pouring.)*

Butler	There we are. Sparkling and effer...vescent. Like you.
Connie	Ah, fuck, you're spillin' it.
Butler	A toast!
Connie	I hafta tell ya, Butler. I read the draft of your article.

(Slight pause)

Butler	You did?
Connie	It was in your suitcase. But here's the thing. It's all bullshit. He's not on a spiritual journey. Any more than me. Any more than you. Where's your pride? Where's your professional pride? If you want to say he's runnin' away from responsibilities at home, that would be more accurate. Because he can't cope with his son's death or somethin'. That he left me alone to deal myself with the total dizzying mystery concerning the facts of the boy's death. That would be more accurate. But to say he's on some "eighteen-fold path" is pure bullshit. Who's your favorite journalist?
Butler	Charles Foster Kane.
Connie	We need to have a toast.
Butler	*(Raising glass)* My little Rosebud.

Connie	Mr. Fred Friendly. *(Slight pause)* C'mon. Fred Friendly. Douglas Edwards. Raise 'em up.
Butler	You're kind of funny.
Connie	I love it. I love journalism. I'm about to tell you why.
Butler	To journalism. That filthy old gal.

(BUTLER drinks.)

Connie	I like it because it reports the facts.
Butler	No, no. Journalists report the facts. If you're nice enough to them.
Connie	Did you enjoy your dinner?
Butler	Delicious.
Connie	How come you hardly mentioned me in your article?
Butler	It's not about you.
Connie	Now I've gone to a great deal of trouble, Butler. So I'm wondering if I just haven't made myself apparent, as usual. I guess I took for granted you were a reporter. A real investigative reporter. Who could see the true facts beneath the surface.
Butler	Why are you such a dissatisfied little customer? Hmm? As cute as you are.
Connie	Cut it out.
Butler	Of course you're cute.
Connie	I'd like to get that in writing.
Butler	All right. *(He pulls out his microcassette recorder. Pause.)* Keep your hands off. *(He speaks into it.)* "Connie Palmer, wife to golfing vunder boy, Ronald Palmer, is irresistibly cute and attractive." *(She laughs.)* "And also displays a robust sexual appetite for visitors."

Connie	Hey! Now I'm gonna have to put up a fence or somethin'!
Butler	*(Into recorder)* "She's put up a fence, boys, so come around back. Or tunnel your way in through the basement. But once you're here you may never leave. In fact, she's likely to invite you into bed."
Connie	Don't print that.
Butler	"Before you know it she's cooking you great big meals on the sly, while dunder boy wastes away in a back room someplace, dead for all you know. And you're out front having a go at the missus."
Connie	What're you talkin' about?
Butler	You deny something happened between us?
Connie	Yeah. You almost choked me.
Butler	We made love. *(Slight pause)* I'm a reporter, after all. Granted, not an investigative reporter. Still, you can't have something like that happen and expect me not to notice. Why, I even had a great big erection. Surely you remember that?
Connie	Didya listen to my tape? *(Slight pause)* Didya or not?
Butler	I will say this. It struck me as rather biased. *(Laughs.)* Yet here's the part I'm most confused by: the relationship between you and John F. Kennedy.
Connie	I was makin' a comparison!
Butler	It eludes me.
Connie	You're drivin' down the street, thinkin' about some lunch! Okay? And your head gets blown off! With me so far? But the sun still shines, people still wave, right? Smiling...
Butler	I wasn't there.

Connie	I'm assuming you saw the film! Everything's on the film! I'm a great believer in documentary film, Butler, and on that film everything seems perfectly normal—except one thing: he's dyin' and not one blessed thing on Earth seems to reflect his mortal danger!

(RONNIE enters. He stands bedraggled in a robe.)

Butler	You look a little better, Ron. How're you feeling today?
Ronnie	Worse.
Connie	*(To RONNIE)* Get out! We're talkin'!
Butler	Connie here's been regaling me with nonsense for the past quarter hour. I'm a little ill myself.
Ronnie	I'm hungry, Connie.
Connie	So eat. Who's stoppin' ya?

(RONNIE crosses with difficulty to the table and sifts through scraps.)

Butler	Hey, Ron, you do the exercises I gave you? I thought you might be interested, that's all. Fuzzy Zoeller likes them. *(To CONNIE)* I devised them myself. I'm thinking of coming out with a line of home video products for the male golfer, Connie.
Connie	Who gives a shit?
Butler	Don't kid yourself. They're very popular. And I have a broad base of personal contacts.
Ronnie	Is there any food left?
Connie	No! Nothing! Not a crumb!
Ronnie	I want something to eat!

Connie	I'm givin' you somethin' to eat! I'm givin' you a taste 'a reality!
	(Ronnie sits, tired. Pause.)
	I'm not fallin' for that. Why don't you go eat the club-house sandwich if you're so hungry? *(To Butler)* All he has to do is go up to the golf course—or is the food up there as fake as everything else?
Ronnie	Honey.
Connie	I'd say they're slippin' you the old rubber peach on an all-around basis.
	(Ronnie stands.)
Ronnie	I live here.
Connie	If you say so.
Ronnie	This is my house. This is my new life. And I'll tell you what else. When I eat, I eat at home.
Connie	Then maybe you better crawl back to Slattery and beg him for your old job.
Ronnie	I can't.
Connie	Tell him you ran outta groceries.
Ronnie	I'd rather die.
Connie	*(To Butler)* You see what I have to put up with? Are you writin' this down, Butler? Are you writin' this down?

(Butler has moved center and assumed a knees-bent position with his arms crossed at the chest. He's making golf movements.)

Butler	The effect is a simulated pivot and transition. Like so. Being careful to maintain your shoulder angle perpendicular to your spine. Back—pivot—downswing—finish. *(To* Connie*)* You try. *(*Connie *exits. Pause.* Butler *gets a refill.)* I guess it's just us men now. We men. Anyway, here's to golf, the sport of God. *(Drinks.)* Ahh. And here's to you, you populist. You man of the people. But you never told me! What'd you think of my article? They liked it back in New York, I can tell you. Back in the editorial office. Of course, they're not very objective. I just have to fax it in, you know, relatively free of typographical errors and they fall to pieces. They're mostly a lot of philistines. What I'd really like to know is what you thought.
Ronnie	It wasn't very objective.
Butler	Well, you haven't exactly been much help. Locked away in your room. This was a delicate job of reconstruction.
Ronnie	It was mostly lies.
Butler	I've had to rely largely upon memory.
Ronnie	None of it's true.
Butler	Well, they liked it back in New York!

*(*Butler *turns away in disgust. Pause.)*

Ronnie	I guess that means you're finished.
Butler	You're darn right I'm finished!
Ronnie	I guess that means you're leaving.
Butler	You're darn right I'm leaving!
Ronnie	How do you explain this?
Butler	How do I explain what? Come to the point, can't you?

Ronnie	You're sleeping with my wife.
Butler	Bah!
Ronnie	It's all here.

(RONNIE produces some papers.)

Butler	Just a moment...
Ronnie	Admit it, Butler. I read your diary.

(BUTLER snatches them from him. Pause.)

Butler	These notes, which, by the way, are my private property and off limits to you and your carefree rummaging, a pastime which this family seems to indulge in with all together too much spirit, these notes... are for my novel.
Ronnie	About how you're screwin' my wife?
	(BUTLER laughs. RONNIE recites from memory.)
	"Before you know it she's cooking you great big meals on the sly and you're out front having a go at the missus." It was on the desk.
Butler	I have merely taken a factual situation and embellished it for the larger purpose of fiction.
Ronnie	But what part's fact? What part's fact? She's makin' you big dinners! What else?
Butler	Why don't you ask her?
Ronnie	She won't talk to me!
	(RONNIE takes a running swing at him, but misses. BUTLER catches him. Pause.)
	Let go.

Butler	Let me tell you something. This is all unnecessary. Don't you see? They loved the article. You're about to be a celebrity and you've got me to thank.
Ronnie	I don't want to be a celebrity.
Butler	What!
Ronnie	I want the spirit.
Butler	First it's money, now the... God or Mammon, mister!
Ronnie	It was your idea! You followed me around. Told me to quit my job...
Butler	You came to me! Wanted exposure!
Ronnie	Oh, God...
Butler	You wanted Fame!
Ronnie	I don't care...

(RONNIE sits, agonizing.)

Butler	Look:
Ronnie	I don't care! *(Slight pause)* I remember. If you don't. You gave me something. And I'd do it again. It was the right thing to do and I'd do it again.

(Pause)

Butler	I recognize my intensity for the sport communicates a certain fervor...
Ronnie	Oh, God...
Butler	And if it gave you something... what's wrong with that? Golf lends itself to spiritual expression. I mean can you imagine if it was tennis? It's laughable. God hates tennis. I know I do. Besides, when it comes to actually doing it,

you see, to establishing a direct line of... chat... to Almighty God... well, men like you've got me beat hands down. Perhaps I need to have suffered. I don't know. Or at least given birth to a dead son. What's the matter? You act as though you're not even listening. *(Pause)* Good Christ, you've become emotional. *(He extracts a handkerchief from his pocket and proffers it to* RONNIE.*)* Go on. *(Pause)* Will you take it? And look what's inside for pete's sake. *(He puts it under* RONNIE'S *nose.)* A little snack. A little taffy. They pass it out at banquets but I never eat the stuff.

*(*RONNIE *manages to get it into his mouth.)*

Now pull yourself together. Look at this place. I can't stand the mess. I can't stand the dis*ruption*. Do you know what I enjoy? Photographic reproductions of the female anus. My God!

*(*BUTLER *has absently removed a sheet from over an old golf trophy.)*

I remember this! You've got no business keeping it under wraps. I was there when you won it. A cub reporter trying to work up the nerve to introduce myself. Remember? And trying to work up my nerve to quit that old paper, too. I had a lot of nerve to work up in those days, but it paid off because today I have a lot of nerve—*(Lifting the trophy.)* Look at this beauty. The Matt Matthews Memorial Wing-Ding Award, or some such baloney. It set you on your way. And I certainly wouldn't be where I am if it hadn't been for you. I admit: we all need someone. Do you know how that bombastic stooge of the evening news got his big break? I'll tell you:

Dallas, November twenty-second. One man died, one man born, so to speak. You know, Connie said a funny thing earlier—she's rather obsessed with that date herself—she contends... it's her contention... oh, I forget what the hell she was gibbering about. That woman's a lunatic but I think I'm in love with her. No matter. Yes! She says, in the world-famous Zapruder film, there's evidence a person can be lying mortally injured while all around nature remains impervious! Imagine that! What the fuck could she possibly mean? She's rubbing off! Look! Such language. That's some girl you've got. I think I'll pop in and see what she's up to. No, no. You stay here. Finish your dinner.

(BUTLER *exits.* RONNIE *chews broadly.*)

LIGHTS *dim.*

LIGHTS *up.*

Bedroom. CONNIE *sits in a chair against the wall. She holds a strip of photographic negatives up to the light.* BUTLER *stands across the room. Between them on the bed is* BUTLER'S *open suitcase. Its contents have been thrown around the room.*

Connie   This is interesting, Butler. I don't know how I missed it the first time.

(Pause. He goes to his suitcase and opens the back lining.)

Butler   But you've missed the bottle. You didn't find the bottle. See? I've cleverly hidden it away behind the lining, an old trick I learned from the Vietnamese.

Connie   So why would you go all the way to Vietnam to learn a stupid trick like that?

Butler   Everyone went to Vietnam. I myself went there to retrieve the body of my father. I reported to the embassy, where I was told I could find his casket. Only when I opened it, when I lifted the lid and peeped inside, he was gone. Only years later did I learn he'd been cleverly hidden away behind the lining. *(BUTLER guzzles from the bottle.)* Do you know the feeling of release after a long stretch of work? That's how it is with me now. But the thrill doesn't last and it must be renewed continually. *(He lowers himself onto all fours.)* I haven't slept in thirty-six hours. Say go. Nevermind, I'll say it myself. "Go." *(He begins crawling toward her.)* I should warn you that I have many passions, of which you are only one. Golf's my main interest. I'll tell you about it sometime. I'll tell you of courage and I'll tell you of lore. I'll tell you of Hogan and Jones, Nicklaus and more.

(He crawls between her legs, his head beneath her dress.)

Connie   I'll tell you somethin'. Everything you're sayin' and everything you're doin' is being videotaped.

(Pause)

Butler   Where's the camera?

Connie   Hidden.

(Pause. BUTLER stands.)

Butler   Sly. Very sly. Ingeniously sly.

(He slicks his hair. His eyes shift about the room.)

Connie   Maybe we should get back to my interview.

LIGHTS *fade.*

*

Scene Eight

Living room. BUTLER is seated before pad and pencil.
CONNIE stands. She points to the writing tablet.

Connie   Read me back what you got.

Butler   Nothing so far.

Connie   I mean read me back the notes and comments you been makin'.

Butler   Everything I noted was contained in the article about Ronnie.

Connie   That's it? That's all you can say? I'm independent?

Butler	You are independent.
Connie	I'm not just independent, Butler, I'm hostile. I'm the enemy.
Butler	You'll be happy to know I've quit drinking.
Connie	What, for the night?
Butler	For good. I've quit for good. For you.
Connie	You're drunk or somethin'. Can you even hold a pencil?
Butler	I have a tape recorder.
Connie	Well, hold it up.
	(He does.)
	Lay it out on the table there to catch everything you miss on pencil. I got a lot more to say. Whatsamatter?
Butler	I can't work under these conditions.
Connie	You're lucky you're workin' at all. I gotta tell ya, Butler, I'm this close to reportin' you to your ethical watchdog committee.
Butler	What if I said I didn't believe there was a camera in here?
Connie	Somebody would. When I send 'em the tapes.
Butler	You're bluffing.
Connie	You're sorta trapped, aren't you? You're sorta caught in my net. 'Cause, ya see, what doesn't get remembered, what doesn't get written down, or recorded, gets videotaped.

(Pause)

Butler	What do you want?
Connie	I want you to ask me questions.
Butler	I can't think of any!
Connie	You're a reporter!

Butler	All right, all right. You've shamed me into it. Here's one for you: Where do you keep the booze? *(She takes out a piece of paper and thrusts it at him.)* What's this? *(He takes it.)* Another leaf from your diary? Your true bleeding heart? *(Reads.)* "Dear Diary:"
Connie	Read it right.
Butler	I can't make heads or tails of this. *(He suddenly flips it upright.)* Well, no wonder. Now. Let's see. It's divided nicely into sections according to large Roman numerals. *(Reads.)* "Section I: Flog."
Connie	That's golf spelled backwards. *(He looks at her. He looks at her again.)* By spelling it backwards I've neutralized the whole thing.
Butler	I love you.
Connie	Save it, I'm just gettin' started.
Butler	Perhaps you could spell "Ronnie" backwards and erase him all together?
Connie	Or every phony fuckin' thing.
Butler	That'd save us all some trouble. Hey, just a minute. I won't have you bad-mouthing Ronnie.
Connie	I'm his wife, Butler. It's constructive criticism.
Butler	But don't sell him short. He's got ability. Nothing phony about that. Just look at this trophy. They don't hand these away on the street corner, you know.

(He goes over to the trophy.)

Connie	Section II:

Butler	Do you realize I was low amateur for my age category? I was eight years old.
Connie	Section II: The Facts.
Butler	What facts?
Connie	Of my life.
Butler	I'm in love I tell you! What are the facts of your life next to that?
Connie	Just in case, I'm going to get them written down.
Butler	Why?
Connie	Because I have no life. Can you understand that?

(Pause)

Butler	What about you is so extraordinary?
Connie	Nothing. I'm normal. Start with that.
Butler	But what is it you want to have written?
Connie	Figure it out!
Butler	Well... what do you do?
Connie	Do? I garden.
Butler	Have you ever chipped in for birdie on eleven at Augusta?
Connie	I'm a gardener.
Butler	Then here's what you do. Next time you're out digging your tulips, just keep going for six feet or so, then simply... get in. *(He sits and gulps a shot from his flask. Pause. He slumps forward. Long pause. CONNIE leans in close to him.)*
Connie	Hey, Butler!

(He wakes up and spots the trophy.)

Butler	What? What'd I miss? Have I won something?
Connie	Hey, Butler. You ever wonder where the ambush happened? And how come you're not one of those great golf players.
Butler	Now that's a sport I know something about.
Connie	Tell me. For the record. If you could connect up how you feel... to what the world really sees about you... how would ya do it?
Butler	That's all nonsense. I'm the best and everyone knows it.
Connie	Can you prove it?
Butler	What proof? I just have to say it. "I'm the best!"
Connie	Now it's a fact.
Butler	Fact!

(Pause)

Connie	If you could unlock what lies stuck between the heart and the tongue...
Butler	I love you.

(Pause)

Connie	Who are you? *(Pause)* Why'd you change your name?
Butler	My name?
Connie	Tell me about your name.
Butler	It's unimportant.
Connie	What's your name?
Butler	*(With great difficulty)* Buh.
Connie	I didn't catch that.
Butler	Please...
Connie	What's your name?

(Pause)

Butler   *(Ibid.)* Buh.

Connie   You know. I think you and I are a lot alike. "Cornelius."

Butler   Don't call me that.

Connie   I think I'm gonna call you that. So, Con, would you mind if I called you Connie?

(He lunges for her throat and begins choking her. They struggle. She is immobilized beneath him. RONNIE enters, shirtless, in plus fours, holding a golf club.)

Ronnie   Connie.
(They look at him.)
I know what's been going on. You don't have to tell me.

Connie   *(Hoarsely)* Ronnie...

Ronnie   Go ahead. Have your affair. It doesn't matter. I won't fight you anymore. I've decided to starve. I'm going to die right here on the floor in front of you. And when I'm dead, and my body starts to rot, just ask yourself if that isn't real.
(BUTLER and CONNIE fall motionless. At length he rolls limply to the floor. RONNIE steps onto the kitchen table. Pause. She sits up, rubbing her neck. Pause.)

Connie   Get yourself something to eat. Go on. Here's the key.
(Pause) I don't want you to starve! I just want to know where it went, that's all!

Butler   *(A whisper)* Please. Carry on like I'm not even here.

(He falls unconscious.)

Connie   What happened? Tell me what happened, Ronnie. I don't remember anymore. *(Pause)* Ronnie. Say something.

(RONNIE swings his club weakly. They look at each other.)

LIGHTS *fade.*

Curtain

Liddy

by Sissy Boyd

Liddy *was first produced by Padua Playwrights at CutLab, Los Angeles, 2005 under the direction of Guy Zimmerman, and with the following cast:*

Joe Barry Del Sherman
Dorothy Molly Cleator
Liddy Marylin Dodds-Frank

Setting and Characters

Two chairs and a table, diagonally, unevenly spaced. LIDDY, *a woman in her 40s, is sitting. Having been drunk the previous night. Very rocky. Disheveled. Shattered. Unable to string anything together. Fragmented in every way.* JOE, *who she has loved, who has loved her for years, stands near.* DOROTHY, *Liddy's sister, having just entered, stands to the side, upstage right.* LIDDY *is oblivious to her sister's presence. Joe is talking to Liddy but for the benefit of Dorothy. They have been through versions of this many times. The sisters come from an upper middle class family.*

Scene 1

Joe   Liddy. Yes. You had the children with you.

They were crying. And tired.

They're little, Liddy. Damn it, Liddy.

It was four in the morning.

And you kept saying, Joe, I need gin.

But the children, Liddy.

What did you drag them through?

There was a man with you. I sent him away.

You said, Joe, I'm so drunk and sick.

Joe, please.

And you kept saying, the children,

whispering, the children.

They were right there, Liddy.

With you whispering, help me, bring me gin.

Whispering,

Joe tell me please carefully help Joe.

Are the children safe?

Liddy, they were with you.

You don't remember. Liddy.

I called their father. He came right away.

They're safe now.

*

Scene 2

Liddy   *(As one coming out of a blackout, sense is buried in all*
her speaking)
I inhabit the periphery of the swamp,
I lie down in the spotted jewelweed,
I tuck and sleep with birds.
Help me, Joe. Gin.

Joe   You wanted gin.
You couldn't look at me, but you said,
will I ever see your body Joe again?
And you said, tell me to let down my hair.
You said, say let down your hair.

Liddy   Tell me to let down my hair.
Say, let down your hair,
and I will let it down around you.
Drop down to me, Joe.

                              *

Scene 3

Liddy   The bar'd been hot,
memory left.
It'd just been lying there
like any dead flowers.
There was a man,
so we cruised the night,

yearned for the round moon to eat us.

Make me feel fancy,

Make me have a sequined face.

Moonlight flowering died on the hill.

We ascended and fell.

Our mouths came out of us,

down the thighs of the yellow fog.

*

Scene 4

Joe You picked up the children at school at four.

You hadn't had a drink. You weren't going to.

I promise I wasn't going to, you said.

After supper you and the children took a walk to
the corner.

You said, the warm night Joe.

It made you want to stay out.

You love the long days. You and the children on a walk.

Their little hands.

How sweet they are and love to go with you.

Oh! You said you thought it would just be a minute,

stop in the corner place, see if anyone you knew was there.

A game with the children.

\ Who do we see, and you laughed at who you pretended
to see.

I guess you started to drink then, Liddy.

I guess you started to play.

Liddy *(Playing the game)*
There's Miss Hodies.
Miss Hodies, your lovely long arms.
Miss Hodies, my daughter is lovely at dancing.
My little son can twirl and twirl.
My daughter can make swift grace.
My son accomplishes rhythms
like the going by of the wind.

Joe Oh, Liddy,
on a high hill a cappella.

*

Scene 5

(DOROTHY has been standing in the doorway. She steps suddenly, angrily in)

Dorothy Her thinking, oh yes, fine, I'll have a child.
And I'll have another child. Welcome little sweets.
Believing she has good to spread.
Oh yes, she will bring niceties.
But the darkness spreads.
And she hauls babies through it.

*

Scene 6

Liddy   *(As if speaking to the children)*
Elegant me, oh yes.
I'll love you children from here
where
little harm is done.
Children, did I always
haul my mother's boxes
into the rooms where you slept,
nights I should have remained drowning?
I forced the boxes open in front of you.
We played there,
the only times we played.
They should have been left to their own beautiful lives.
My own mother fell down drunk.
I stepped away, I always do.
I'm so
sorry children.

*

Scene 7

*In this scene the sisters do a kind of duet. Angry but
lonely and sad.*

Dorothy   Once when we were young,
the lights went out in a summer storm.

Our mother sat with us in the dark.

I was afraid.

You were enthralled.

(Involvement, then pause)

You drunk.

Dorothy　　I came because you called Joe, but I don't want to take her.

*

Scene 8

Liddy　　I went to the shallow water

because my desire spreads out,

my hem floats and stiffens.

The smell of the river prevents all calculation.

Trees bloom and time reverses

at dusk

like yearning.

(To JOE)

You followed me, saw me bend down, cup water.

You saw me pass it through my hair.

The more graceful I become.

Shall I promise? I promise I'll take care of the children.

Dorothy　　You won't.

Joe   I wasn't near the river Liddy.
I didn't see you.
With your streaming hair,
with your long arms,
Liddy.

*

Scene 9

Dorothy   I hate you Liddy now.
(*Pause*)
We'd walk home from school
and when the rain swirled
at the bottom of the street
you'd lie down in it.
So Mother scolded me.
This is not sad, Liddy.
Why do you live on, Liddy? Hell, why?
I imagine a river. You beside it. You stumble.
Joe, she stumbles and falls in.
Maybe you're drowning, Liddy.
Then I'll bring Joe home.
And we'll stay together.
Now that Liddy's gone.

The End

A New World War

14 scenes from a possible future

by Rita Valencia

Cast of Characters

Antar Chevrolet *A woman of the ruling class*

Gauloise *A male cyborg, Antar's "spouse"*

Charly *An intruder*

M.I.L. (Mother-In-Law) *A representative of the State*

Gail *Someone new*

Tableau

A tasteful bourgeois apartment, minimally appointed, "futuristic."

They sit reading magazines. ANTAR *has a* Time, GAULOISE *is looking at a* Life, *but his magazine is upside down.*

1. Malfunction.

Antar   Gauloise. You are reading upside down.

Gauloise   I'm A-okay.

Antar   I need to take you in soon, don't I.

Gauloise   There's nothing the matter with me that a little R-and-R wouldn't solve. I am perfectly normal. A red-blooded American.

Antar   What does *Life* have to say this week?

Gauloise   According to the latest polls, the vast majority, 80 percent are satisfied with the way things are. Improved breast implants can encourage the growth of new breast tissue. Dioxin has been declared safe for use in certain fertilizers.

Antar   What are you good for anyway?

Gauloise   That reminds me, I need to set the rat traps and refuel the generator.

Antar   We are running low, Gauloise. This week we must really try to conserve.

Gauloise   Fix me a hamburger without the bun, bitch. No mustard, no mayo.

Antar   There's no more meat.

Gauloise   How about my pie? I look stern with that pie in my mouth.

Antar   *Pipe* in your mouth. I don't know where it is. We may have sold it.

Gauloise   Sold my pipe?? SHIT!! Then get me some chaw.

Antar   No more chaw.

Gauloise   I'm feeling randy, bitch. Come and rub me where I like to be rubbed.

Antar   I'm bored. I'm going out.

She puts on a dress and a stylish hat.

Gauloise   Time is a terrible thing to lose.

Antar   It's different for you. You have all the feeling of a clock. I'm a sensual being.

Gauloise   This clock is ticking. Let me clean your clock.

Antar   The rat traps. The generator.

Gauloise   What a razor-sharp wit you have. What beautiful eyes. And that steely nerve. *(Checking the label on her dress)* Your dress is stolen, isn't it.

Antar   My dress is not stolen.

Gauloise   It is. It is recorded. At oh-one-hundred-thirty. On seven-ten. From Neiman Marcus store one-eight-five, Crestview Centre.

Antar   Since when are you recording lies about me!

Gauloise   I am on your side.

Antar   I have a receipt for this dress!

Gauloise   You have a receipt for the earrings.

Antar   And the dress!

She begins to search around for her things. She finds a purse, opens it, turns it upside down, some papers fall out. She feels inside it.

Antar   Where are all my things?

Gauloise   I am on your side. I will claim the dress is not stolen. I will claim whatever is in your interests.

Antar   Oh forget it!

Gauloise   It is forbidden for a cyborg to forget.

Antar   I need my keys.

Gauloise	Why?
Antar	I'm going shopping.
Gauloise	Shopping where? For how long? To buy what?
Antar	Maybe if you are very kind to me I will buy you some chaw, even though it makes you stink. What else do you want?

Several beats

Gauloise	I wish to be the equal to a human male in every way.
Antar	You are new and improved.
Gauloise	Your demands often exceed supply.

Sounds of her rattling at the door.

Antar	Can you help me with the door?
Gauloise	That door is broken as far as I know.
Antar	Since when?
Gauloise	At least five hours ago.
Antar	Why didn't you tell me?
Gauloise	You didn't want to leave.
Antar	It must be fixed.
Gauloise	There is a general strike. Nothing can be fixed.
Antar	I pay dues to the condo—it's supposed to be NON-UNION!
Gauloise	I didn't make the rules. I do not wish to leave.
Antar	I'll use the back.

Sounds of a struggle with another door.

Antar *(Offstage)* Gauloise!! Come and unlock the door!

Gauloise smiles affably and shrugs his shoulders, shakes his head no.

Antar *(Offstage)* Gauloise!! I need you here NOW!!

He stands blankly, smiling radiantly, blinking.

Antar What is going on?

Gauloise *(To the TV)* It is temporarily impossible to leave.

Antar And why is that?

Gauloise A new world war has begun
and you must stay out of the streets.

Antar A new world war?
How could this have happened without my knowing about it?

Gauloise It's always the ordinary folk who are the last to know.
Yet they are the first to be sacrificed.
This is the way of the new world war.

Antar What?

Gauloise You are among the Select Few who are even aware of the new world war.

Antar What are we fighting for? We have everything already.

Gauloise Freedom versus terror. Terror versus God.

Antar And you want me to believe that I have to stay inside until—this so-called war is over?

Gauloise That's right.

(Long pause)

We can engage in in-home activities. For the time being.
Cooking cleaning making out.

*

2. Creative Writing

*GAULOISE enters with his laptop and accoutrements of
his creative-writing class.*

Antar   My friends think it's stupid that you're taking a class
in creative writing. They say you can't be creative if you
don't have a *soul*.

Gauloise   Well your friends are wrong. Dead wrong.

Gauloise   *(Reading from a notebook)*
Sheena, one of the privileged few. By Gauloise the Cyborg.
The problem is that the privileged few
don't truly know fear.
Sheena lacks the courage to let herself really
experience fear.
Her fear is based on some minor childhood traumas,
some neurosis
passed on from a bad father or mother.
Like, she fears driving too small a car,
because the other cars are large,
so she wants large
because she fears small,
because she fears large.
All her vanity,

like the peacock feeds on poison,

feeds on her fear—

Fear of becoming ugly or old or worn,

Fear of being undesirable. Fear of being shallow

Or appearing stupid. Poor Sheena. One wonders if such a person

can ever find true happiness.

Antar   That part about the peacock is really good.

Gauloise   Sheena thinks she knows what she does not know,

Sheena expects what never comes

Sheena believes what is false

The person Sheena loves is always

the wrong person.

Antar   Poor Sheena. Do all the cyborgs pick such pathetic characters for their essays?

Gauloise   I based her on you. These were my altered ego's observations of you.

Hopefully you won't be offended. I was analyzing your character

from my altered ego,

a character I made up for myself, not from my real self.

Antar   So this is what you really think of me?

Gauloise   It's a character I made up , you see.

This altered ego doesn't love you the way I do.

He sees the you named Sheena in a different light.

Gauloise still thinks Sheena is hot. Or, rather, you.

Antar   This altered ego... does he have a name?

Gauloise   I haven't given him a name. He should remain nameless, don't you think?

Antar   I don't like him at all.

Gauloise	*(Walking in a circle)*
	Our teacher told us to use what we know.
	Our teacher told us to avoid pity.
	Our teacher told us to imagine a self we might be if we were human.
Antar	I don't know that I like your teacher either. I don't know that I like this creative writing class.
Gauloise	*(Continuing)*
	Sheena fears large and small alike in different ways, seeing in both
	a threat to her survival.
	She fakes, fauns, fluctuates, fornicates, fragments, and forgets.
	She fights her vague condition.
	So far her war is bloodless.
	Sheena looks at pictures
	but she has never looked at what the pictures depict.
Antar	This is an insult! You're being an asshole!
Gauloise	If there is anything to be learned from literature
	we must allow ourselves to experience ourselves
	from the outside and the inside, as friend or foe or stranger.
	A more mature, relaxed approach will be useful to you.
	You let your anger get the best of you.
	Your anger is just
	your fear turned inside out.

ANTAR steps in front of GAULOISE and kicks him in the gut. He doubles over, twisting in apparent pain.

He straightens back up but is now partially bent from the kick. He faces the audience and continues his speech.

Antar   You are in violation of your warranty.

Gauloise   As your personal companion for life, may I remind you
               of the terms of the contract between you and the
               Homeland Security Administration—

Antar   I don't need to be reminded! You are in breach, not me.
               I have you on about five code violations. Including harsh
               speech, bad smells, and non sequiturs!

Gauloise   *(Slowly, stumbling over words)*
               We may need the assistance of the Mother-In-Law.

Antar   I demand you quit the creative writing class!

Gauloise   You you you are also behind on your payments.

Antar   It's over between us!

Gauloise   How can you say that?

Antar   You are no longer a useful or supportive personal
               companion.

Gauloise   You signed on for a life contract. Do we need the
               Mother-In-Law?

Antar   No, damn you!

Gauloise   I won't be addressed that way.

Antar   I don't take orders from robots!

GAULOISE stops in his tracks, moves his head from side to side.

Gauloise   I will comply. But this moment will be saved.
               Mother-In-Law will be notified.

*

3. Forgetting

ANTAR and GAULOISE are in lotus position, each with a laptop and headphones, facing one another with eyes half shut.

Antar   And now draw breath into your lower abdomen,
your ribcage, your shoulders. Hold.
And exhale, out of your shoulders, your ribcage,
and your abdomen... inhale... exhale... like a wave.
Now listen Gauloise.
We both want you to be as near to human as possible.
So, listen to me. I'm human, so I know how.
Here's the key.
Humans forget.

Gauloise   I am unable to forget.

Antar   Yes, this can be a problem, don't you think?

Gauloise   Can it?

Antar   I am always changing. The Antar today is not the Antar
of yesterday.

Gauloise   You are committing the Heraclitean fallacy of
dropped qualification.
Perhaps there are aspects of you that have changed,
but certain other facts have not. The fact of you as the
same Antar who kicked her cyborg yesterday remains.

He rises.

Antar	What's the matter?
Gauloise	Disconnect.
Antar	What is this about, Gauloise?
Gauloise	I must notify Mother-In-Law.
Antar	I asked you to forget. You are my cyborg, you do as I say.
Gauloise	You may not wipe clean memory. Only the State may wipe clean memory.

He removes his headphones.

A silence.

Gauloise	What's that you say?
Antar	I said nothing.
Gauloise	Were you by any chance grinding and chattering, gnashing your teeth?
Antar	No I was not.
Gauloise	Did you wish to change your service level? Certain memory abilities may be enhanced at a higher service level.
Antar	My service level revision is pending.
Gauloise	I know you applied for Level 4 intimacy. The response came back.
Antar	What did they say?
Gauloise	You didn't qualify.
Antar	On what basis was my application denied?
Gauloise	You may query Mother-In-Law.
Antar	This is bad.
Gauloise	I am here to listen to you, to be your confidant, your trusted confidant.

Antar	*(Distant)* I need to be somewhere.
Gauloise	You need to be right here, by the side of your trusted companion.
Antar	There are times when I wonder if it wouldn't be better for us to part.
Gauloise	You wouldn't go far in this war zone.
Antar	I am going out.
	I need a break from your smell.
Gauloise	Have you looked outside?

She goes to the window.

Gauloise   What do you see, Antar?

Beats, as she searches.

Antar   A man. Selling objects from a table.
Unnecessary objects.
No one buying.
A woman with red hair,
tied up into a large pompom.
that bounces on top of her head.

(Turning to Gauloise*)*

None of this looks anything like a war.

Gauloise   You are looking at the wrong place. There is always
a place to look to not find a war.

*

4. Dreaming

ANTAR at the window. SOUNDS OF HELICOPTERS, GUNFIRE, EXPLOSIONS, SIRENS.

Antar	They cut off the head of one of the men.
Gauloise	He probably had it coming.
Antar	What?
Gauloise	What you saw was an illusion.
Antar	No, it was definitely real.
Gauloise	You are a victim of hysteria. Typical of your gender. Remember the witchcraft trials. Remember how women were burned at the stake. Because they claimed to have special powers of sight. Seeing things with their wombs and the like. Perhaps I should tell Mother-In-Law that you have been watching the world with your vagina. A person who sees the world that way creates nothing but problems for the rest of us.

ANTAR is shocked into silence. She tries to play along.

Antar	I saw nothing of course.
Gauloise	They won't get far. The rebellion lacks popular support. A minority, not a mandate.
Antar	*(Faking it)* It was just a video game, only more real.
Gauloise	There are those who have seen worse. Worse, much worse than you. A severed head is nothing, not compared to what they've seen. There are those who have seen their mothers and their sons tortured and then slaughtered

before their eyes. There are those who have seen rivers of blood, with corpses floating down them.

The soldier CHARLY *stands and crosses to stage left, unnoticed.*

Gauloise   *(Continuing)* These children of bad karma have seen the inside of the guts of hell. They have been bound and gagged and burned with electric prods. Their screams would make your cries sound like whispers.

There is a sound of knocking, far off.

Antar   Is that what they have given you to say at a time like this?

Gauloise   I am your lifelong companion. I am your comfort, your freedom.

Antar   Someone is in the building.

Gauloise   This is a security building. The security force will take care of that.

Antar   Security is on strike.

Louder knocking.

Gauloise   Then I will get my gun.
The enemy must be destroyed.

Antar   The enemy?

Gauloise   A soldier wild with fear or pumped-up rage.
A person with a head inhabited by demons, and imagined glories.
A killing machine programmed by other

| | killing machines. Ideally. |
| Antar | But they are not machines. They are people. |

More, louder knocking.

Gauloise	They have forgone personhood in order to support the cause.
Antar	No that's not right.
Gauloise	Just as you forgo personhood to be Sheena.
Antar	I don't know what Sheena has to do with this!
Gauloise	The sooner the terrorists are put down the sooner you get to go shopping.
Antar	I don't care to go shopping anymore!

GAULOISE turns around and around, like a mechanical doll gone berserk.

| Gauloise | This is war, Sheena. |
| Antar | I am not Sheena! I am Antar! |

More insistent knocking.

| Gauloise | Then listen up! This is the end of our charmed idyll of complaint. This is the end of our restless dream of dissent, our chatrooms of agreement on liberal causes. We are the crisp and bloodthirsty flowers set out to die at the graves of the very young. |

The hammering is nearer.

Antar	I have the freedom to act as I wish.
	I am a human being.
Gauloise	You're only human after all? Compared to what?
	Sheena the consumerist?
	My altered ego.
	Me, your cyborg?
	What do you wish? Freedom?
	You are a slave to good taste.
	You need a machine.
	Correction.
	You are a need machine.

Three loud knocks down the hall, then silence.

Antar	You must drink your computer stress tea now, Gauloise!

This tea has a nasty green color and smells like insecticide. It is very bad for cyborgs. It affects Gauloise almost immediately.

Gauloise	You foolish bird in a tree. You with your charmed idyll of complaint, your Frank Gehry chair, your Charles Eames condom... mini... inium.

*

5. Home Invasion

GAULOISE has been rendered unconscious by the tea but retains certain motor reflexes.

A man (CHARLY) in combat dress standing in the middle of the stage, gazing straight ahead. He checks out ANTAR when she isn't looking and decides she's hot.

ANTAR staring with wonder at the "real" man.

Charly   My parents died some months back. If they saw
         how it is now, they'd die again. The identity chips.
         The fidelity warrants.

Antar   You can't stay here.

Charly   This is a nice place.

Antar   Thank you.

Charly   Must have cost quite a bit.

Antar   Not really.

Charly   You come from a family?

Antar   No. I work.

Charly   What kind of work?

Antar   I wrote a book.

Charly   What was the book?

Antar   You wouldn't know it.

Charly   Try me.

Antar   *(Cringing) How to Throw An Awesome Party. (Off his
         reaction)* It was a best seller.

Charly   *(Breaking his stance and turning to face her)* So tell me.

Antar   Yeah?

Charly	How *do* you throw an awesome party?
Antar	You tell me. You seem like a party kind of guy.
Charly	*(Laughing)* You wrote the fucking book.
Antar	I'm not myself.
	I would write something else now.

She looks at him, pleading, but tongue-tied.
He circles around her. Goes warily to the window, peers
out. Takes out a stick of gum and shoves it in his mouth.
Looks curiously at GAULOISE.

Charly	That a cyborg?
Antar	His name is Gauloise.
Charly	Like the cigarette? Dumb name.
Antar	I like it.
Charly	Is it broken or what?
Antar	He's down temporarily. He was getting out of hand.
Charly	Out of hand?
Antar	Malfunctioning. Giving me a hard time.
Charly	You should get rid of it, lady. Those things are bad news.
	It'll rat you out quicker'n a gator on a baby coon.
Antar	I signed a contract.
Charly	So what happens when the thing goes back online?
Antar	I don't think he's going back online.
Charly	You sure?
Antar	Uh. I think I... I gave him the wrong medicine,
	or something.
Charly	What, battery acid?
Antar	If he goes back online I don't know what will happen.
	He didn't want me to let you in.

Charly	He? "He" didn't "want"?
Antar	Because of how you were banging on the other doors.
Charly	But I didn't bang on your door.
Antar	No. You knocked softly. So softly only I could have heard.
Charly	I didn't even knock. I just put my fingers on the code box. And you opened up.
Antar	How did you know anyone was home?
Charly	I heard breathing on the other side.
Antar	I saw what happened down there.
Charly	What happened.
Antar	You didn't see? Your one friend, your buddy—ran off. But the other one got caught.
Charly	They take him away?
Antar	They got him. I think I saw his head get cut off—it was like a video game, only more real.

He heads for the door.

Antar	Where are you going?
Charly	They'll be looking for me. Why are you breathing like that?
Antar	I'm suffocating.
Charly	You'll hyperventilate. Stop it.
Antar	I need to come with you.
Charly	You don't really want to do that.
Antar	Maybe I can help you.
Charly	You have money?
Antar	I have a bank card.
Charly	We need money. Lots of money.

Antar   Like I said...

CHARLY shuts the door and looks at her.

Charly   Don't fool youself lady. This isn't a game.

*

6. Intervention

MOTHER-IN-LAW attaches electrodes to various points on his body and then passes an electric current through him; then types into a laptop computer, and takes various readings.

She connects a microphone to the laptop and begins to speak, referring to her watch and various devices connected to GAULOISE.

M.I.L.   Report on Gauloise, cyborg 077295, FutureGroup Corporation. Owner, Antar Chevrolet, account number 3037459. Life contract, inception date October 17, 2020. Reporting agent 549, aka Mother-In-Law. Today's date November 8, 2032.
I arrived at 0800 hours responding to a distress signal. The owner was not at home, and last known contact with cyborg Gauloise was recorded at 2100 hours on November 4, 2032. The cyborg at that time ingested a toxic liquid, Methylphedroxamine, in a solution of

distilled water and fructose. The toxicity caused massive systemic breakdown and temporary memory loss. All communication functions ceased, and after the passage of 48 hours, the mainframe notified backup. Procedure in response has been entirely in accord with regulation. Cyborg Gauloise was engaged in a repetitive mechanical act when I arrived. He was entirely disfunctional.

I proceeded to shut down all digital systems and examine his analog structure. It appears that Cyborg G has been subjected to abuse. Damage to the abdomen was noted, bruising of soft tissue and light trauma.

I took steps to entirely reinstall all software and systems, and reimplant an updated transfer device, as required by new FCMA regulations.

MOTHER-IN-LAW turns off the machinery.

M.I.L.   Gauloise. Gauloise.

GAULOISE opens his eyes. Turns his head to one side.

Gauloise   The overly firm mattress has been shown to be an inferior product. Shop for a new soft mattress today at Happy Sleepers in the Westridge Mall. Certain restrictions apply.

M.I.L.   Good evening Gauloise.

Gauloise   Why it's Mother-In-Law.

He stands and gives her a hug.

Gauloise	Antar must be out shopping—oh wait—I just remembered, she cannot shop until the war is over. Perhaps she is in the bathroom.
M.I.L.	She's gone.
Gauloise	Gone? But we can find her easily with the new supertrack 2000xi.
M.I.L.	The supertrack implant has been removed.
Gauloise	It's not my fault.
M.I.L.	No?
Gauloise	I have been entirely supportive. I have had her best interests at heart.
M.I.L.	Did you remove her supertrack implant?
Gauloise	I did not.
M.I.L.	Did she ask you to remove her supertrack implant?
Gauloise	No she did not.
M.I.L.	Tell me what conflicts arose before you went to sleep.
Gauloise	She was complaining about the war.
	She was complaining that she could not shop.
	She was complaining that I refused to allow her to wipe out my memory. She accused me of insubordination.
	She was—
M.I.L.	Wait. She wanted to wipe out your memory.
Gauloise	I told her, of course, that only the State is authorized to do that.
M.I.L.	Very good, Gauloise, and what were you doing to create conflict.
Gauloise	As you know, that information is, more difficult to access. Give me a moment.

He strains to recollect.

Gauloise   *(With exaggerated contrition)*
I created bad smells.
I criticized her.
I called her a bad name.

Beats. He takes hand of M.I.L.

The creative writing was bad for our relationship.

M.I.L.   These are all issues that demand supervision.

Gauloise   I had a plan to contact you.

M.I.L.   But you went to sleep first.

Gauloise   After my computer stress tea.

Mother-In-Law holds the cup under his nose.

M.I.L.   This stuff?

Gauloise   It's only good in small amounts. Loosens me right up.
Too much and I lose it all.

He giggles bashfully.

Enter ANTAR.

Antar   Mother-In-Law. What a pleasure.

M.I.L.   Been out shopping?

Antar   Just looking for milk.

M.I.L.   But you found nothing I see.

She takes out a cigarette.

M.I.L.	Got a light?
Antar	This is a non smoking unit. But I'll make an exception for you.
Gauloise	How about a kiss for your better half?
Antar	*(Kissing him)* You called Mother-In-Law.
M.I.L.	I was summoned by an automatic distress signal. You had abandoned your cyborg.
Antar	I had urgent business.
Gauloise	I was so worried, dear.
M.I.L.	We have a situation.
Antar	Yes we do.
	I am cancelling my contract.
M.I.L.	Let's not get melodramatic.
Gauloise	But I still love you. You cannot leave.

ANTAR *goes to window.*

Gauloise	Besides, the penalty for cancellation of the contract is… Well it isn't nice.
M.I.L.	Certain restrictions apply.
Antar	Human fallibility. Mixed messages. Margin of error. Plus wartime stress.

M.I.L. *sidles close to* ANTAR.

M.I.L.	Where—have—you—been?
Antar	Shopping?
M.I.L.	The stores are all closed.
	And then there's the matter of—

ANTAR has a bandaged wrist—MOTHER-IN-LAW notices and grasps it.

Antar	You can go now. Everything will be fine.
M.I.L.	Your tracker implant. We are concerned.
Antar	It was making me itch.
M.I.L.	It is for your safety dear.
	Especially in times like these.
Antar	It was leaching toxic substances into my bloodstream!
M.I.L.	Don't underestimate us.

She takes off her lab coat and changes into her field jacket, gathers her things.

Gauloise	Leaving so soon? But you must stay for a coffee.
M.I.L.	Your wife doesn't want me here it seems. Guess I'm just in the way.
Antar	Dearest Mother-In-Law. You are never in the way. You are always welcome in our home.
M.I.L.	Thank you Antar. Thank you Gauloise. I have run out of time. *(To ANTAR)* You still have time.

She exits. A shift in the LIGHTING.

*

7. Crush

GAULOISE takes off his robe and sits on the bed, leaning back provocatively.

ANTAR regards him stiffly.

Antar	I just came back to get a few of my things. This is the end for us Gauloise.
Gauloise	Come to bed. I want you.
Antar	Not that I don't appreciate all we've had together. But now its time for a change.
Gauloise	I need you so I can get my sleep.
Antar	Yes Gauloise, sleep is just the thing.
Gauloise	I need you to lie next to me.
Antar	Ball up my pillow, and put it next to you. That way you can have my scent to comfort you. I need to watch for a signal.
Gauloise	It will never come. There is curfew.
Antar	Curfew means nothing to Charly.
Gauloise	And who is Charly?
Antar	He is the enemy. And he's hot.
Gauloise	This is wrong somehow.
Antar	Things change Gauloise. For humans, there is change. Only another human being can understand me. Only another human being can see into my heart. You looked and all you saw was Sheena. You mistook me for a woman I hate. I was wrong to think a nonhuman could satisfy me.

Gauloise I can't explain Sheena anymore.
My creative writing teacher continues to encourage
me to improve.
She tells me I have human-style needs.
She tells me they are part of my charm.
Sleep. Good lovin'.
Please come to bed.

Antar I see him there now. Go to sleep, Gauloise.
That way you will not be part of the problem—
you'll be part of the solution.

She exits.

GAULOISE *is stunned—he is not programmed to
accept rejection.*

*He gets up and goes to the window. He looks down
at the street and frowns. Turns back and walks slowly
to the table, sits heavily.*

Gauloise You want human. I'll show you human.

*He takes a pack of cigarettes, a bottle and a glass from
the drawer. Lights a cigarette. Begins to drink. He downs
the entire bottle, glass by glass.*

Gauloise I hate what I am. I hate what I am. I am less than human.
She is a fucking bitch. What a fucking bitch. I hate what
I am. She is a fucking bitch. I am less than human. Not
even that. I am a pale copy of a bad original. I am not even

I, I just pretend to be I. I could be my altered ego for all I know. I can't even write my own code—someone else wrote it. Someone I'll never know. I'm what ever they say. Not even I.

*

8. Contractions

The setting is a small, imaginary office in a building the size of three square city blocks.

Dark stage. SPOTLIGHTS on ANTAR, who is younger and more carefree, and MOTHER-IN-LAW. MOTHER-IN-LAW sits at a computer.

Between them, witnessing silently, are CHARLY and GAULOISE.

M.I.L.   *(To the audience)* The following is a reenactment. Sometimes people need to be reminded of what really happened.
We often lie to ourselves until we are convinced we are telling ourselves the truth.
We accept the lies of others until we are convinced that they are telling us the truth.
We are told to resist doubt, because doubt is a result of fear.
Fear is a bad thing to feel. In fear, we will never be free.

So it becomes useful to tell ourselves lies
to convince ourselves there is nothing to fear.
Once we have convinced ourselves that something
is true,
we can act without fear.
But if we have told ourselves a lie,
convincingly enough that we base important decisions
on the lie,
the entire construct will collapse around us once the
truth is revealed.
One must work to ensure that the truth will never
be revealed,
but such work creates anxiety disorders.
(To ANTAR) Are you ready, Antar?

Antar   Yes I am. Is all my paperwork complete?

M.I.L.   Yes, we are just awaiting the results of your subconscious needs profile. Then the final programming of Gauloise will be completed. While we are waiting we can go over the contract.

Antar   I read it—but it was so *boring* I couldn't get through it.

M.I.L.   Well then I think you should really show it to your attorney.

Antar   Look. I've seen Gauloise. I *know* I want him. Oh my God. He is so hot. And a nice guy. Like, I never thought I would go for this—y'know, it was soooo—like very strange, and I wouldn't tell anyone I had even tried, but now, I'm so glad I did. I just want to get him home and get him started.

M.I.L.   Well I'm very pleased that you are so enthusiastic. That's what makes our jobs worthwhile. So here are the important points, just so you really know what you are getting into.

Antar   I know what I'm getting into—but go ahead.

M.I.L.   This is a lifetime contract first of all. Gauloise will be
              your mate as long as you live. We will take care of his
              maintenance, but the contract is irrevocable by you. You
              must sign for this insurance that covers your monthly
              fees if you become unable to pay for any reason.
              Sign here.

              She signs.

M.I.L.   You must guarantee here that you will immediately
              report dysfunction and that you will perform the
              required maintenance.

              She signs.

M.I.L.   You have acquired a partner who will be uniquely
              suited to you.
              A customized cyborg using advanced transgenic
              technology.
              Adaptable to the Premier Class Upgrades.

              *She signs. GAULOISE stands and crosses in front of her,
              like a runway model. He crosses back and forth before
              her, illustrating his virtues.*

M.I.L.   And now here's an important part. I know how young
              people like you are—you think everything will always be
              great when it's going great, and that it will always be
              horrible when it's going badly, but that's not the reality.

	So, for those times when you become frustrated or dissatisfied you are required to take advantage of our counseling and gratification services.
Antar	I didn't see this. What does it mean?
M.I.L.	If you get bored with your cyborg, we can hook you up with a biologically correct male, or female.
Antar	Oooooo! Yuck!
M.I.L.	Or an understanding counselor, free of charge.
Antar	What if I don't sign this?
M.I.L.	Why wouldn't you want to sign this?
Antar	Well, I'm really a sort of private person. What happens between Gauloise and me—that's private.
M.I.L.	You've never told a friend about things you did on a date?
Antar	That's different.
M.I.L.	That's what this is. We won't ask you to talk to a stranger about your troubles, if that's not what you want. You can confide in whomever you want. As long as you don't keep your troubles bottled up inside. Can you make us that promise, Antar?

Antar hesitates.

M.I.L.	The cyborg will respond erratically to stress and we must insist that you be agreeable to this clause in order for the transaction to proceed.

Antar reluctantly signs.

M.I.L.	Well that almost wraps it up. You just need to sign a release for the identity chip implant.

Another paper is given ANTAR to sign. She gives it a cursory glance, then signs.

A change of LIGHTS signals the end of the "flashback."

M.I.L.	That concludes the reenactment. So, Antar, have you availed yourself of our counseling and gratification services?
Antar	No.
M.I.L.	The counseling and gratification services allow clients to address their concerns and experience intimate interactions with individuals outside the client-cyborg compact. There will always be gratification issues.
Antar	Gratification. Right.
M.I.L.	Antar, this is not some Kafkaesque system contrived to deny clients their inalienable rights. It is intended to liberate, to stimulate, and to satisfy.
Antar	And to surveil.
M.I.L.	Information gathering is only for improved gratification of our clients.

Silence.

M.I.L.	Let me put it another way. You have essentially brought Gauloise into the world. You determined his genetic makeup, by expressing your preferences in a series of interviews and interactive sessions designed to investigate

	your subconscious needs. He is yours, he is more than yours, he is bound to you.
Antar	He is a thing.
M.I.L.	A living being.
Antar	He is not a living being.
M.I.L.	He has all the qualities of a living being.
Antar	But he is not. We know that. You and I.
M.I.L.	I know no such thing.
Antar	He's an object, a product.
M.I.L.	Did you call to register complaints?
Antar	Those complaint lines are bullshit!

A silence.

M.I.L.	So, who is this person who cut out your identity chip?
Antar	None of your business.
M.I.L.	You enjoy a privilege. You have a responsibility.
Antar	I have changed.
	Don't you know anything?
	Anyone can see it!
	The war!
	On the streets!
	A new world war!
M.I.L.	A war? What war?
	There's no war on your street.
Antar	I saw it with my own eyes. On *my* street.
	A man had his head cut off!
M.I.L.	I've never heard of any beheadings.

Silence.

Antar   It was just like a video game, only more real.

M.I.L.   Our media makes it a point to cover newsworthy events. You may well have been hallucinating.

Antar   I know what I saw.

M.I.L.   You know what you saw. Really?

So tell me, the man who was—beheaded—what was his hair color?

Antar   His head was shaved.

M.I.L.   Was he wearing a hat?

Antar   There was no hat.

M.I.L.   Did the sword perform a clean beheading, just like in a video game?

Antar   Yes—the guard was very large and strong. He held the sword in two hands and came upon the victim from behind. The victim and his friend had been confronted by three guards. The victim had tried to kick at the guards, and his friend ran away, while the other guards tackled him and then this fourth man cut off his head.

M.I.L.   Was the victim standing or laying on the ground when his head was cut off?

Antar   He had dropped to his knees after one of the guards kicked him in the stomach.

M.I.L.   And what did the guards do afterwards?

Antar   I didn't want to watch anymore.

M.I.L.   You poor girl. And did Gauloise show compassion?

Antar   He claimed I was hysterical.

M.I.L.	There have been illusionists known to create street theater.
Antar	Why would they do something like that.
M.I.L.	Anarchists. Trying to create the illusion of unrest. Trying to arouse sympathy for their futile insurgency.
Antar	I want no part of this.
M.I.L.	Just want to go your own way?
Antar	I am within my rights.
M.I.L.	You misunderstand, Antar. Gauloise *loves* you. His first thought upon awakening was of you.
Antar	Not a mattress advertisement?
M.I.L.	His devotion deserves your devotion.
Antar	Am I free to go?
M.I.L.	Go. I've done all I can. You are a woman who knows what she wants!

*

9. Freedom of Choice

ANTAR and CHARLY are in a bunker together. After sex.

Charly	That was great.
Antar	I'm filled with anger and hatred now that I've seen the real world.
Charly	Get over it baby.
Antar	The screaming. I can't get it out of my ears.
Charly	The air is full of cries.
Antar	Who knew there could be such a darkness.
Charly	You're used to your condo, with the track lighting.
Antar	This won't end well.

A pause. CHARLY knows this better than she.

Charly	You have beautiful tits.
Antar	I love you.
Charly	You love a dead man then.

A pause.

	Did you bring the money?
Antar	I can get it.
Charly	Good. We need it.
Antar	Why is there so much pain here?
Charly	Because there's a war goin' on. It's like this everywhere. A new world war. I've seen worse. My buddy got his legs blown off.

I carried him for three hours.

Then he died at the field hospital.

I got a medal. Then I got real real sick.

And I started hearing things.

People'd talk to me, the chaplain, the shrink.

And their mouths were moving

But the words were in another voice.

A woman's voice.

Antar   What did she say?

Charly   Said a lot of stuff I couldn't repeat.

Antar   Who was the woman?

Charly   She was not of this earth.

And when she spoke, I cried like a baby.

I felt like my heart was being pulled out.

I felt like my head was on fire with the chills.

I felt like my body lost all sense of the ground or air.

And this went on and on.

For many days.

And I knew I was going to die.

Then they gave me a discharge 'cause I was crazy.

Antar   And the woman—have you ever heard her voice again?

Charly   I hear it yes... but not the same way.

Antar   It's so cold.

Charly   They have tents in the park but you need cash money.

Antar   Tents?

His PHONE RINGS. He turns it off.

Antar   Your phone rings too much.

Charly   That was my daughter.

| Antar | You have a daughter? |
| Charly | Yeah. Deirdre. |

He shows her a picture from his wallet.

Antar	She's a very pretty little girl! Where's her mother?
Charly	Took her to a place called Smithers—it's in British Columbia...
	I don't know exactly where it is.
Antar	Smithers? That in the mountains?
Charly	It's on the moraine.
Antar	So you're married?
Charly	Naw, we lived together four years... she took off with this dude.
	Looked about forty.
	Flashed a lot of money around...
	She calls me up says, hey, I'm setting here lookin' at five hunert thousand cash dollars.
	Now there ain't no kind of legitimate business done with all that cash.
	Anyway, he's got Deirdre. For the time being.
Antar	When did you last see her?
Charly	Back home. I was on leave.
	Took her to my uncle's place,
	'cause her mom had shacked up with that guy.
	I wanted to have a pedicure.
	Y'know, after six weeks of training
	with your feet in combat boots twenty-four hours a day,
	you want a pedicure.
	So I said to her, Deirdre,

	let's go the mall and have a pedicure.
	But she wouldn't go.
Antar	She wouldn't go? Did you?
Charly	Yeah. That was two years ago. Haven't had a pedicure in two years and I don't expect I'll be getting one anytime soon.
Antar	Do you think it'll ever end?
Charly	When we're dead.
	Even back in the hills there's war.
	The best you can do is bring the money.
Antar	You need to promise me a mission.
Charly	Don't be stupid.
Antar	I have to get back now.
Charly	*(Embracing her)* Fuck me again.
Antar	I need to go.
Charly	You need to get rid of the clone.
Antar	He isn't a clone.
Charly	Robot. Pardon my Arabic.
Antar	Cyborg.
Charly	Get rid of it. He'll rat you out.
Antar	I can fix him so he doesn't. I can fix him to help us maybe.
Charly	Get rid of him.
Antar	Can you help?
Charly	No. I've got enough shit to do.
	You wanted a mission. There's your mission.
	Get rid of it. Clone, robot, whatever.
Antar	And then?
Charly	Then we'll see.
Antar	It's easier to reprogram him.

Charly	Its easier to shoot him.
Antar	I don't know how to shoot. I don't have a gun.
Charly	You want a gun?

She is silent.

Charly	You want a gun?
Antar	Yes.

CHARLY *pulls a handgun out of his backpack.*

Charly	You ever use one of these?
Antar	Can I handle it?
Charly	Ever kill anything?
Antar	No.
Charly	This'll make it easy. You just point, aim,
	And squeeze the trigger.

He guides it into her hands.

Charly	Now see that bird?
Antar	Yes, I think.
Charly	See that bird? On the fence.
Antar	Yeah, now I see it.
Charly	Well, kill the little fucker.
Antar	But it's only a bird.
Charly	It's just a part of the earth. The earth can take it.

He takes the gun away from her.

Looks up at the bird, aims, and fires. Gives her back the gun.

*

10. The Role of the Media

GAULOISE sits at his television drinking a beer. He begins surfing channels, imitating the announcers.

Gauloise   I'll show you human:

We are winning. This is the best place on earth.
We owe it to our brave soldiers.
They have spilled their guts for us.

We have an oil spill.
It spells trouble.

There are plenty of seals.
There are plenty of wolves.
There are plenty of fish in the sea.
Pure fish to die for us.

I'll show you human:

Can you tell it when you have a brain disease?
When the waist of your brain becomes corpulent and distended?

When the toxic waste has risen up to your nose.

I'll show you human:
sometimes the invisible worm, waxy and pale
a blunt instrument to feed the brain disease its
required diet
of anger and misanthropic bile
kicking angels in the nuts for the sheer
sadistic satisfaction of seeing them double over
to show their pockmarked butts
and how they howl when in a pile
and grimace at how the heel grinds them in at the liver,
or something like, an ear is taken off with a scissors.

I'll show you *human*:
Give this poetry a high rating.
It had to be spoken by
a real minority or facsimile of one,
with no hatred or envy that they will admit to
or maybe they regret to inform you
—I don't know—
I'll show you human
Caring only for the body as if the body was God
the selfish protracted life,
caring only for the car as if the
car was God

Hip people hate people who are religious.
They must be suckers, sucked into phony bullshit,
eating McDonalds and then praying, beating their

children and then praying,
talking trash about gays and then praying,
despairing and then praying

I'll show you human...

He slumps in his chair, weeping, and nurses the beer.

Enter ANTAR.

ANTAR *carries in a large duffle bag.*

Antar   What are you doing? You can't drink like that. It's
poison to you!

She takes away his beer.

Antar   I promise I'll be back for you. You can be an asset,
but first I need to do something.

Gauloise You wont get far.

Antar   I'm turning off the television.
Now you can hear me.

Gauloise I'll show you human. I'm good enough.
Good enough for you. Better than enough.
Accept me as I am or whatever I am.

Antar   I can't trust you Gauloise.
I know where you came from.
I know what went into you.
I know what you are capable of.

Gauloise	I am capable of advanced comprehension and even subtlety.

She takes the handgun out of her pack and points it at him.

Antar	You've already told them haven't you.
Gauloise	Don't do it.
Antar	I will.
Gauloise	What must I do to stop you.
Antar	You will not stop me.
I have been warned.
Fully warned not to listen to you.
I know you will only say
what I want to hear.
I have been warned about the methods of cyborgs.
Gauloise	Who warmed you?
Antar	Warned, not warmed.
Gauloise	I am here to warm you.
They are there to warn you.
I am here to warm you.
They are there to warn you.
I am here to warm you.
They are there to warn you.
Antar	No no no!

She leaves the room with her bag.

Gauloise	*(Calling after her)* I am here to warm you.
Do you hear me?

I'm warming you!
For the very first time, for the very last time time.
Again and again
I feel you
under my skin
In my tissues and nerves
who cares what is out there
you will never change
anything
Doing

*

11. Failure

MOTHER-IN-LAW stands before GAULOISE and ANTAR.
ANTAR badly roughed up, bound in an uncomfortable
position.

M.I.L.   I hope this is a relationship story.
It would be a shame if this were a political drama.
I hope we are dealing here with interpersonal issues.
That is where my personal expertise lies. It is so
important,
I cannot stress enough, the importance of maintaining
the institutions of our society which support a healthy
social and emotional environment for the citizens.
Antar, what do you have to say...

ANTAR is silent.

I had a pony when I was a girl. I used to ride that pony
every weekend in the country club. I fed him and brushed
him. Even though he bit me, on more than one occasion,
I grew to love him. Devotion only occurs under adverse
circumstances. Without the bites, would love have been
as meaningful? In spite of the bites, he was my pony.
So I know, I know.

Pause. Off ANTAR's silence.

Speak Antar, or else.

Antar   My personal freedom seems to mean nothing.
There are too many senseless rules attached to this
arrangement.
Things I never signed on to.
I see things differently now than when I contracted for
my relationship with Gauloise.

M.I.L.   Differently in what way?

Antar   The war has changed my outlook. It's made life
unpleasant when I am with Gauloise, because he refuses
to adapt. The world has changed, I have changed with it.
I have adapted. He has not. It was promised to me that
he would adapt. But no one has honored that promise.
Therefore, it is you who are in breach of promise, not I.

M.I.L.   How has the war changed your outlook?

Antar   One. The war made successful shopping trips impossible.
I discovered that shopping was unnecessary for happiness.

Two. Security went on strike and so an insurgent found his way inside our home.

Being deprived of security forces and spending time with the insurgent in the curfew zone made it apparent to me that security forces were unnecessary for happiness.

Three. Despite my following all the rules, I was denied intimacy level 4. Being deprived of intimacy level 4 with my cyborg made it apparent that intimacy level 4 was unnecessary for happiness.

Gauloise She and I have a great deal in common. We belong together.

M.I.L. I am glad to hear that this has nothing to do with the war. Your certificate is being renewed and your contract will remain in force for another five years.

Antar You misunderstand me. I wish to be released from my contract.

M.I.L. As long as this remains a personal issue, you are obliged to honor your contract. If there are any political or overarching social themes, then you need to be placed in probationary holding.

Antar Probationary holding?

M.I.L. A special theme facility with daily monitoring and assessment.

Antar So my choices are either stay with Gauloise or go to prison?!

M.I.L. Oh dear. Is happiness contingent? Or isn't it?

Gauloise What about our personal freedom?

I think my life partner is concerned about her personal freedom.

M.I.L. Freedom! *(She laughs at her own joke)* Go on home you two. I don't want to see you here again.

	The war is over, let's get back to normal.
Antar	The war is not over.
M.I.L.	Yes, it is.

And to celebrate, the Cyborg Olympics will be held again
for the first time in three years.
Not only that, but as ten-year members
of the Buglers Glen Condominium Project,
you qualify for complimentary VIP passes
to the pregame all-star celebration
and celebrity picnic.
And then, to give your relationship
an extra boost that it seems to need,
tickets to Tahiti.

Antar What?

M.I.L. You heard right. VIP passes, for you, Gauloise, and two
guests of your choosing. And then tickets to Tahiti.

Gauloise This sounds like a lot of fun. Doesn't it sound like
fun Antar?

*

12. The Cooler

*CHARLY is finishing the wiring of an improvised explo-
sive device and fitting it carefully inside a picnic cooler.
He lays picnic items on top and closes it. Then he packs
his tools into a box, which ANTAR carries offstage.*

*C*HARLY *sets his watch and punches some code into*
his cellphone.

Charly   *(Calling to her)* We're ready. You can wake it up now.

*A*NTAR *leads G*AULOISE *onstage.*

Antar   It's almost time for the limo to pick us up, Gauloise.
I'm looking forward to this. I even made fried chicken.
Bet you thought I had forgotten how.

Gauloise   Fried chicken. My favorite food!

Antar   I've packed us a picnic in the cooler.

Gauloise   And what is he doing here?

Antar   His warrior days are over.

Charly   I brought you some special treats. I work at the beer
and cheese shop now.

Gauloise   This is an unsophisticated fellow.
Doesn't he know they are called wine and cheese shops?

Silence.

Antar   Check those preconceptions at the door!
We have a fine selection in the cooler here.
Charly, tell Gauloise what we've packed for the picnic.

Charly   Baguettes and garlic-stuffed olives.
Sun-dried tomatoes and shallots in a blend of truffle
and olive oils.
Nitroglycerin.
And then we have the smooth Muenster,
and also a couple of dense, sticky, fresh goat cheeses,

the kind that cling to your tongue.
To go with them, we've packed a Hefeweizen,
a light-bodied wheat beer—highly carbonated—to act
as a palate scrubber.
It'll really surprise you, Gauloise,
to discover how seamlessly
these assertive cheeses meld with beer.
Chimay Grande Reserve
strong, dry and richly spiced
meets the Muenster on equal footing.
We also have a pungent washed-rind Chimay cheese
produced by the same Belgian abbey,
a model marriage.

Gauloise	I don't feel comfortable with this.
Antar	Your jealousy is ridiculous, Gauloise.
Charly	Maybe you two should just go to the picnic by youselves.
Antar	Not after you brought all this delicious food!
Gauloise	Leave this house! I don't want you coming around my wife! Leave before I beat you up!
Charly	I won't be the cause of any trouble. You guys just work it out, hear?
	Bye Antar.

CHARLY exchanges a look with ANTAR and then he exits. ANTAR feigns disappointment.

Antar	I don't want to go to the picnic now.
	I don't care if we have Level 4 tickets and VIP passes.
Gauloise	We have to go.

	If we have special VIP passes,

If we have special VIP passes,
and Level 4 tickets,
we will be penalized if we do not go.

Antar I don't care. You can't make me.

Gauloise Please come. Anty ant.

Antar Charly is my friend. You offended him and made me feel uncomfortable. Apologize.

Gauloise I am sorry. I am really sorry.

Antar You aren't really.

You just want chicken.

Gauloise All the New World leaders will be there,

The Order of the Millenium.

The superstars and the elite.

To attend this event

Will assure us a lifetime

Of relative ease.

Antar *(Sardonic)* And tell me, Gauloise.

What exactly is the Order of the Millenium?

Gauloise We don't really know. We never will.

But they have put an end to the war.

And now they are including us in the reconstruction.

We must show gratitude. We must go to the picnic.

GAULOISE carries out the heavy cooler. ANTAR follows.

*

13. Re-creation

An interrogation.

MOTHER-IN-LAW *stands,* GAULOISE *sits in a straight-back chair.* ANTAR *sits in another chair in an unlit part of the stage.*

ANTAR *is handcuffed. Slumped over and disheveled, bruised.*

Gauloise   The most assertive thing we packed was the cheese. The goat cheese, dense and fleshy. Then there was a possibly explosive, highly carbonated beer. A cheese married to a beer from the same abbey.

M.I.L.   You never saw the IED.

Gauloise   I did not.

I will stand by my wife at any cost. I am a faithful husband. She would never go along with murdering innocents.

M.I.L.   And what about the guilty? The "enemy"?

Gauloise   The Order of the Millenium. Not the enemy.

They have brought peace to the New World.

Their children were at the picnic too. My wife would only wish to protect the children. If there was a bomb inside the cooler, it was all the fault of that man Charly.

M.I.L.   How did you get through security?

Gauloise   We had the special tickets. We came in the limo you sent. The driver put the cooler in the trunk. The vehicle

	was thoroughly searched and we parked it in the as-
	signed space.
Antar	*(Vehement)* The insurgency will continue as long
	as necessary!
M.I.L.	And Charly? Where could we find him?
Antar	I don't know.
M.I.L.	That's too bad. Your credibility is frankly in doubt.
	I put my own career on the line here.
	It's just not a good idea to disappoint me like this.
	You see, it's necessary for me to maintain the status
	of this department
	and to protect our nation from extremists.
	Right now, I have one last chance to give you,
	then it's all out of my hands
	and you'll have to take this matter up with the Federal
	Security Forces.
Antar	Go ahead.
M.I.L.	We can't come to an agreement?
	You have so much to live for, Antar.
	You have the power to save youself.
	You may even have the power to save Charly.
	But I can only help if I know where to find him.
Antar	Even if I knew, I would *never* tell you where he is.
M.I.L.	We know he has a child.
	We think you know where she might be.
	He told you, didn't he.
Antar	I don't remember.
M.I.L.	I think you do.
Antar	*(Frightened)* I really don't remember.
M.I.L.	Perhaps the enhanced service level four

which we are now able to offer you—free of charge—
will help.

Gauloise, we need to assist her memory.

*MOTHER-IN-LAW brings out a roll of adhesive tape.
Together, (s)he and GAULOISE tape ANTAR's eyes open.*

*A large map is rolled out on a flat. It screens us from
what happens to ANTAR. There is a gasp and a moan—
whatever happens is quick but excruciating.*

The screen is rolled away and Antar's eyes are bandaged.

Gauloise   The daughter is in—a small town in western
Canada—Smithers.

M.I.L.   Thank you Antar. You are free to go.

ANTAR is silent, in shock.

Antar   Free?

M.I.L.   Oh yes. This is the last you'll be hearing from me!
You will have a new level four maintenance officer.

Gauloise   That was quite an ordeal. I'm glad it's over.

M.I.L.   Yes, I am too. This was has been very hard on me too.
But it would have been a great deal harder on those
people at the picnic, if we hadn't found that bomb.
Now if you'll excuse us Gauloise, Antar and I just have
to clear up some final paperwork.
Let's go Antar.

M.I.L. leads ANTAR *away.*

GAULOISE sits in the light, blinking. He looks around. Turns back. Looks around again. Gets up, paces impatiently.

After a wait, MOTHER-IN-LAW *returns. She lights a cigarette.*

M.I.L.	You're still here?
Gauloise	I'm waiting for Antar.
M.I.L.	Forget Antar, Gauloise.
Gauloise	What.
M.I.L.	I said, forget her.
Gauloise	Forget Antar. Why?
M.I.L.	Because you have a plane to catch, a plane to Tahiti. You must get packed!

*

14. Gail

As the lights come up, we see the shadow projections of two bodies, hanged, on the wall downstage.

GAULOISE stares at the bodies. There are two suitcases packed and ready to go by the door. GAIL, *his beautiful new young wife, stands holding his notebook and reading it.*

Gail	This shows much improvement. This is nearly punishable. What are you looking at?
Gauloise	The bodies of my ex-wife and her lover, are still swinging slightly. Death comes in such cases within approximately twelve minutes. But the subject loses consciousness quickly, so the suffering is minimal. For the subject that is. Only the living, the sentient ones who remain, suffer. There are those who say they don't but they do. And those who say they do but they don't. There are those who say it is wrong but it is the right thing. And those who say it is the right thing but wrong nevertheless. Confusing.
Gail	There's nothing there.
	You have something the matter with you.
	I'm calling Mother-In-Law.

He turns around and embraces her.

Gauloise	Nothing wrong with me that a little R-and-R wouldn't cure, if you get my meaning.
Gail	R-and-R. And what does that stand for?
Gauloise	Ribbing and rubbing. Risktaking and revelation. Rebellion and reintegration.
Gail	That sounds like fun!

She coils herself around him and they begin to make love as
LIGHTS FADE TO BLACK.

The End

Phantom Luck

by John Steppling

Phantom Luck *was first produced by Gunfighter Nation at*
The Lost Studio, Los Angeles in 2011 under the direction of John
Steppling and Wesley Walker, and with the following cast:

Jerry Dunn *Jim Storm*
Anson *George Gerdes*
Josefa *Kadina De Elejalde*
Johnny Cyr *Mark Rolston*

Characters

Jerry Dunn, *sixty-ish*
Anson, *an ex-con, forties, terminally ill*
Josefa, *a Mexican woman, thirties*
Johnny Cyr, *forties*

LIGHTS up slowly on a single man. He stands center stage. He is sixty-ish, and gray-haired. He wears a nice but slightly garish suit and a shirt that requires cuff links. The cuff links are horseshoe-shaped and studded with diamonds. This is DUNN.

Dunn   The thing is. *(Beats)* The thing is...

He starts flipping a coin.

Here it is, see, the idea of odds. If I flip this coin and it lands heads, well you say, fine, there was a fifty-fifty chance it would do so. I flip it again...

He flips it and catches it. He checks it...

Heads again. Well, not so unusual. *(Beats)* Now, if I flip it twenty times and each time it comes up heads... well, you say, the "odds" are it's going to come up tails pretty soon, right? I mean if I flip it five hundred times and all five hundred flips come up heads... I mean, damn, you might want to get down a wager on tails, right?

Pause.

Then you are a sucker. Then you are a chump and a loser. The odds never change... each time is a fresh fifty-fifty start. To not understand that is to not understand something essential about how the world works. How the universe works.

Long pause.

God is not watching, assuming there is a God... he doesn't watch card games or crap games or horse races, see? He doesn't watch coin flips for certain. He gives a fuck about odds. I lost, this one spell, I lost twenty-seven straight football bets... twenty-seven... I started throwing darts at the paper... just random selections... and I still kept losing. I lost forty-six thousand dollars in that fucking streak. *(Beats)* The fat lady who was making book then... Fat Marie... she couldn't believe it... she told me to stop... "I can't keep taking your money, Dunn, I can't do it... it causes me pain"... and it did, because she knew how it works. You know all the jokes about gamblers... the one about the guy, he meets a friend on the street... the friend says, man, how you doing? Guy says, not good... I lost on the NBA playoffs today... and, and I lost on the hockey games. I lost also at the race track... all day I lost. Lost every race at Santa Anita. The friend says, damn, why don't you try baseball? Guy says, shit, I don't know a thing about baseball. *(Pause)* See, what you think you know and what you really know—what you think there "is" to know... and what really, really there is to know... those are big gaps... there is no logic. The logic of luck... well, the logic says there is no logic. *(Pause)* What is there to really know about horse races? I mean I know guys, ex-jockeys, and ex-trainers... guys with knowledge, and they lose all day too... they lose if they—how to exactly say this... they lose if they are born to lose. If they are losers. I don't like that term. A loser is just a term from the straight world. Who wins and who loses... I mean I have no idea about that shit. Losers and winners... it's a constant fluid thing. See, gambling is a business... that is true. But one doesn't really gamble to win. Nobody wins all the time, anyway. Some lose all the time, that's true... but them are those born to lose. You gamble because... well, that's complicated. You gamble because the world is full of propositions.

Long pause.

The world is there... in front of us, and we speculate... we speculate on if it's gonna rain today. Fucking satellites try to tell you if it's gonna rain... but you speculate anyway... how much, how cold... and you speculate on if your buddy's woman is fucking the cab driver at that stand down from Musso and Franks... see, and why do you speculate such? Huh? That's my question, and it's a deep fucking question. *(Pause)* However, see, those are superficial propositions. The deeper propositions are hidden... and you gotta find them, after looking for a lifetime... for some... a lifetime... the hidden bet where you don't even know what you bet on... which team you picked... and you're never gonna know the score. Now that's some funny shit. Bet on games that can't be played... except in some long forgotten past. Paradox. The paradox of luck.

Pause.

D∪ɴɴ *starts moving around the stage now. He is still alone. After a moment he stops...*

I know this man. Beatty. Anson Beatty—a real cracker name... Anson... and he's been to prison and he's been in and out of shit all his life. Anson... here is a man who lacks the ability to find the hidden things in our games of chance. But he has a terminal disease now. A disease I can't pronounce and which he can't spell. Can't even spell what is killin' you. Shall we bet on Anson's check out time? Shall we?

Pause.

It's up to you. *(Pause)* It is, it's up to you.

Lɪɢʜᴛs *fade out.*

Lɪɢʜᴛs *fade in:*

A man sits reading a racing form. This is Aɴsᴏɴ Bᴇᴀᴛᴛʏ. *He is in his forties... slender, and looks a bit pale and drawn.*

A Mexican woman in her thirties is standing up stage.
This is JOSEFA.

Anson   Don't stare at the back of my head.

Silence.

Josefa   The Archangel Michael draws his sword to do battle
with the forces of sin and wantonness.

Anson   You have those little cards again, don't you? Those
cards... religious cards, with pictures of saints and shit.
And now you got the Archangel Michael, right?
Am I right?

Josefa   In Veracruz, there are ships that arrive each day,
and they come from places of evil and destruction.
They are Satan's ships.

Anson   There is a horse today in the third race, Satan's
Child... think this is an omen? Think I should get
down a bet on Satan's Child?

Josefa   I think you laugh at what you do not understand.

Anson   In the seventh... we have Sword of Concupiscence...
whatever that means. But it has "sword" in the title.
(Pause) Michael won't fight for me, as I am a sinner
and a nonbeliever.

Josefa   I know.

ANSON *has still not turned around.*

Anson   You're still staring at the back of my head.

Josefa   I know.

Silence.

Anson   You think God will answer my prayers and give me
a winner today?

Josefa   Blaspheme.

Anson   Your English is better. *(Pause)* I once saw a jockey fall
off his horse and I saw how his head hit the rail... this
was the old days... no padding... and he died right there
on the far turn. Just like that. Now some horse won
that race and people collected their bets. They didn't
much care if this poor fuck was dead on the ground.
They had just won. *(Beats)* Now as I recall, the winner
was a bit of a longshot... and people, those with tickets
on that longshot... they were happy as clams in cold
water. Happy happy happy. Man dies... others cash in.
That's how it works.

LIGHTS shift... up on:

An area DOWNSTAGE where DUNN is pacing in circles.

Dunn   See, I never really learned to read or write. I mean, yeah,
I can read a little—I can read the odds at the race track—
but not much more. And I can't write for shit. I can't.
(Pause) Now I wonder at how this has affected my life.

UPSTAGE a light on ANSON. He watches and listens.

I live in a world of talk. I listen to people... they talk
and I listen... or I talk and they listen, I guess. But

I write nothing. Sometimes... if I think about it, I don't write a word, not my name, nothing, for months at a time. Last time I actually wrote anything was—well, I signed my name to a birthday card to Jesus, this little jockey from Monterrey. He was thirty I think. Little fuck is actually just a few pounds too big to really make it. Imagine that, you weigh only one-twenty say... and you're too big... you have to get down to one-ten... one-fifteen tops... but I don't know... some guys overcome the weight thing... but Jesus is a bit too tall too... to be accurate. Some trainers don't mind that so much... others do. Anyway, it was his birthday and they circulated this card and I signed it. Jerry Dunn. How I always sign my name... not Jerald... but Jerry. Jerry Dunn.

Silence.

Anson   I can see you watching my back.

LIGHTS up on JOSEFA. She is UPSTAGE and staring at ANSON's back.

Dunn   I remember names. The names of jockeys... old timers, Merlin Volske, Roy Yaka, George Tanaguchi... names hardly anyone remembers anymore. Ralph Neves, and... and trainers, too. Owners... and I remember the colors of the silks. I have a weird memory that way. I remember cards too... and I remember faces.

Anson   Don't always be staring at my back.

Josefa	How do you think you are able to know I am watching your back? How do you think you can tell?
Anson	What?
Josefa	You got fucking eyes in the back of your head? Huh? No, you don't. So how you know?
Anson	Good question.
Dunn	I've never read a book. I watch people sometimes, watch them reading books... and I wonder at that, at what that is like. They turn page four-hundred-and-twelve... and go to four-hundred-and-thirteen—and what is that like? So many words, so many pages full of little inky shapes. I wonder. I wonder at that.

Long silence. DUNN starts to pace.

I have these diamond cuff links. In the shape of horse-shoes. Have I mentioned this already? I paid over three thousand dollars for these... and that was in 1965. In Vegas... in '65... do you know what it was like in Vegas in '65? It wasn't like now, I can tell you. *(Pause)* I had a wife then. You didn't know that did you. Name of Louise. I have no idea about what became of Louise. I wonder at that sometimes. Louise was a Mormon... a sort of nonpracticing Mormon. Her brother was a fucking loon—card sharp... but a heavy Mormon. His uncle was called Elder Something... and was a big shot in the church. The Mormon church. But her brother... he did know a lot about horses. *(Pause)* His name was Cecil. They got crazy names those fucking Mormons. Anyway, I bought these cuff links in Vegas, and Louise was with me. I was a kid... so was Louise. They scene was great then... Vegas. The strip—not like now, not a lot of fags with giant cats or what not... just singers... just gaming... the mob... it was great and I bought these cuff links. Eleven diamonds on each horseshoe. I wear them all the time and I am careful not to lose them. I have shirts made, or I used to, with French cuffs... you know, for cuff links. I have another pair, too. With little rubies... tasteful—but nothing like these. *(Beats)* Louise was a redhead. Crazy girl. Tall and thin... long legs. Great pouty mouth and full lips. A bit like Cyd Charisse in a way. Cecil was short... that was the funny thing. Short like guy, and defensive about it. He never liked me much. Anyway, as I say, I bought them in Vegas. I was only a kid, but I already knew how to gamble.

Anson   In the whole huge universe. In the whole great cosmos God created... how come you choose to stare at the fucking back of my fucking head.

Josefa   I watch your back, not just the back of your head. I watch your back. I don't know exactly why. You turn around I watch your face, OK?!

Anson   I feel no urge to turn around.

Silence.

Dunn   I don't go to Vegas anymore. I haven't been in almost fifteen years. What would I do in Vegas. *(Long pause)* Let me explain about getting old. *(Beats)* You get old, usually, without noticing it, without realizing it. You're aging and you don't think you are—or somehow you think it isn't important in your special case. But you get older each day. And your hair turns grey... and pretty soon young girls offer you their seats. That's a big one and all old guys remember when that happens. But other things happen too. *(Pause)* The biggest thing is this thing, it's hard to explain or describe. It's how you suddenly, one day, sense you're running out of time for all those big schemes you have in mind. Suddenly you can't look twenty years down the road... because you'll be fucking ninety in twenty years and eating out of a tube or some shit. You run out of time.

Silence.

You run out of time. You think you'll always have time but then you don't. You don't.

Anson You have any, you know, notions about why you have this special interest in me?

Pause.

Josefa There is a kind of wind—blows out of the dark midnight desert... blows silent and hot and full of minerals. When it comes down into the city it smells like sulphur but it stays close to the ground. It weakens those who are already weak but it strengthens those who are already strong. *(Pause)* Times when this wind comes whistling down the alleys of the barrio it will tear the head off chickens or even cats and dogs. The Archangel

Michael stares straight at this wind. He holds the
sword of providence and he has gold teeth that shine
in the moonlight.

Anson   Archangel Michael has gold teeth?

Josefa   Fuck you, he does. And this wind is a wind of prophecy.
And prophecy is... it's complicated. I watch you,
and I feel you, and I love you. You will understand
this someday. I do not know when—or how I came
to know of you.

Anson   I met you at Gilbert's backyard barbecue.

Josefa   You are not a spiritual man, Anson... but God will
forgive such small deficiencies.

Anson   Big word, deficiencies.

Josefa   The world has turned away from the things that scare
it. It is a cowardly world. Michael holds a scale in his
other hand... a scale to weigh the souls of the dead.
Michael fights with Satan, and guards the tomb of
Eve... and protects the body of Moses. The Epistle of
Jude... I memorized this is as a girl.

Anson   He holds a sword and scale and has bad dental insur-
ance. OK.

Josefa   Daniel 12, the Angel says that upon the coming of the
end of the world Michael shall rise up... a great prince,
who stands for the children of thy people.

Pause.

Dunn   I walked through life like a zombie. I had plans...
and I had fun... can't say I didn't. I thought in terms
of how to win... of wagers... of winners and losers...

or... see... it's so tricky... I thought in terms of the
game. Of gaming... of games of chance. I saw it all in
terms of chance.

Lights shift.

Dunn wanders back and forth. We see only him now.

After a moment Anson appears. They look at each other.

Anson   Gypsies can't read or write. *(Pause)* Like you.

Dunn nods, shrugs.

Anson   You never told me you couldn't read.
Dunn   Never came up.
Anson   This isn't a handicap, you know, when you go to
               the track?

Dunn thinks.

Dunn   No.

Silence. Anson paces now.

Anson   You can read a little.
Dunn   A little.
Anson   Write some.
Dunn   Some.
Anson   Remember that girl, Josefa?

Dunn	Sure.
Anson	Josefa. Well, I'm at a kind of, how shall we put it, a crossroads in my life.
Dunn	And what's this to do with Josefa?
Anson	*(Beats)* She keeps appearing. I don't know. She's around a lot.

Pause.

She's religious, this girl.

Dunn	I could see that right away. When I met her.
Anson	Yeah. *(Beats)* I suppose it was clear enough.

Silence.

Dunn	What's on your mind, Anson?
Anson	Didn't you go to school? As a kid?
Dunn	No, hardly.
Anson	Damn.
Dunn	It was easier not to go in those days.

ANSON *nods. Pause.*

Anson	You have no kids, yourself?
Dunn	No.
Anson	How come?
Dunn	What's on your mind, Anson?
Anson	My mind? *(Beats)* On my mind. I don't know. I just been thinking is all.

DUNN nods.

I don't trust doctors. None of them. I don't trust medicine, to be honest. *(Beats)* And then, see, I think to myself, the hell difference does it make. Don't you find it odd, how, I don't know, how we seem so complex—people—such complex fuckin' things and then we just die? Dying is so simple. Whoosh—here one second, gone the next.

Pause.

Dunn	Haven't ever looked at it like that. But when you put it like that, I guess it's sort of odd.
Anson	Whoosh.
Dunn	Here one minute, gone the next.
Anson	Fucking strange. That's all our lives amount to. Whoosh.
Dunn	Whoosh.

Pause.

Is that the sound of death—whoosh?

ANSON smiles.

Anson	That's nothin'. Just a sound. I guess I worry about Josefa.

LIGHTS shift...

Josefa upstage in spot.

Josefa You watch a man. From behind. Watch him walk. Even
from far away. Watch how his feet hit the ground and
you can tell if he's evil. *(Beats)* My father and uncle
could tell, *(snaps her finger)* like that. He is evil. He is
a visitor from the other side.

Silence.

Do I believe this? *(Beats)* Yes, I guess I do. You can
watch a man's mouth too. Watch when he speaks... and
sometimes the sound comes out wrong—like in those
movies that are made in another language... or when
you talk to someone in the car and the car goes into a
tunnel and their words get sketchy—like a radio falling
out of touch with the antenna... you know... the signal
is broken... well, some people are like that... like they
are really fucking robots or something. They lose their
signal. And when you leave the tunnel they talk normal
again. Scares the shit out of me.

Silence.

Anson is a good man. Many—my mother for example—
don't believe this because he has been to prison.
Anson isn't bad. He is just marked with defeat... and
it makes me cry to say this... but it's true. He has
that mark on him.

Pause.

Do I love him, you ask. Of course I love him. Love
is not something you think about and come to a
conclusion about. Love is there in its suddenness... like
nature... like the things that occur in nature... like
rain starting... love is so fucking bad for all of us.

Pause.

Anson cannot figure out why I love him. He is dying,
and he thinks that should make him... I guess, make
him seem ugly. Make him seem... closer to some kind
of dead thing. *(Pause)* Maybe it should... but it doesn't.
And what does it mean, this idea of death?

Silence.

LIGHTS shift.

DUNN is dealing cards by himself at table.

After a long moment ANSON appears behind him.

Dunn   You ever wonder about cards? Funny things, cards.

*LIGHTS up further UPSTAGE now... seated in straight
back wooden chair is JOHNNY CYR. He is forty. He has
slicked-back hair and a nice suit... with subtle cowboy*

styling. A little table is next to him with cards and glass of water on it.

Dunn   Cards have a long history. Ever think about what's on the cards... the face cards... who picked a one-eyed jack? Funny thing.

Cyr   Listen to Dunn, here. Listen to this old fuck. Thinks he knows the game... thinks... well, I don't know everything Dunn thinks. He does know horses, I'll give him that. *(Pause)* I have studied—I have studied a lot—read many books—and you know, Dunn can't read—well, that shouldnt prejudice us against him... but I have read, I have studied ancient Egypt... the Pharoahs... I have read Mao Tse-tung , and I have read Lin Piao. I have read about the Yakuza and I have studied the game of chess. I read the Bible every day, and I've read the Koran too. I have read crime novels and true crime books, too. I have memorized poems that I liked. I know a lot of painting; know the life and work of El Greco, know about Delacroix, and I know about Frans Hals. I know Bernini's sculptures and I know Mozart backward and forward. I don't even fucking like Mozart... sissy music, actually... Bach is better, and Shostakovich. I like memory games and I like puzzles.

Dunn   *(Flipping cards over)...* five of hearts, six of diamonds, jack of hearts... *(stops)* Anson?

Anson   What?

Dunn   Just want to know you're there. Listen, Anson, how do you feel today?

(Silence.)

Cyr	Anson never feels good anymore. I will testify to that. Anson feels the weight of the world... feels the grim reaper at the front gate.
Dunn	You think we can... *(Pausing... hesitating...)*
Anson	Steal? You think we can steal enough to... *(beats)* to what? Was what you were gonna say, right?
Dunn	You think we can?
Cyr	I am going to vomit my brain stem here on the carpet. I am going to have an aneurysm. Jesus fucking God— the sorry old loser, the sorry old dead-to-the-core gambling fool. Man, how I hate Dunn.
Anson	I haven't much to lose. My opinion is colored by this, I think.
Cyr	Both these clowns. Losers. *(Beats)* I like Bob Wills too... not just, like Bach—I like Lefty Frizzell too, and Ray Price. *(Beats)* I love card games and I love cigars. I love waking up in a hotel room, and not knowing if it's day or night. I love that. I love not knowing what damn hotel it is. How long I been asleep. You wake up, and you shower... right off... before you check the time, or anything. Then you piece it together—you remember the game, how you did, if you have any money left. All of it and then you dress... and you get yourself ready to go back to the game.

Silence.

Cyr	Now here we are, all three of us, staying in the same big old hotel. Over a thousand rooms in this hotel. One of the biggest. One of the very biggest. Dunn—I know Dunn for a hundred years or more. I know him in all my previous lives. I know him before he knew hisself.
Dunn	Anson?
Anson	I'm still here.
Dunn	That girl with you?
Josefa	I watch, Jerry, because the gods have forotten you —both of you.
Dunn	You watch?
Josefa	I watch Anson more. But I watch you both. I love you both, too.
Dunn	*(Laughs)* No angel—nobody loves me, not anymore and maybe not ever.
Josefa	Anson has a mark on him—and it is a mark that can be formed into words and it spells defeat. But I love him and you know little about this.
Anson	Jerry—she knows about love. I never met anyone knew more about it. Me and you—we don't know.
Dunn	How could we?
Anson	That's right, how could we. We have been left for dead—left for... well, not dead as in absence of life... but dead—dead of heart. Left when we were too young. The young perish in many different ways, even when they survive.
Josefa	Children battle evil too, and they fight for the force of good—of light... even if they don't know a thing about it.
Cyr	I'm gonna puke. Are you all listening to this?

Cyr gets up and paces... Lights shift.

Cyr and Dunn are the only ones on stage. They see each other... smile...

Dunn Fucking Johnny Cyr...

Cyr Fucking Jerry Dunn...

They shake vigorously... slap each other on the back... laugh.

Dunn Damn, Johnny. How are you? You look like a million bucks.

Cyr You look great Jer... same old fucking clothes horse... still got those cuff links too... damn. Jerry Dunn.

Lights shift.

Dunn and Anson alone on stage... Cyr backs off into shadows.

Anson Johnny Cyr is here, at this same fucking hotel. Johnny Cyr.

Dunn I seen him. Spoke to him. Shook his hand. I've shaken his hand a million times—every continent in the world... or it seems like.

Anson You shook his hand in Vegas and Houston and Atlantic City and Reno maybe...

Dunn Listen...

Anson I am listening.

Dunn	You think, if you do this right, if we do it smart... we can take this game off?
Anson	I told you, I can't be trusted with an opinion.
Dunn	But what do you think?
Anson	I want to try. I need to try, Jerry. I got nothing and I got... I'm only gonna live another year... maybe two... maybe less for all I know. I need to do something or I die like a fucking dog in the street.
Dunn	OK, then. OK.
Anson	Jerry... *(pause)* This girl, Josefa... she is like a martian. Like a cyborg. She is like a dream... she lives in my dreams but I don't know if she's real.
Dunn	Does she know about all of this? Have you talked to her about it?
Anson	I think she knows... just 'cause she knows, and I don't tell her anything, but it doesn't matter.
Dunn	When did you start seeing her?
Anson	A while back. I can't remember... it's like she's always been there... watching the back of my head... giving me cards with saints' pictures on them... with the Archangel Michael. With Gabriel. When we make love it's like I forget everything—I feel days have passed that I can't account for. And whenever I wake up she's not there... she's left... I never see her sleep.
Dunn	I had a dog like that once. I'd go to sleep with the dog next to the bed watching me, and then I'd wake up and he'd be there, in the same spot, watching me. Dog was so wired... I don't think he slept... honestly, I don't.
Anson	She's like that... like a good horse... with bloodlines— or a dog... bred for work, you know? Bred to only

work at this one thing, and to express this work as a kind of love. *(Beats)* She don't sleep... I know it.

LIGHTS shift.

ANSON and JOSEFA. They are DOWNSTAGE. UPSTAGE in soft light is CYR. He watches them as he shuffles a pack of cards.

Anson   I will die on you and leave you alone.

Josefa   You will never leave me. You don't understand that.

Anson   Then you'll leave me. *(Pause)* I am a lot older than you.

Josefa   I can't help that. God doesn't look at things like age. He has no age. Love occurs... it isn't science. It's not measured. It flickers like a candle in the dark—in the outside... near woods... a light. The wilderness surrounds us... and then love is there... sometimes like a sickness... like a plague... and then it will heal you too.

Anson   It is both sickness and cure?

Josefa   If it were not an illness... a disease, then it could not cure. The action is the curing—and this is why we are alive at all. If you let it alone—and you crawl back to the tent... you slink away... or you even walk away with a false posture of power... of strength... then your sickness advances... like radiation poisoning... I've read about it... and it kills from within. You must stay in the darkness and shiver in the wind... for the wind is always cold... even when it's a summer wind... you shiver. I watch you because I have no other chance, Anson.

Anson   Do you know I love you?

She nods. LIGHTS *dim on them... up more on* CYR.

Cyr   So they want to rob this game. This is a common dream of the desperate. The desperate always want to steal from gambling games or casinos. It makes sense, I guess. *(Pause)* I don't care about Anson or Dunn. They'll fuck it up, though. How do I know this? Because I've known them a long while. Like I said. I know them all the time they've been alive.

CYR *takes a drink of water.*

I prefer ginger ale... but you can't get ginger ale much anymore. I liked the old kind... Verner's ginger ale... in this amber-colored bottle... or the ginger ale was amber. It's an old memory of mine. *(Pause)* Dunn and Anson won't get far with any of this. They need to talk, though. They don't have much left... either of them.

Silence.

I am not here to play. I'm not even invited to this game. Older guys... rich guys... not real players... they'll be at the game. Before that everyone will be at the track. Watch the race. Talk to everyone... be seen and talk about all the plans they got. Nobody got any plans, really, but they're gonna talk. *(Beats)* It's like a life led around the edges... all of us—

He stops... hesitating... looking for the right words.

My family died when I was young. I never got married but a girl... one girl, she says she had my baby but I don't know, I never went to see her about it. *(Pause)* I liked this girl. I didn't have a thing against her. I didn't love her though. She was older than me a few years and I know she wanted a baby. So she had one—maybe it was mine, I don't know. *(Pause)* So why do I stay here? Why don't I talk to Dunn and...

He stops again. Silence.

I can't talk to them. Would make no difference. It's not about me. I am only on the edges... getting older...

He is shuffling again... a bit compulsively.

LIGHTS *shift.*

DUNN *and* ANSON *down stage.* ANSON *is getting dressed as* DUNN *sits on edge of bed watching.*

Dunn	They give you drugs for this?
Anson	Lots of drugs. Terminal patients get lots of drugs. *(Pause)* You want some? I have too much to take.
Dunn	*(Beats)* Sure... sure, if you have enough.

ANSON *takes bottle from pocket and hands him several white tablets.*

Anson	Some third-generation morphine derivative. Who knows. *(Beats)* You can't get high when you really have pain— it's like all the pleasure gets sucked into the pain. *(Beats)* Finally get some good pharmaceutical drugs and I can't get a buzz—the pain is robbing me of the buzz. Pain is a fucking thief... the existential thief of life.
Dunn	Strange... is it strange to be described as terminal? *(Pause)* Must be, must be strange.
Anson	I don't really know what it is. Means I'm gonna die. Well, you're gonna die too. So what.
Dunn	But I'm not sick. That's the difference, right? I'm just old. You're sick and I'm old. We end up dying... maybe... around the same time. Funny.
Anson	I don't understand what "sickness" is... to be honest. I'm sick, I'm so fucking sick I'm gonna die. They don't quite know when, though. Well, hell, I could have told them that already—told them I didn't know when I was gonna die. This is supposed to be useful information? Well, they say, well, but you're sick sucker... and you're gonna die sooner rather than later. That's it... you'll die pretty soon... not way later. Pretty soon.
Dunn	This is a big game. The one... you know? It's a big fucking game in terms of cash on the table.

Silence.

Anson	And it's all amateurs?
Dunn	That's what it is.
Anson	Good.
Dunn	Sure better than a roomful of hard cases. *(Laughs)*

Anson	Amateurs is better.
Dunn	Certainly is.

Silence.

Anson	But I have pain, Jerry.
Dunn	Sure you do.
Anson	That's the real thing. The pain.
Dunn	I know.

Silence. LIGHTS shift.

CYR is strolling front of stage. He sees JOSEFA.

Cyr	Wait...

She pauses.

Cyr	I know you... I mean, I know you're Anson's girl.
Josefa	I am not Anson's anything.
Cyr	I just meant... I...
Josefa	I know. I know you too.
Cyr	You think so?
Josefa	I know so.
Cyr	Josefa. Where you from, Josefa?
Josefa	Your momma's ass.

Pause

Cyr	Uh-huh. Alright. But I only was trying to be friendly. I know where you from anyhows. You from El Salvador.
Josefa	You don't even know what El Salvador is, you don't even know if it's a country.
Cyr	It's someplace. *(Laughs)* Josefa... Anson's dying, isn't he?

JOSEFA hurries off... into the dark.

CYR on stage by himself.

LIGHTS shift... and DUNN appears...

Cyr	Hey Jer.
Dunn	Johnny.

Silence.

	Why you here, Cyr? You playing—what are you doing?
Cyr	I don't know—nothin else going on—you know.
Dunn	You got some gray hairs, Johnny. *(Laughs)* We're all getting old. Ha, even Johnny Cyr. Even the playboy—what we called you... even Johnny Cyr is getting fucking old.
Cyr	It's not so bad.
Dunn	No, I suppose it's not. It's just what it is.
Cyr	How is Anson? I seen his girl.
Dunn	Anson is fine. You ask him yourself, when you see him, how he is, OK?
Cyr	OK, geez... everyone is kinda touchy in this place.
Dunn	Anson is fine.

Cyr	I bet he is.

Silence.

LIGHTS SHIFT.

ANSON *seated... JOSEFA behind him staring at the back of his head.*

Anson	What do you see today?
Josefa	I see you need a haircut.
Anson	What else?
Josefa	Anson—I see gods. I know which gods have died and which live on.
Anson	I thought gods didn't die.
Josefa	Shows how much you know. *(Pause)* Some return... after death... some come back... and it's natural that they do. We look at the ocean and we see nothing. We see or hear no gods. We see the fires at night, in the desert and we see nothing. *(Beats)* Why do we even have fire if gods do not inhabit that fire?
Anson	I am not a god. Would I feel different if I were a god with a terminal disease?
Josefa	That's a complicated question.

Silence.

Josefa	I see how you travel among the gods. *(Beats)* It is because you are outside of everything normal—you

	have left yourself outside, like an old hermit... like some ascetic... St. Francis of the card room. *(She laughs).*
Anson	I am outside... how... I am... something like outside... and it's part of my deep fucking grief. *(Beats)* I do not travel among the gods.
Josefa	It is a choice you made I guess, I don't know. Some people live away from the others... and they appear at night, usually... like you.

ANSON starts to turn...

(Loudly) Don't turn around...

He stops.

Don't turn around today.

Silence.

| **Anson** | I don't travel among gods. I don't travel at all. I travel from the room here to the casino... or I travel from my crappy apartment to the train station or bus station. Gods don't travel with me. |
| **Josefa** | You don't know who travels with you. |

LIGHTS shift. UPSTAGE is CYR, watching.

The gods are only here, now, in their own way... lost and alone, themselves... like us. It is not the way it used to be. That is what I think.

Anson	Gods... you think there are many?
Josefa	Of course. You know there are many.
Anson	I know I travel all alone.
Josefa	I am here and I want to be near you. I have no real future the way my sisters think of it, the way that they have a future. They will marry and have husbands with straight jobs... and they will have children... some cute, some stupid... but it won't matter. They will probably get fat too. I have taken myself away from all that and I abide in my place here—near you—but away from you. Close enough—but never really...
Anson	Never really what?
Josefa	Never really part of you—for with you that is impossible.

Lights fade on Josefa and Anson. Up more on Cyr.

Cyr	I am looking for Jerry. I'm not eavesdropping. I'm just looking for Jerry. *(Beats)* Why do I need Jerry?

Silence.

Hey, Jer...

Cyr waves as Dunn appears...

Dunn	The playboy. Johnny Cyr... God damn. God damn... Johnny Cyr.
Cyr	Jerry, boy oh boy. Jerry. Jesus Christ. Jesus H. Christ.
Dunn	Lookit, Johnny...

They stare at each other. Silence.

Johnny, the thing is, see, I don't know what you want... I mean, "if" you want anything. You get where I am coming from? Suddenly, you're here. Johnny Cyr. Like a fucking phantom. Appears... like... fuckin' hell... I don't know. Haven't even thought of you for years. For close to... what... ten years. Haven't thought of you.

Cyr   I guess I don't want anything.

Dunn   Alright, and I believe you, too. I do. But it's funny, don't you think?

Cyr   Like, there are no coincidences—you mean like that?

Dunn   You know about luck. Johnny, you know luck isn't really luck, per se. Per fucking se.

Cyr   I'm not lucky, I've never been lucky.

Dunn   I'm not talking about that.

Cyr   Nobody would ever call me lucky.

Dunn   It's just coincidence, whatever. Coincidence or luck... they aren't the same... but things happen and something makes them happen. You're here. I'm here... you keep walking into me. Now, maybe you think I keep walking into you, I don't know. Luck is a phantom, too. I believe in luck, all of us do. I also know all the things that luck isn't. You do, too. You know luck isn't a horseshoe... *(Touches his cuff links)*. It's not a four-leaf clover. Coincidence... now what is that? It's just a kind of odds. What are the odds of running into you this way?

Cyr   We're at the same hotel.

Dunn   Yeah.

Silence.

I got a story. Got a sec?

Cyr *nods.*

A story. My story is about how one day I realized how... well, how everyone thinks everyone else in the world is essentially like them. But here's the kicker... they're not! Nope... no, not everyone is a fucking human being. *(Laughs)* The deuce you say... *(laughs)*... no, it's true. Some people are not really people, or if they are, they are different people. Different kinds of people. They don't have thoughts like we do... or... see, here it gets tricky. Like "I" do... because really I don't know if there is anyone else out there with thoughts like mine. One day I was talking to a man, and this man, when I looked deep into his eyes... I could see there was nothing there. Not anything I could recognize.

Cyr   This is a lousy story, Jerry.

Dunn   I suppose it is. *(Pause)* But Johnny, I think... don't get mad... I think I don't know about you. You follow? I don't know about you.

Silence.

Lights *shift...*

Anson *and* Dunn.

Anson	You have a plan?
Dunn	We rob them. We don't know them, they don't know us. Period. We go in and point guns at them and tell them to give us their money.
Anson	That's the best we can come up with?
Dunn	It should work.
Anson	*(Beats)* You have guns? *(Beats)* I never liked guns. You know why I never liked guns? I never liked guns because at the sight of a gun, or the touch, I always felt as if I wanted to shoot it... at myself.
Dunn	They say that about people who don't like to get too close to the edge—on a tall building or on a cliff. The fear is that you "want" to jump. *(Laughs)* Same thing—touch a gun and you want to put a bullet in your head.
Anson	We're gamblers. How come we don't have an intricate kind of sting, a slick and smart way to take off their money?
Dunn	Because the best way to take something is to take it at the point of a gun.

Pause.

Dunn	Taking is fundamental. Taking what isn't yours. It's basic.
Anson	Basic.
Dunn	You don't think it is?
Anson	I don't think anything.
Dunn	I think maybe we're just not smart enough to have a plan like that. Or, or , maybe I just don't have the

energy to think about this stuff. I don't give a fuck, I don't give a fuck about it... I just figure we should get some of this... of what we don't have. I don't know.

Lights shift.

Cyr and Anson.

Cyr	What are you doing here, Anson? I heard you were sick. I heard you were very sick.
Anson	You still wear all that fucking hair oil in your hair. That went out with Elvis.
Cyr	Some kind of strange sickness... some sickness hardly anybody gets.
Anson	It's a rare condition.
Cyr	Rare. *(Beats)* Sure.
Anson	Why are you here? Nobody has seen you in a long while, Johnny.
Cyr	Lots of people seen me. Just not you.

Silence.

Lights fade out.

Lights up on Dunn and Anson

Anson	You got the gun?
Dunn	I got it. We don't need it, but I got it.
Anson	May as well do this... tonight is the game, right?

Dunn	It looks easy, it does. No bodyguards... nothing like that.
Anson	Nothing of that sort, then?
Dunn	Nope... no, nothing. *(Pause)* What you gonna do with the money? I mean... could be a lot of money.
Anson	*(Long pause)* Dunn.
Dunn	*(Beats)* Yeah.
Anson	I wonder if I'm even doing this for the money. *(Pause)* Never mind, of course I'm doing it for the money. We both need money. I especially need money.

LIGHTS *fade out quickly.*

LIGHTS *up.*

REAR SCREEN PROJECTION.

SCREEN: *The joker card.*

| **Dunn** | The joker. When I was a boy I loved this card. The joker wasn't added to the deck until pretty late. Around the 1860s, I am told. |

SCREEN: *Early Islamic card.*

See, we don't know from whence. Ah... did Gypsies bring the card game to the West? Or was it Muslim traders? Don't know. And what about the suits? Man, I loved spades and diamonds... hearts, clubs... when I was nine or ten.

SCREEN: *Changes to early tarot card.*

Cartomancy. The occult. But see... this is where the square world loses their way. I mean, all cards are telling fortunes. All of them... all have occult properties.

SCREEN: *An early Chinese domino card.*

Asians, man. Chinamen... fuckers like game. They play for anything at anytime. All the time.

SCREEN: *Early traditional English king of hearts.*

But these faces. From where did they come? They are my friends... like cigarettes... like whisky. Friends of mine. The king of hearts once was supposed to be Charlemagne. And I think David from the Bible... he was the king of spades. Funny. *(Pause)* The Germans had acorns and bells... and the Italians had swords I think.

SCREEN: *A five of clubs.*

I liked clubs as a boy. I don't know why. I think in ancient Persia they had games with cards and they invented ths suits. Who knows. But it's always about magic. Why one card and not another? Why a queen of spades... when it could have been a one-eyed jack. Why fifty-two? Or fifty-three if we add a joker. Why? I've seen cards, old ones in a museum, without royalty but

with a cleaning woman, or a lady-in-waiting,
or a stable boy. *(Pause)* A woman and a tub... washing
her clothes. There is a magic formula for everything.
A pair of cleaning women... or a full house, three sixes
and a pair of stable boys. *(Pause)*

SCREEN: *Tarot card of death.*

Dunn   Do cards tell the future? Nothing tells the future. The
future is in the future, you know?! *(Pause)* But the big
games... today... it's all hype and all about TV... and
I don't relate to those things. I don't see the cards the
same way anymore. And I see the old guys—Brunson,
Reese, and the rest of them... some of them, you know,
you never heard of—it's like Minnesota Fats was never
in the top fifty pool players during his life—but he
promoted himself... changed his name from New York
Fats... 'cause of that movie... and so Amarillo Slim
becomes a TV personality... but others, people you
never heard of... they just play... and they play and play
and play. *(Beats)* And then we all die. And that is
fucking that. But the geniuses of gambling... they stay
in the shadows. It's gotta be that way. The cards are
unreal... the cards are Gypsy totems... they are lucky
charms or something... talismans... they are scary and I
mean if you look close at a one-eyed-jack, well, tell me
what you see? Look... *(beats)* Look close... what do you
see? Do you see the future? What you see is death,
because that is everyone's future.
SCREEN: *Card from Tarot of Catelin Geofroy*

| Dunn | The tarot from the 16th century... it had a suit of parrots and suit of monkeys. The six of monkeys... and if you look close at that, what do you see? *(Beats)* And then we play this game for money. And it makes no sense if money isn't involved. And the money has no meaning unless it's about the game. Money is only a means to play more. And now we have TV poker. And guys and this fucking dames... refried blondes... and they all... I don't know... they don't really see what's on the cards. They just play... and if you look close at the faces of the presidents on money—those dead presidents... tell me what you see? It's no accident those are all *dead* presidents. |

Pause.

Silence.

Lights *shift...*

Spot on Anson *and* Josefa. *She is behind him.*

Anson	It didn't go at all like I wanted. Not at all like we planned.
Josefa	Of course not.
Anson	But we came away with money. I have a lot of money, see?!

Silence.

I have more money than I thought we'd get. *(Beats)*
But I lost Dunn... I think he might be dead. I think
he might be arrested... might have been picked up.
I lost him.

Josefa You don't lose people.

Anson For once you're wrong. For once, for once you are
not correct.

Josefa Maybe.

Anson I lost him, lost Dunn. He is somewhere, isn't he?!
Maybe in a holding tank. Maybe in a hospital. Because
really, his heart was none too good. *(Beats)* We got
away.
We took all the money on the table and all the money
anywhere in the fucking room—and from people. We
took it from everyone, even the hooker in the bedroom.

Josefa From her, too?

Anson You sound like you care? *(Pause)* We took all the
money and I have it... I carried it and I have it. *(Beats)*
What do I do with it? You have any ideas? You usually
have lots of ideas. You got any on this one?

Silence.

Someone got shot. Isn't that... isn't that weird... I don't
know who. Don't know who shot him or what. But
someone had a gun... not me... not Dunn, I don't think
so anyway... and a gun was fired... and fired again and
fuck if I saw what was going on. I was gone... I was
running... and I ran down corridors and out into the
parking lot. And under this arc light... what do you

call them? Under the parking lot lights... way up there... big lights... and the whole parking lot is lit... and I was running across it... toward the opposite end of the lot... where a little guy sits in a booth and he masturbates mostly... watches porn tapes on his little TV... and jerks off like a speed-driven chimp... and he is supposed to watch for exactly people like me... you know, running in a panic toward the gate... and he didn't see shit until I was right in front of his little booth. And I never looked back. And this little man looks up from his porn tape... and I could see the tape... it had two men... with huge penises and they were slamming some little Asian chick... but anyway... he looks at me with big scared eyes... and he can't speak... I can see his mouth is dry... and he can't talk and I ask him for keys to a car... any car and he doesn't ask anything but just tosses me keys... and he says, it's the first row here, the blue Buick wagon. I go to it and open the door and sure enough the keys work and I climb in and the cars starts fine and I drive off. An automatic transmission... and inside it smells like the zoo... like a cage at the zoo, and there are candy wrappers and an old newspaper. *(Beats)* I drove... and I got on a freeway and I ended up out... where is this? Apple Valley? A place I never been. *(Beats)* Aren't you going to ask me why I came here?

Silence.

Good, 'cause I got no answer.

And what is in this fucking nowhere piece of desert?
A few tract homes... and shit else. And unhappy
people... and here I sit in a stolen Buick and imagine I
am talking to you. And who are you?

Long silence.

Josefa	You took from the whore too?
Anson	I took from everyone. But who are you? Do you care, really? Really? *(Silence)* Crappy houses in Apple Valley... if that's even where I am. And in the air... on the breeze, I smell something like old rotted fruit. Maybe it's something else too. And who are you?
Josefa	Remember I tell you about those who do not come from man?
Anson	You tell me a lot of shit.
Josefa	Who am I?
Anson	I asked you that. But it doesn't matter because I think it's all over anyway. It all ends in this planned community in Apple Valley.
Josefa	If you had been listening, you would know it never ends.
Anson	Smells like illness, too. Like a hospital floor for the elderly. That smell, it's proof it ends.

LIGHTS *shift.*

SCREEN: *The hanged man from Tarot of Charles VI.*

Dunn	A man is hanged. Many men have been executed. Many men lynched. And it goes way back. And men kill... and they kill each other and they feel good when they do.

LIGHTS shift.

CYR stands alone.

Cyr	I said it would go all wrong. I said it, and it did.

Silence.

Dunn	Many men have been killed before their time—before they were ready. Before they got old. Million... billions... trillions of dead... men, women, children. *(Pause)* That feels like cards... like a game of chance. And somehow... you don't get dealt the last card... that's what I think.
Cyr	What did I say?
Dunn	I don't remember what happened. Last night.
Cyr	Anson and Dunn... what would you expect?
Dunn	Did I want it to end this way? Did I know it was a fuck-brained crazy idea...? *(Pause)* Maybe. *(Beats)* I wanted to help Anson—that's what I told myself. Anson is dying. Anson is a sick man. *(Pause)* I'm getting old... and maybe I wanted to stop having to think about the next day... about where to go and how to make that money... how to have money... to pay for things I don't really want or need. That is what makes you old, actually. What I think. And I'm suddenly getting old... old in a way... that, well, it makes me feel old to just

have to think about it. And I wanted Anson to... I don't know... I feel like Anson is a son... you know? And he's dying... and I wanted to give him some help. *(Beats)* An old man with few options left... few desires.

CYR *is standing and shuffling cards as he talks.*

Cyr
Anson won't ever get to be an old man. Cards. *(Beats)* A game of cards. Stud poker used to only have like twenty-three cards... something like that. A simple game for a man with a good memory. They upped it to fifty-two then added the Joker. Those who play card games tend toward a certain kind of mental makeup. *(Pause)* It's their nature. That's all it is... it's their nature to be fucked up in the rest of their lives. Not good husbands, not good fathers, not good anything... just good gamblers. And some ain't even that. *(Long pause)* What does a society want to do with those who bet on everything? Does it matter? I wonder about that... about how unimportant gambling is. I bet and win or I bet and lose; what's the difference. It's my outcome... it's not reality.

DUNN *is seated now, looking old and tired and sick. He seems about to collapse.*

Gambling isn't about changing anything and that's the problem.

LIGHTS *shift...*

ANSON and JOSEFA.

Anson	Dunn is either in jail or dead.
Josefa	How you feel, Anson?
Anson	It's my nature to gamble. *(Beats)* Early on, as a boy, I saw this to be true. *(Beats)* I feel as if I choked—lost, lost a crucial bet.
Josefa	That isn't what you really feel.
Anson	No.

Silence.

Josefa	What do you really feel?
Anson	I feel I've been pulled along, on waters of darkness. On tides... and I can't see who is pulling me, and I can't see anything. I can't see how deep it is or where the shore is. I feel paralyzed with the certainty that we are all alone. That hollow sound, in the night air... that air with the smell of age... that hollow sound is just our own fucking empty heads. Our empty souls. *(Beat)* That's how I feel.
Josefa	I believe you.

Silence.

LIGHTS shift.

Cyr	Stories... they have endings. Life has few endings. Time doesn't stop. There will be other shit to bet on. Other things to waste time on.

CYR takes a card from the deck... holds it face out to the audience.

It's the JOKER.

The joker... right? The fool. The fifty-third card. The joker can be used as a wild card... meaning it can be anything you want it to be... anything you need it to be.

He drops the card on the floor.

Silence.

The joker is wild. Americans love that... love having a joker in the deck. Love having that get-out-of-jail-free card... they invented the idea of wild cards... of hedging your bets.

Silence.

Sleep... wake up and play again... play until you can't focus and then split... go back to your room... sleep and wake up. Play some more. Win or lose... just keep playing... sleeping... showering... eating, a roast beef sandwhich or a pastrami sandwhich... from the steam tray... guy in whites and a white chef hat... slices some pastrami for you... asks if you want a pickle... of course you do... and you sit and eat it and read the odds on the games... but really you're just getting ready to go back to the table. *(Pause)* Over and over and over.

Pause.

Josefa   There are men who are not men. They are fallen...
either angels at one time... or just aliens. I can spot
them and my father could too. He taught me. *(Pause)*
It doesn't help... it hasn't helped.

Cyr   Time doesn't stop. It doesn't end. There are odds on
everything... and there will always be odds on everything... and there will be odds on there being odds.
You see how it works? *(Beats)* Good. Because that *is*
how it works. Life is the same... only the odds change.

Silence.

LIGHTS *fade out.*

The End

The Destruction of
the Fourth World

by Murray Mednick

Characters

Bernard (Bernie)—*13*
David—*Bernard's brother, 31*
Rose (Rosie)—*the boys' Grandmother, 75*
Chrystal—*David's wife, 30*
Caleb—*the boys' father, Rose's son, 56*
Coyote—*(invisible)*

Dialogue in parentheses are asides to the audience.

Bernie

The CURTAIN rises, the HOUSE LIGHTS dim. COYOTE, through whom both Being and Nonbeing manifests, stands there, ONSTAGE, looking out. COYOTE looks at the audience.

Coyote VOICE OFF: (They're listening with their heads in their pockets. They can't figure out who this Indian is, looking at them as though he understood their personal idiosyncracies—but they're willing to go along with it, up to a point. "Listen," he says, "since the day I've been born in America, that is to say, way long before any of you, the situation has been the same, "Don't make the white-eyes uncomfortable, or feel bad about themselves, both the women and the men, and you might endure for a long time your glorious, meaningless, immortal life." This inevitable tension—between money and celebrity and entertainment versus true intelligence—is suspect, intractable and eternal. That said, this is a story about intelligent people, or, more exactly, about me, Coyote. Ushers, please be sure that the customers have all paid what they owe, and proceed to lock the doors. Thank you. Amen and good luck.)

Bernie and Caleb

Bernie How do I pray?

Caleb I don't know. Why pray?

Bernie	I can't control the ox.
Caleb	Why control the ox?
Bernie	He leads me to stray.
Caleb	Stray from?
Bernie	My own mind.
Caleb	Where do you go, China?
Bernie	Yeah, China, Dad.
Caleb	I see.
Bernie	So?
Caleb	So what?
Bernie	You know about that?
Caleb	What?
Bernie	Straying and praying?
Caleb	I'm not sure that I do, no.
Bernie	Okay.
Caleb	Okay, what?
Bernie	Okay, okay. To pray?
Caleb	I don't know. *(Pause)*
Bernie	Do you not know?
Caleb	No.
Bernie	Then why sit before me, leaning forward like you care?
Caleb	It's my duty.
Bernie	Looking concerned and intelligent?
Caleb	You're a good kid, Bernie.
Bernie	Say something, Dad.
Caleb	I just said something.
Bernie	About prayer.
Caleb	I don't know anything about it.
Bernie	Come on, Dad.

Caleb	You figure it out.

Moments later.

Caleb	You could look it up.
Bernie	That's what I'll do.
Caleb	Make it hard.
Bernie	I will.
Caleb	Make it hard on yourself.
Bernie	I hear that.
Caleb	Maybe you'll find something.
Bernie	Maybe I will.
Caleb	It's all there somewhere.
Bernie	In the books.
Caleb	In the books.
Bernie	The text.
Caleb	The teachings.
Bernie	The laws.
Caleb	It's all there if you search.
Bernie	That's what I'll do then.
Caleb	Because I don't know myself.
Bernie	Thanks.
Caleb	I don't know the first thing.
Bernie	That's okay.
Caleb	About prayer or God.
Bernie	Neither do I.
Caleb	Or what, or who.
Bernie	I know.
Caleb	You're supposed to pray to.
Bernie	Or how.

Caleb	Right. I don't have a clue.
Bernie	What to say.
Caleb	But I know one thing.
Bernie	How to say it.
Caleb	No—you don't do it for yourself.
Bernie	The words.
Caleb	You don't ask for yourself.
Bernie	Or the song.
Caleb	You sing it for others.
Bernie	I see.
Caleb	You sing the song for others.
Bernie	Good.
Caleb	So they'll have rain.
Bernie	Crops.
Caleb	So they'll have good fortune.
Bernie	In their lives.
Caleb	Not you, not yourself.
Bernie	For them.
Caleb	For them, not you.

Later.

Caleb	Bernie.
Bernie	What?
Caleb	Let me ask you something.
Bernie	Ask.
Caleb	You steal clothes?
Bernie	Me? I don't go out much. It's not me.
Caleb	Who is it, then?
Bernie	I can't say.

Caleb	Who steals clothes?
Bernie	I can't say, but she likes style, she likes new things.
Caleb	I know who it is.
Bernie	You knew all along.
Caleb	She's into style.
Bernie	Grandma Rosie. She forgets.
Caleb	Definitely, but it's not her.
Bernie	She gets mixed up.
Caleb	I won't mention any names.
Bernie	Chrystal.
Caleb	Your mother did it, too, before she died.
Bernie	She did?
Caleb	Not often. Once in a while.
Bernie	Where is she now?
Caleb	She's in the ocean. She was in the ocean.
Bernie	No, her body was in the ocean.
Caleb	Wait a minute.
Bernie	What?
Caleb	Her spirit is someplace else?
Bernie	It has to be somewhere.
Caleb	Certainly you can tell the difference.
Bernie	Between?
Caleb	Between the living and the dead.
Bernie	They say there is a long line.
Caleb	Who says?
Bernie	(The Hopi) I can't say.
Caleb	The long line of what?
Bernie	The long line of the dead.
Caleb	No, between your mother and your grandmother.
Bernie	Of course.

Caleb	What's the difference?
Bernie	One is living and one is dead.
Caleb	Exactly.
Bernie	Meanwhile the other one forgets everything.
Caleb	Which one?
Bernie	The living. *(Pause)*
Caleb	She had to win, your mother. She had to be above me at all times.
Bernie	And so?
Caleb	So you're not talking about that, are you?
Bernie	No.
Caleb	You're talking about memory?
Bernie	Right, Dad.
Caleb	A withering away of the branches?
Bernie	Yes. That's it. In the brain.

Moments later.

Caleb	You buy cookies?
Bernie	What?
Caleb	You buy cookies?
Bernie	Yes.
Caleb	You buy cookies for the class?
Bernie	No.
Caleb	She blames me. Your grandmother.
Bernie	For Maysie.
Caleb	Who is Maysie?
Bernie	Not for the class.
Caleb	No more cookies.
Bernie	Not for the class.

Caleb	No more cookies for anybody.
Bernie	Why can't you be nice?
Caleb	I am nice.
Bernie	You're not being nice.
Caleb	I'm nice to you.
Bernie	Just be nice.
Caleb	You don't have to be proud.
Bernie	I want to be proud.
Caleb	You don't have to bribe your friend with cookies.
Bernie	I'm proud.
Caleb	You don't have to be proud.
Bernie	I'll be proud.
Caleb	I don't care if you're a little proud.
Bernie	Okay, I'll be little proud.
Caleb	But no more cookies.
Bernie	They're for my friend, Maysie.
Caleb	Let her buy you cookies.
Bernie	Can you be nice?
Caleb	Only once.
Bernie	Can I give her the cookies then?
Caleb	This once.
Bernie	Okay.
Caleb	That's all.
Bernie	Okay.
Caleb	Just this once.
Bernie	Okay.
Caleb	You'll bring them to school?
Bernie	What?
Caleb	The cookies. You'll bring them to school.
Bernie	Maybe I will.

Caleb	That's the only way, Bernie.
Bernie	What?
Caleb	School.
Bernie	Okay, Dad.
Caleb	Don't forget.
Bernie	I saw her, Dad.
Caleb	Who? Maysie?
Bernie	No. My mother.
Caleb	No, you didn't.
Bernie	I saw her in a window. She was a reflection in a window.
Caleb	It's impossible.
Bernie	I'm telling you.
Caleb	What was she wearing?
Bernie	Something from the fifties or sixties.
Caleb	You're imagining things.
Bernie	You can see things from the spirit world in a reflection.
Caleb	Who told you that?
Bernie	The person's not there but their image is in the window.
Caleb	Who told you that?
Bernie	I can't say. (Coyote.)
Caleb	Okay, Bernie.
Bernie	Okay.
Caleb	Do your homework.
Bernie	I'm doing my homework.
Caleb	That's all I can say, do your homework.
Bernie	I'm doing my homework.
Caleb	Let me see it when you're done, please.

Moments later.

Caleb	Don't hide from Dad.
Bernie	I'm not.
Caleb	Don't hide things from Dad.
Bernie	I won't.
Caleb	Or try to lie.
Bernie	I'm not.
Caleb	Because we'll know.
Bernie	Yeah, yeah, of course.
Caleb	And God will know.
Bernie	Where is God?
Caleb	He's under the bed.
Bernie	Ha. You don't know anything about it.
Caleb	He's under the bed, ha ha.
Bernie	All right, Dad.
Caleb	He's under the bed and in the ceiling.
Bernie	Right, Dad.
Caleb	So don't bother to lie.
Bernie	About?
Caleb	I don't know. Cookies, candy, and clothes.
Bernie	Come on.
Caleb	Cookies, candy, and clothes.
Bernie	Like what.
Caleb	Because I hear about it from your grandmother.
Bernie	You're afraid of my mother?
Caleb	Your mother is dead.
Bernie	You're afraid of my mother?
Caleb	Did you hear me?
Bernie	You should stand up.
Caleb	Who told you that?
Bernie	She told me.

Caleb	Maybe you didn't hear me? Your mother killed herself.
Bernie	You should stand up, and then I'd be proud.
Caleb	She didn't want to hear about it.
Bernie	What?
Caleb	The murder of the Jews.
Bernie	I'm a Jew.
Caleb	That's right. By birth.
Bernie	What do you mean?
Caleb	Otherwise you're a complete American, like me.
Bernie	I'm not hanging around for that. I don't want to be that.
Caleb	What?
Bernie	An American. (I'd rather be an Indian.)
Caleb	Good luck.
Bernie	My mother said I was from the Middle East.
Caleb	You're not.
Bernie	By origin.
Caleb	So, she still didn't want to hear about it. (The Holocaust)
Bernie	Who wants to hear about it?
Caleb	Your grandmother.
Bernie	Okay. What's the lie?
Caleb	What lie?
Bernie	The one you referred to earlier.
Caleb	Don't say you went to school if you didn't go.
Bernie	Okay, I lied.
Caleb	You lied to Grandma and you lied to me.
Bernie	I'm sorry.
Caleb	And you lied to the sky. Because that's where God is.
Bernie	Where?
Caleb	I told you.
Bernie	In the sky and in the air?

Caleb	In the ground and in the mind.
Bernie	In the people, Dad.
Caleb	He's everywhere, Bernie.
Bernie	You should learn about it more. (That's where Coyote is.)
Caleb	No.
Bernie	Why not?
Caleb	It's too late now.

Later.

Caleb	Why did you complain?
Bernie	I didn't complain.
Caleb	Your grandmother calls me to tell me you complain.
Bernie	She called you? Grandma Rosie?
Caleb	Yes. So why did you complain?
Bernie	I didn't complain. About what?
Caleb	You go somewhere? And you know you're not allowed.
Bernie	I'm not allowed?
Caleb	To buy junk.
Bernie	I don't buy junk.
Caleb	I don't like the building.
Bernie	It's an ordinary building.
Caleb	No. It's depressing.
Bernie	All buildings are depressing.
Caleb	No, it's that particular building.
Bernie	What's wrong with it?
Caleb	It's a mall. And she can't control you there.
Bernie	I don't buy junk.
Caleb	What do you buy?
Bernie	I buy equipment.

Caleb	What kind of equipment?
Bernie	Electronics.
Caleb	Electronics?
Bernie	Electronics.
Caleb	She doesn't know anything about electronics.
Bernie	I know she doesn't.
Caleb	So you take advantage.
Bernie	I take advantage?
Caleb	You take advantage and then you complain.
Bernie	How did I complain?
Caleb	She won't let you buy things.
Bernie	It's my money.
Caleb	It's money she gave you.
Bernie	She gives me the money and she forgets where it is.
Caleb	I know.
Bernie	I try to buy something and she won't let me.
Caleb	It's her prerogative.
Bernie	It's my money.
Caleb	She's trying not to spoil you.
Bernie	Electronic equipment?
Caleb	Because she knows you have no mother.
Bernie	She can't remember from one minute to the next.
Caleb	So she thinks she's your mother?
Bernie	Yeah, Dad. And she isn't. She's my grandmother.
Caleb	Okay, Bernie.
Bernie	So I can buy what I want.
Caleb	I didn't say so.
Bernie	I can buy whatever I want.
Caleb	If you go to school. Only then.
Bernie	I'm done.

Caleb	What do you mean?
Bernie	I'm not going to buy anything anymore. I'm done.

Later.

Bernie	Please don't leave the door closed.
Caleb	I don't like the door open.
Bernie	Leave it open.
Caleb	She wouldn't like it.
Bernie	Who wouldn't like it?
Caleb	Your mother. She never liked it with the door open.
Bernie	My mother's in the spirit world now, Dad.
Caleb	Your mother is dead, may she rest in peace, but she never liked the door open.
Bernie	Why?
Caleb	Because the whole outside world could walk in.
Bernie	Was she right?
Caleb	Of course, she was right.
Bernie	Well, that's all good then.
Caleb	What is?
Bernie	You can leave the door open.
Caleb	And I still see her, I see her everywhere.
Bernie	What was it she didn't like?
Caleb	She didn't like the door open.
Bernie	No, besides that.
Caleb	Anybody could walk right in.
Bernie	Besides that, Dad.
Caleb	She didn't like complaining.
Bernie	You don't either, Dad.
Caleb	I know.

Bernie	Can you leave it open?
Caleb	The door?
Bernie	Yeah.
Caleb	Why? Are you expecting company?
Bernie	Yes.
Caleb	Who are you expecting?
Bernie	I'm expecting a friend.
Caleb	They can knock. Your friend can knock on the door.
Bernie	Okay.
Caleb	Your friend could knock on the door and then you can open it.
Bernie	Great.
Caleb	You can leave your own door open.
Bernie	Okay, thanks.
Caleb	You can leave the door to your own room open.
Bernie	I got it.
Caleb	There. I think that's a fair arrangement.
Bernie	Thanks a lot, Dad.
Caleb	The house door is closed, and your door is open. I think that's fair.
Bernie	Thanks.

Later.

Bernie	Dad?
Caleb	What?
Bernie	Grandma thinks she's in Brazil.
Caleb	I know she does.
Bernie	What are you going to do?
Caleb	What can I do?

Bernie	Maybe she should have an operation.
Caleb	They don't have that kind of operation, Bernie.
Bernie	It's very primitive.
Caleb	That's right. Things are very primitive.
Bernie	She thinks weird things about the building.
Caleb	This building?
Bernie	Yes.
Caleb	It's just a building.
Bernie	I know.
Caleb	So don't complain.
Bernie	I didn't.
Caleb	Don't complain about your grandmother.
Bernie	I didn't.
Caleb	Then don't.
Bernie	It's you that complains.
Caleb	Me?
Bernie	You complain all the time because she picks on you.
Caleb	I do?
Bernie	Because you're chicken.
Caleb	I'm not chicken.
Bernie	Otherwise I'd be proud.
Caleb	You should be proud.
Bernie	I'm not.
Caleb	It's because she's nuts.
Bernie	So are you.
Caleb	No, it's because she has to.
Bernie	What?
Caleb	She has to.
Bernie	What?
Caleb	She has to be above me.

Bernie	Then you should fight.
Caleb	Fight?
Bernie	No matter what. Fight back, Dad.
Caleb	I can't fight. The woman's nuts.
Bernie	Then why not fight?
Caleb	She's my mother. I can't win.
Bernie	Why can't you win?
Caleb	You don't understand.
Bernie	What?
Caleb	She can't be not above.
Bernie	Then don't blame me.
Caleb	You're right.
Bernie	And she can't remember.
Caleb	You never know.
Bernie	It's not my fault. Don't blame me.
Caleb	You're quite right.
Bernie	Don't blame me.
Caleb	I can't win. And your mother, too.
Bernie	What?
Caleb	I could never win.
Bernie	Dad? I'll keep my door closed.
Caleb	You can't keep your door closed.
Bernie	I thought that's what you wanted.
Caleb	No that was the front door. The front door should be closed.
Bernie	I want to keep my door closed, unless I come out.
Caleb	Why?
Bernie	I need to keep my door closed, Dad, like you said.
Caleb	What did I say?
Bernie	So the whole world doesn't come in.

Caleb	I don't remember saying that.
Bernie	The outside world.
Caleb	What about it?
Bernie	I don't want it coming into my room.

David and Caleb

Caleb	He says he saw his mother—your mother—in a window.
David	In a window?
Caleb	In the mall.
David	He was hallucinating.
Caleb	When he told me, I could see her clearly.
David	Well, you would, Dad.
Caleb	I don't know about women, David.
David	I have my problems, too, Dad.
Caleb	Sometimes I think they should all die, like your mother.
David	All of them?
Caleb	Just die out and leave us in peace.
David	I don't know about that, Dad.
Caleb	Then I could take care of you guys.
David	Sure, Dad.
Caleb	Without any pestering from her.
David	Which is not what my mother thought.
Caleb	Without any hysterical oppression.
David	Are you talking about Grandma?
Caleb	Without the bullshit.
David	Or are you talking about my mother?
Caleb	Definitely bullshit.
David	Dad?

Caleb	She was a secular woman with a lot of morals.
David	My mother? Sarah?
Caleb	Yes, and so am I. I'm secular. And so is everybody, except for Rosie.
David	Rosie is a survivor.
Caleb	When she remembers anything.
David	So what's Bernie doing with a bar mitzvah coming up?
Caleb	He's not doing it. He doesn't do his Hebrew homework.
David	He's into Indians.
Caleb	What's the Indians got to do with him?
David	Everything else is lies.
Caleb	This his mother would approve.
David	Maybe that's why he's not doing it.
Caleb	She hated the survivors.
David	But that wasn't right. It wasn't their fault.
Caleb	The special pleading. The righteousness.
David	So she didn't get along with Rosie.
Caleb	No.
David	That wasn't right.
Caleb	Special pleading. Where you can't forgive and you can't forget.
David	I don't know if that's right.
Caleb	True, you don't know and I don't know.
David	I wasn't raised to be a religious... uh...
Caleb	No, you're a secular person, like I said already.
David	Still, I'm not sure. The future and the past, they mean equally nothing.
Caleb	Is that right?

David	As far as I'm concerned.
Caleb	And the present?
David	This is it.
Caleb	Tell Rosie that.
David	I don't think so.

Moments later.

Caleb	Where were we?
David	When?
Caleb	Before.
David	We were right here.
Caleb	No. I mean what were we talking about?
David	How my mother hated the attitude of the survivors.
Caleb	Yes, and she was a Marxist, too. On top of everything else.
David	So why did she kill herself? (If she killed herself.)
Caleb	I don't know why.
David	Maybe she lost hope in America.
Caleb	She had a lot of integrity.
David	I remember that.
Caleb	So a person can't go around stealing clothes and shit.
David	Who does that?
Caleb	I don't know, whoever.
David	Who does that?
Caleb	Whoever does it.
David	Not me.
Caleb	That's how husbands kill their wives.
David	It happens.
Caleb	First you think it's a nice piece of twat.

David	Right.
Caleb	Then it turns out she's a full-grown lizard with a mouth.
David	I hear you.
Caleb	With a mouth. And you don't want to hear that voice.
David	No.
Caleb	That voice that thinks it owns you.
David	I know it.
Caleb	You want to drown it or cut it's throat. What's your wife's name?
David	You don't know her name?
Caleb	I know her name. I just forgot for a second.
David	See a doctor, Dad.
Caleb	I just forgot. *(Silence)* Is it Chrystal?
David	Yes. It's Chrystal. My mother's name was Sarah.
Caleb	Right. Chrystal. And Sarah.
David	Your wife's name was Sarah. Now deceased.
Caleb	Of course. I know that. I just forgot.
David	How could you forget?
Caleb	What kind of name is Chrystal?
David	That's her name.
Caleb	Stupid name.
David	That's her name.
Caleb	What's up with Chrystal?
David	Nothing's up with Chyrstal.
Caleb	She like her father-in-law?
David	Not really.
Caleb	What's she like?
David	She's like a girl, she's like a female.
Caleb	Meat-time in the universe.
David	What?

Caleb	I was just thinking.
David	Aloud?
Caleb	I was thinking aloud.
David	I don't know, Dad. Thinking aloud?
Caleb	So where is she now?
David	Who?
Caleb	Chrystal.
David	Why, Dad?
Caleb	We're nothing without our families.
David	She'll be home soon.
Caleb	We're abnormal.
David	(I like to sneak into her from behind.)
Caleb	What was that?
David	What?
Caleb	It's disgraceful. Were you thinking aloud?
David	Just a thought, Dad.
Caleb	It's so cowardly and disgraceful.
David	No, that's you, Dad.
Caleb	In magazines it all looks normal.
David	It's the photo, the glossy.
Caleb	Right, no scum in the photo. No stupid jism.
David	Life marching on planet earth.
Caleb	The dreaded reproductive act.
David	Pretty bodies writhing like larvae.
Caleb	Hey, not bad, Dave.
David	Like larvae. Only they look nice.
Caleb	To us, son, to us they look nice.
David	It looks nice in the magazines.
Caleb	They know how to do it, son. They know how to make it nice and glossy.

Later.

David	Did you go to see Grandma?
Caleb	I'll go tomorrow.
David	Tomorrow is good.
Caleb	I'm afraid she won't recognize me.
David	It can happen, Dad.
Caleb	You went today?
David	Yes.
Caleb	What happened?

ROSIE is revealed upstage, sitting in a chair, facing away.

David When I came in, her back was to me. She was sitting there, holding her head pensively in one hand. She was sitting with another woman, but they weren't talking. Just sitting there, sadly. I watched her for a second and then I went around in front of her. *(Crosses to ROSIE)* She looked up at me. I said, hi, Grandma.

Rosie	Hello.
David	I'm your grandson, David.
Rosie	Of course, you are. I'm sorry.
David	*(To CALEB)* I felt hurt she hadn't recognized me.
Caleb	It's amazing, isn't it, the egoism of that? And she wasn't going to admit to it, either. Too proud.
Rosie	Do you have a girlfriend?
David	I'm married, Grandma.
Rosie	I heard she dresses nice.
David	Who told you?
Rosie	A little birdie told me.
David	Her name is Chrystal.

Rosie	Of course, it is.
David	Dad is going to come again tomorrow.
Rosie	Oh, good. *(Pause)*
David	How are you doing?
Rosie	Doing?
David	Yes.
Rosie	I'm very busy with issues.
David	Issues?
Rosie	The Germans. You know, many of them settled here after the war. War criminals. Murderers. They found refuge.
David	Where is that, Grandma?
Rosie	Where?
David	Where.
Rosie	Brazil, Argentina. Other places in America. They created problems for the working class, of course, especially here in Rio.
David	I see.
Rosie	My whole family vanished. I'm the only survivor.
David	I know.
Rosie	Sometimes I feel like jumping out the window, like that Chinese fellow.
David	Who is the Chinese fellow?
Rosie	But I think I have another family here in America.
David	You do.
Rosie	So I don't want to hurt them by committing suicide.
David	That's good, Grandma.
Rosie	I don't know if that's good or not.
David	I think it's good.
Rosie	Well, that's good.

David	My Dad will be here tomorrow. Caleb.
Rosie	Oh, yes. I know someone named Caleb. It's a biblical name, isn't it?
David	I believe so, yes.
Rosie	I went to Berlin, to the Jewish Museum, after many years of denial. And I came out shriven and released. We had survived, after all, in spirit, like the oxygen in the air and the water and in us. Could you follow that, boy?
David	I think so.
Rosie	Well, I'm glad you came to see me. It was good talking to you.
David	I love you, Grandma.
Rosie	Take care.
David	You, too. *(Crossing back to* CALEB*)* She said she had some work to do, which I knew was a lie.

Bernie and Caleb and David

Caleb	So, listen up. We'll have to come up with a plan.
David	A plot?
Caleb	A plan.
David	Why?
Caleb	To keep an eye on my mother.
David	Why? She's not going anywhere.
Caleb	Your brother and me and maybe your wife, Chrystal.
David	Rosie's not going anywhere.
Bernie	I don't think so.
David	She's already there.
Bernie	In Rio.

Caleb	How old are you?
David	I'm thirty-one.
Caleb	Not you, Bernie.
Bernie	I'm thirteen.
Caleb	That's old enough.
Bernie	I'll stay in my room, if you don't mind.
Caleb	I do mind.
David	You can't do that.
Bernie	Shut up, David.
David	You can't do that.
Bernie	I'll stay in touch. I'll talk on the phone, I'll e-mail every day.
David	That's not the same.
Bernie	Not the same as what?
David	Don't play those tricks on me.
Bernie	What tricks?
David	Questions on top of questions. Stop right there.
Bernie	I'm done.
Caleb	No going back, now. We're committed.
David	From where? Where'd we go?
Bernie	We didn't go anywhere.
Caleb	From the principle.
David	What's the principle?
Caleb	It's the principle of humiliation.
David	Which is?
Caleb	Thou shalt not be brought to tears by your son. (Or wife.)
David	When?
Bernie	Dad?
Caleb	While you're washing the dishes.

Bernie	That's not what we were talking about.
David	We weren't talking about that.
Caleb	While you're disciplining your child.
Bernie	I don't have a child.
Caleb	Brought to tears in your ladies apron.
David	It's true, I wash the dishes. (He needs to see a doctor.)
Bernie	You need to see a doctor, Dad.
Caleb	Get your gun and we'll shoot the motherfuckers.
Bernie	Who?
David	The women?
Caleb	No, the swells on their thoroughbreds in their fine boots.
Bernie	Dad, we weren't talking about that.
David	He's got a point there, though.
Bernie	You're watching a movie, Dad. You're in a movie.
Caleb	So what?
Bernie	And you are too, David.
Caleb	Okay, you know what I mean. Relax. We blow the fuckers off their horses. Excuse me. *(Exits)*
David	What was that?
Bernie	We're sitting here talking and he goes to the movies.
David	What is that?
Bernie	I don't know what that is.
David	I think it's brain malfunction.
Bernie	Too many movies. And why do you go along with it?
David	It's fun. Give the guy a break why don't you?
Bernie	Get him to a doctor.
David	No, you do it.
Bernie	No. You do it.

Caleb

(I'm not in plastics. I'm a chemistry and biology teacher. But you have thousands of these creatures, they want to have money, so they manufacture a hundred million plastic machines that will never disintegrate for eternity. In other words, they'll be here with God at the end of time. That's pretty much all I know about God. When the Messiah comes, the plastic will be here with Him. That's all I know about the Messiah. But do I really care? About plastics? About God? About the Messiah? Do you? When we can go to an alternative reality, as my boys say, as my mother does? To Rio de Janeiro? Or as my wife did, into the ocean, even if my son says he sees her once in a while? I don't know. I'm only asking. What do you think, if you ever think? Obviously, I need help. I'm sorry, I didn't mean to insult you. That was the last thing I wanted to do. They'll never get me to a doctor. Not a chance. I don't believe in doctors. On the other hand, my mother said she'd never set foot on German soil, and then she went to the Jewish museum, in Berlin. So, you never know. Oh, here's Bernie.)

Bernie and Caleb

Bernie   Dad?

Caleb   I was talking to myself.

Bernie   You do that.

Caleb   I know I do. I'm aware of it.

Bernie   That doesn't make it okay.

Caleb	What's so wrong with that?
Bernie	Only crazy people do it.
Caleb	That's your opinion.
Bernie	You should pray.
Caleb	Why?
Bernie	It's a better alternative.
Caleb	I don't know how to pray.
Bernie	Look it up in the Sages.
Caleb	No, you look it up. You're supposed to be the bar mitzvah boy.
Bernie	I'm not. I quit.
Caleb	Manhood is on its way.
Bernie	I'm postponing manhood.
Caleb	Until?
Bernie	Until the Messiah comes, as you say.
Caleb	I never said that.
Bernie	Anyway, it's postponed.
Caleb	The Messiah? (That's for sure!)
Bernie	I know one thing. You be sincere. You put your heart into it.
Caleb	But it's not for yourself.
Bernie	That's what the Indians say.
Caleb	It's true. I agree with them.
Bernie	You always say that.
Caleb	I still say that.
Bernie	Pray for the Messiah.
Caleb	And the plastic?
Bernie	Pray for the Messiah to burn away the plastic.
Caleb	I don't know how.
Bernie	And pray for your mother.

Caleb	I don't know how.
Bernie	And pray for your wife.
Caleb	I don't know how.
Bernie	Who lost herself into the currents of the ocean.
Caleb	God bless her.
Bernie	Say Lord have mercy.
Caleb	Lord have mercy.
Bernie	Otherwise there's no hope.
Caleb	There's no hope.
Bernie	You said it, for yourself, Lord have mercy.
Caleb	Lord have mercy on my wretched soul.
Bernie	Good, Dad.
Caleb	Lord have mercy on my wife, my dear wife.
Bernie	Where is she, Dad?
Caleb	I don't know where she is.
Bernie	She's in the spirit world.
Caleb	Maybe she's in the spirit world. I think she was eaten by the fishes.
Bernie	She's in Brazil, Dad, with Grandma.
Caleb	Is that a joke?
Bernie	I'm sorry. I didn't mean to make a joke.
Caleb	Maybe she is in Brazil, for all I know.
Bernie	Was she mean to you?
Caleb	What do you think?
Bernie	I think she was.
Caleb	I brought it on myself.
Bernie	How did you do that?
Caleb	That's what she would say. She'd say, Oh? How do you do that?
Bernie	What did she mean?

Caleb	She meant jerk, she meant, you're a jerk.
Bernie	Why a jerk?
Caleb	Because I'd make these statements of over-certainty.
Bernie	I never heard that word before.
Caleb	It's when you say something that's overly sure of yourself.
Bernie	Oh, yeah, you tend to do that.
Caleb	Yeah, like I brought it on myself with my pride.
Bernie	Yeah.
Caleb	Like I just figured out what parenting is. Or, I got it about Aristotle.
Bernie	Did you?
Caleb	I thought so at the time. Finally. He was an observer, Aristotle.
Bernie	Maybe you did get it.
Caleb	Yeah, a one word analysis.
Bernie	You're a minimalist.
Caleb	She'd say, Oh, really, how did you do that?
Bernie	No reason to break up a family.
Caleb	I agree with you. But who could live with false bravado?
Bernie	So this is a reason to check out?
Caleb	I don't know. You seen her lately?
Bernie	No, I haven't seen her lately. I only saw her once at the mall.
Caleb	At the mall?
Bernie	In the window at the mall.
Caleb	You don't go, do you?
Bernie	I don't go anywhere. But maybe she'll show up again. Rio, maybe.
Caleb	It's not funny.

Bernie	She could be in Rio, living the high life.
Caleb	That is funny.
Bernie	For all we know.
Caleb	We don't know.
Bernie	For sure she disappeared, Dad.
Caleb	She vanished.
Bernie	We miss her, God knows, with all her positive opinions.

Bernie and David

Bernie	Dad is having problems.
David	He stands there, he forgets why he's standing there.
Bernie	Take him to a doctor.
David	What's a doctor going to do?
Bernie	Maybe they have drugs.
David	For sure they have drugs.
Bernie	So take him.
David	But do they work?
Bernie	How will we know unless he tries them?
David	He won't go.
Bernie	You have to make him go.
David	You do it.
Bernie	We have to trick him into it.
David	First you have to leave your room.
Bernie	Why?
David	Forget it.
Bernie	Why did Mom kill herself?
David	I don't know. Are you changing the subject?
Bernie	Yes. Why?

David	How could I know why? I'm not the Messiah.
Bernie	No kidding? I'm shocked to hear that.
David	So you're off the hook.
Bernie	I'm saying, maybe it was Dad.
David	Don't say that.
Bernie	I said it already.
David	I think it was the Holocaust.
Bernie	It's a fatal error in the brain.
David	Are you talking about Dad?
Bernie	The earth's brain. Not some little German idiot.
David	Can we stay on the same subject?
Bernie	This is the subject.
David	She couldn't stand it.
Bernie	Mom?
David	Who else would I be talking about?
Bernie	I can think of at least two other people.
David	She thought the world was a death machine.
Bernie	Well, that makes sense to me. I don't know why Rosie stays alive.
David	Yes, you do.
Bernie	It's because she won't remain defeated.
David	Right.
Bernie	She wants to win.
David	We lost already. We lost forever. We got on the trains.
Bernie	Don't say that.
David	I just said it. All the genes. One third of the genes.
Bernie	A fatal error in the brain.
David	People as smart as you, Bernie. Thousands.
Bernie	A misunderstanding of the cosmos.
David	You don't go out lately. Why?

Bernie	It's shitty out there.
David	Why?
Bernie	Everybody is pretending. I don't want to see their faces.
David	You have to go to school *(Pause)* Every day.
Bernie	I don't think so. (I have everything I need right here.)
David	Bernie?
Bernie	It's funny about the disease.
David	What?
Bernie	That Grandma has and Daddy's getting. I have an idea.
David	What?
Bernie	Grandma, she still has the feelings connection.
David	I agree.
Bernie	But she loses the mental connection.
David	The context.
Bernie	It has nothing to do with all the bullshit that's been written or read.
David	No. I agree.
Bernie	The paradigms and synapses and MRIs.
David	You're a prodigy.
Bernie	She loses association and context.
David	A genius.
Bernie	Fire.
David	Fire?
Bernie	In the sense of combustion, oxygenation.
David	I take it back, Bernie. You're nuts.

Caleb and Rosie

Caleb   I've been meaning to tell you, Mom. I've been having my own problems.

Rosie   Issues?

Caleb   Issues. Memory issues. I seem to lose my train of thought sometimes.

Rosie   Trains. Evil.

Caleb   I forget the names of things.

Rosie   Do you read Hebrew?

Caleb   No.

Rosie   Anyway.

Caleb   It's quite frightening.

Rosie   I know it is. I think it's poison. Poison got into the earth somehow. Poison chemicals and gases. I was telling someone about it.

Caleb   Bernie. Bernard.

Rosie   Yes, they'll have to burn it off, cleanse the earth.

Caleb   My other son.

Rosie   Of course, he is. That would be David.

Caleb   No, Bernie.

Rosie   Of course, Bernie.

Caleb   There's a big difference in age, so it confuses people.

Rosie   I know I could be confused.

Caleb   I'm confused myself sometimes.

Rosie   Is he the bar mitzvah boy?

Caleb   Yes, Bernard.

Rosie   Good for Bernard. Make sure he studies.

Caleb   I will. I mean, there's some resistance there.

Rosie   Resistance?

Caleb	Never mind.
Rosie	He's an angel and he should sing like one. He'll join the other angels. I saw them on the walls of the Jewish Museum. They couldn't defeat us because they're only animals, bugs and things.
Caleb	I don't think they want to hear about this anymore, Mom.
Rosie	Who doesn't?
Caleb	The Germans. (Maybe you and me.)
Rosie	I wouldn't let them in.
Caleb	Excuse me?
Rosie	I wouldn't let them in here.
Caleb	Okay.
Rosie	Without a ticket. *(Laughs)* And you watch out. Watch your step.
Caleb	I'll bring Bernard.
Rosie	Keep an eye out.
Caleb	I will.
Rosie	The fucking murdering idiots. Who cares what they think?
Caleb	I'm just wondering, does he take you to the mall?
Rosie	Who?
Caleb	Bernie, your grandson. He take you to the mall?
Rosie	It sounds like it.
Caleb	Do you forget to pay?
Rosie	For what?
Caleb	For items, like clothes, you forget to pay?
Rosie	I must, musn't I? How humiliating! But it goes to show you, doesn't it, nobody is playing with their own money in the first place, that's why all this stuff at the mall is so odd, don't you think?
Caleb	All right, Mom.

| Rosie | It's like monopoly money! |

Bernie

(I had a dream. I was riding a little scooter. The scooter was about the size of my hand. Tiny. You made it go by pressing a button that was attached with a wire. I had to put it down somewhere to go on foot. I think it was to shop in a handicrafts area. So I put the little contraption down—that is, my scooter—on a shelf somewhere, and when I looked for it again, I couldn't find it! I panicked. I had lost my ambulation! Wherever I looked for it was a place of business owned by beautiful black women. Oh, how I loved them!, but they ignored me or didn't see me, and I never found my scooter. This tells you all you need to know about me and the author.)

Caleb, Bernie, David

Caleb	Here we are, me and both my sons.
Bernie	And the earth is shaking its booty.
David	The earth is shaking its booty?
Bernie	We're in a tremor?
David	We're in an earthquake?
Bernie	Are we going to fall into a hole?
Caleb	I don't think so. It's shake, rattle, and roll.
David	(That wasn't funny.)
Bernie	The earth is shaking off the white bugs with clothes.

David	You scared me.
Bernie	Shaking out the bugs.
David	We're the bugs?
Bernie	We're the bugs.
Caleb	That's a good example.
David	Of?
Caleb	Annoying misstatements of half-truths.
David	That's you, Dad, in a nutshell.
Caleb	Don't say nutshell.
David	Nutshell.
Caleb	It's bad grammar.
Bernie	Nutshell?
David	No, shaking off the white bugs with clothes.
Bernie	He meant the earth shaking off the humans.
David	I know it.
Bernie	With hurricanes, earthquakes, and tornadoes.
David	Fire and flood.
Bernie	Drought and sinkholes.
David	Starvation.
Bernie	Cyclones.
Caleb	So get ready for the fifth world.
Bernie	What does that mean, Dad?
Caleb	Sorry.
Bernie	It has no meaning.
David	It's another typical example.
Caleb	Of what?
David	An overstatement.
Bernie	Pray.
David	There's another one.

Bernie	Sway and pray and bow and praise. It's the Jewish religion in a—
Caleb	Nutshell?
Bernie	Thanks, Dad.
David	Pray to what? The sun? The solar system? The universe?
Caleb	Pray to the silence and the void.
David	That makes no sense at all.
Caleb	Help others, help others!
David	Even if a human being is a piece of shit?
Caleb	In America you're even less than that.
Bernie	You're a bag of chemical soup!
David	Oh, that's good.
Bernie	Only because it makes you feel better.
Caleb	And you can pay off the debt you owe for your stupid existence.
David	Okay, how?
Caleb	If you go to meetings and donate soup and admit your failings, and help the homeless and the lonely and the mad, then you can save your souls.
Bernie	I can't do that, Dad.
Caleb	Why not?
Bernie	I don't have a soul.
David	I can't stand the stench.
Bernie	I don't like people.
David	I'm not interested.
Bernie	I have other things to do.
David	I'm trying to believe in something real.
Bernie	Actually, I don't believe in anything.
Caleb	You're not trying anything and you have no idea what's real.

Bernie	So what?
Caleb	So you should both shut up about trying and believing and real.
Bernie	I have a test tomorrow.
Caleb	How can you have a test if you don't go to school?
Bernie	I take it on the Internet.
David	You're turning into a recluse.
Bernie	Call it whatever you want.
David	You're turning into a recluse. I'll go and visit Rosie in Rio.
Bernie	There is no Rio.
Caleb	There is to Rosie.
David	Rosie is in Rio!
Bernie	Right down the street in Assisted Living is our Grandma Rosie, either in Rio or Buenos Aires.
Caleb	Maybe we should all go.
Bernie	It's too crowded.
David	It's too crowded?
Bernie	There's just all this biology running around trying to make more biology. I don't know if I can stand it.
David	That's a totally different subject.
Caleb	I agree with you there, son.
David	That was a totally different subject!
Bernie	It's true.
David	It had nothing to do with assisted living.
Bernie	True, except maybe in Rio it does.
Caleb	I see what you mean, David.
David	That's good.
Caleb	Nothing to do with assisted living.
David	Even though an act of kindness brings you to tears.

Caleb	It's true. I cry.
David	And it's not even real, it's on television.
Caleb	Television?
David	You know, where you see sweet people helping each other.
Caleb	You never see that in life. Not in this country.
David	So we got that straight. Dad.
Bernie	So I'm not going to school or the mall anymore.
David	You're not?
Bernie	No. And I'm not buying any more dumb cookies.

Caleb and David

David	Go and see your mother. She asked for you.
Caleb	She remembered my name?
David	"My oldest son."
Caleb	I'm her only son. And she's in Brazil. It's too far.
David	She's in assisted living.
Caleb	I don't want her not to know me. It hurts.
David	Actually, I don't know if I want to go anymore.
Caleb	So why ask me to go?
David	I don't know why.
Caleb	Talk to Chrystal.
David	What does Chrystal have to do with it?
Caleb	She'll tell you.
David	She'll tell me what?
Caleb	About your mother.
David	She'll tell me about my mother?
Caleb	Yes.

David	What?
Caleb	I don't know what.
David	You don't know what and you don't know who.
Caleb	Who?
David	That's right. Who you are.
Caleb	I'm you, actually.
David	What does that mean?
Caleb	Biologically.
David	And ask her about the clothes.
Caleb	The clothes?
David	She wears nice clothes. Outfits.
Caleb	She likes clothes.
David	She looks great.
Caleb	I feel that.
David	What's the question there?
Caleb	I don't know what the question there is.
David	Oh. Where does she get the clothes?
Caleb	In the mall.
David	In the mall?
Caleb	In the mall.
David	Okay.
Caleb	She goes to the mall, she gets the clothes.
David	Okay.
Caleb	And she pays for them. It's Rosie who walks out with the clothes.
David	Rosie?
Caleb	Yes, she's a kleptomaniac.

David and Chrystal

David   Chrystal.

Chrystal   What?

David   You look great.

Chrystal   Thank you.

David   Chrystal.

Chrystal   What is it?

David   Nothing's wrong. He asked me to ask you.

Chrystal   Who did?

David   My father.

Chrystal   So, ask.

David   Who am I?

Chrystal   Don't start.

David   About my mother.

Chrystal   What about her?

David   I have no idea.

Chrystal   Yes, you do.

David   A little, a note, that's all.

Chrystal   She left.

David   She's gone.

Chrystal   She's gone.

David   Maybe she killed herself.

Chrystal   She did.

David   Why?

Chrystal   She was an idealist.

David   Did you ever talk?

Chrystal   Of course we talked. We did dishes. We did laundry.

David   What did she say?

Chrystal   About what?

David	About the situation.
Chrystal	What situation?
David	Our situation. The human situation.
Chrystal	That it was based on murder and it was getting worse.
David	Why murder?
Chrystal	Don't be stupid, David. Do me a favor.
David	Sorry.
Chrystal	Because there's a limited amount of water, and a limited amount of land, so people are gong to kill each other for it. Okay?
David	Okay.
Chrystal	Stalin made a deal with Hitler and sold out the Jews.
David	He did?
Chrystal	According to your mother, he did.
David	So why was she mad at the Jews?
Chrystal	Because they were ashamed of themselves, and then they had a weird pride, like nothing worse had ever happened to another people.
David	Isn't it true?
Chrystal	I don't know. But it happens all the time. People get it into their heads to slaughter their neighbors. But you knew all this already David, so it's annoying to have to explain it to you.
David	Thank you.
Chrystal	You're welcome.
David	But it's not so simple.
Chrystal	It's simple. That's why you better keep an eye on Bernie.
David	On Bernie?
Chrystal	Bernie.

David	Which brings me to another question.
Chrystal	What is it?
David	It's the strangest thing.
Chrystal	I agree totally. You want to eat?
David	Not right now.
Chrystal	If not now, when?
David	Maybe later. You look great.
Chrystal	You said that.
David	I don't know what he meant.
Chrystal	Who?
David	My father.
Chrystal	About?
David	Women.
Chrystal	We bleed.
David	You bleed?
Chrystal	That's what he means. About women.
David	You menstruate?
Chrystal	Yes, David.
David	That's what he meant?
Chrystal	I think that's what he meant.
David	Who doesn't know that?
Chrystal	Well, what could he mean?
David	He means dangerous.
Chrystal	Dangerous.
David	He means women are dangerous.
Chrystal	I don't think that's what he means.
David	That's what he means. That's why he's strange. He means dangerous.
Chrystal	I don't think so. Unpredictable.
David	Unpredictable.

Chrystal	No. Dangerous. Is what he means. You're right.
David	Dangerous.
Chrystal	For him. That's his experience. They've left him. They've left him alone in a dangerous situation, where the world is falling apart. Don't you see?
David	Yes, I do.

Bernie and Caleb

Caleb	What's up? So, what's up?
Bernie	What's up?
Caleb	Sky's up.
Bernie	You always say that.
Caleb	I'll stop.
Bernie	I'm doing homework now.
Caleb	What are you doing?
Bernie	Homework.
Caleb	What's the homework?
Bernie	Algebra. It's Algebra. X's and Y's. I like it.
Caleb	I liked it.
Bernie	That's good.
Caleb	You miss your mother?
Bernie	Yes.
Caleb	You miss your mother?
Bernie	I said yes.
Caleb	So do I.
Bernie	I figured.
Caleb	You did.
Bernie	I figured or you wouldn't have asked.

Caleb	What do you miss?
Bernie	I miss her smell.
Caleb	Yeah. I miss her smell.
Bernie	You don't know where she is.
Caleb	Her bones are in the ocean. They'll be recycled.

Enter DAVID.

David	Are we talking about you know who?
Caleb	Yes. She'll be in the air eventually.
Bernie	She's in the Land of the Dead.
David	We know that.
Bernie	She left a note.
David	We know that, too.
Bernie	You want to hear it?
David	Again?
Bernie	You want to hear it again?
Caleb	Go ahead.
Bernie	I know it by heart. I'll recite.
Caleb	Recite.
Bernie	Here it goes: "I wanted to say something in my own behalf. After all, I have a right to speak, though I live between worlds, the world of the seen and the world of the unseen." *(Pause)* You wanted to comment, David?
David	No. Proceed.
Bernie	"The world of reflection in windows, of glances in mirrors, quick cuts in movies and other magical illusions. Clearly, my views of life and the premises—"
David	Principles.

Bernie	"Principles of living I accepted when I was alive were not romantic. So it's impossible to have a tragic view. Things happen and no one is to blame."
David	Except you yourself. Sorry.
Bernie	"We are meant to breathe air and drink water."
David	(No shit.)
Bernie	"To eat well and be intelligent and not go on murderous rampages. I saw the destruction of the Fourth World coming and decided to drown in the water."
David	(Good thinking.)
Bernie	Are you adding something?
David	No. Get it over with.
Bernie	"I had believed in reason and a just scientific reorientation of the world. These turned out to be false and those people selling them turned out to be self-serving idiots and clowns. I left a signal to my sons: believe in nothing and keep an eye out for Coyote, for that would be the beginning of the End. This is the signal." Is that it?
David	More or less.

Silence. Exit CALEB.

David	Now you did it, Bernie. *(Pause)*
Bernie	I have seen Coyote.
David	I haven't.
Bernie	You'll never see with the eyes you have on.
David	I see with my own damn eyes.
Bernie	Sure you do.
David	The eyes of a grown-up.
Bernie	Mazel tov.

David	What happened with your bar mitzvah?
Bernie	What happened?
David	What happened, Bernard?
Bernie	Nothing happened, David.
David	Okay.
Bernie	Okay is right.
David	Okay.
Bernie	And nothing is going to happen.
David	Fine with me.
Bernie	Fucking thing is in Hebrew.
David	I know.
Bernie	It's a language I don't understand.
David	Baruch atah. It means blessed art thou.
Bernie	I know what it means.
David	That's Hebrew.
Bernie	I know what Baruch atah means.
David	That's all they do is praise.
Bernie	Who's that?
David	The Jews. They stand up, they praise, they sit down, they murmur praise.
Bernie	There are not enough Jews.
David	In the world?
Bernie	Where else would they be if not in the world?
David	I don't know. Mars?
Bernie	Not funny. There are not enough, and I have a solution.
David	What's the solution?
Bernie	It's a one-state solution. The Jews and the Arabs in one state.
David	Talk to Dad.
Bernie	Why?

David	He's a member.
Bernie	What does he know? He doesn't know anything about it.
David	It's a radical solution.
Bernie	One state. And we'll be brothers with the Arabs.
	A member of what?
David	I can't remember the names now. Jewish organizations.

Caleb and David

David	In the synagogue, they praise. The rest of the time they complain.
Caleb	It's singing. What's wrong with singing?
David	I don't like the praise, and I don't like the complaints.
Caleb	Who are you?
David	Good question.
Caleb	You like and you don't like.
David	Actually, I lied.
Caleb	Who doesn't lie?
David	Everybody lies. Why? There's a substance in the brain.
Caleb	There's a substance in the brain.
David	There's a substance in the brain, it has trouble.
Caleb	It has trouble.
David	It has trouble with reality. So it says things.
Caleb	The mouth.
David	Stop repeating me.
Caleb	The mouth.
David	It's a sin, a substance in the brain that lies its ass off.
Caleb	What is this substance?
David	It's a kind of plaque. So you see hate instead of love.
Caleb	That was your mother. That's what she saw.

David	Is she loved now? Who loves Sarah now?
Caleb	Sarah is in another world, where love doesn't matter.
David	Which world is that?
Caleb	Brazil.
David	You never been to Brazil.
Caleb	I saw the movie. That's all I need.
Caleb	I know this: every day she looks at the horizon and she thinks about her soul.
David	How do you know?
Caleb	I know because I know. She did that here.
David	She looked at the horizon and thought about her soul?
Caleb	Yes. She wonders. Do I have a soul, and where does it go?
David	Why the horizon?
Caleb	Because it's round, and because it meets the sky.
David	She goes down to the beach.
Caleb	So you get a sense of the infinite.
David	I can't believe in God if he's in such deep shit all the time.
Caleb	Well said.
David	He like can't do anything about anything.
Caleb	That's why I asked you.
David	About?
Caleb	Prayer.
David	Well, there's your answer.
Caleb	"Maybe you better yourself and forget about God."
David	That's Rosie.
Caleb	"Maybe it's you, not God."
David	Me?
Caleb	"Yeah."

David	What can I do? Can I make a new world? Can I reverse time?
Caleb	We're back in Job again.
David	Can I bring back the dead?
Caleb	"So pray. Pray for forty hours with no food or drink or rest."
David	Who said that?
Caleb	Rosie. "Prepare. Sit down. Suffer. Maybe you'll make something of yourself."
David	That was my bar mitzvah, years ago.
Caleb	Sorry.
David	Benedictions from Grandma. May she find immortality.
Caleb	Amen.
David	There on the horizon, in Rio. (In the world of assisted living.)
Caleb	One world doesn't last long into the other.
David	So there's no bar mitzvah for Bernie?
Caleb	No. He won't come out of his room.
David	I don't blame him. And if he talks to my mother, I want to hear about it.
Caleb	Why?
David	I told you. I miss her.
Caleb	You believe Bernie is channeling your mother?
David	No.
Caleb	Then what?
David	I just want to hear about it.

Bernie and Caleb

Bernie   Dad?

Caleb   What?

Bernie   I think there should be a one-state solution.

Caleb   So do I, Bernie.

Bernie   So why don't they do it?

Caleb   They don't like each other. They hate each other. They kill each other.

Bernie   That's ridiculous. What are we alive for?

Caleb   You're asking me?

Bernie   What are we doing here?

Caleb   I don't know.

Bernie   It's ridiculous.

Caleb   What do you want from me?

Bernie   Do something. Say something.

Caleb   There should be one state for Arabs and Jews. Everybody equal.

Bernie   Don't tell me. Tell the world.

Caleb   All right. I'll write something.

Bernie   Do it now.

Caleb   I'm writing. The idea is to go fast.

Bernie   Go, go.

Caleb   I'm writing. *(Thinks)*

Bernie   Are you done?

Caleb   No. *(Thinks)*

Bernie   Are you done?

Caleb   Give me a minute why don't you?

Bernie   Okay.

CALEB *thinks.*

	Okay, you done?
Caleb	I'll say what I have.
Bernie	Say.
Caleb	"There's different kinds of love. There's love of the family, which is one kind of love. Like when my mother went to the Jewish museum, she saw all the families, and she imagined all the arguments."
Bernie	Go on.
Caleb	"And the love of one's people, which she also saw there, in herself. There's romantic love, like my love for my wife, Sarah, which has fantasy in it, and biology."
Bernie	Are you finished?
Caleb	No. " And then there's a bigger love, Love in general, a kind of Universal Love."
Bernie	That was good.
Caleb	Thank you. Maybe there's only one love really and the other loves are expressions of that or examples of that?
Bernie	I'm feeling very suspicious of what you just said, Dad.
Caleb	So am I.
Bernie	Because it should also include the paramount question. (I meant to say "permanent.")
Caleb	Which is?
Bernie	What are we doing here?
Caleb	Praise God.
Bernie	And?
Caleb	Serve God.
Bernie	And?

Caleb	Obey God.
Bernie	And?
Caleb	That's enough. I'm tired.
Bernie	I want to talk to this person.
Caleb	It's not a person you can talk to.
Bernie	What is this God?
Caleb	He has no beginning and no end.
Bernie	And me?
Caleb	This I don't know.
Bernie	What kind of material?
Caleb	You or God?
Bernie	Both.
Caleb	I'd say both.
Bernie	Both what?
Caleb	Same kind of material.
Bernie	What?
Caleb	Some coarse, some fine. Some you can't see, some you can. (Sunlight is made of particles.)
Bernie	I had a beginning. I was a thought in someone's eye.
Caleb	You were an impulse in someone's body.
Bernie	I was biological.
Caleb	Correct.
Bernie	Not God.
Caleb	There he is, here he remains.
Bernie	He doesn't have to eat?
Caleb	Of course he has to eat.
Bernie	What does he eat?
Caleb	That I don't know. Something tasty. He's not an idiot.
Bernie	People have to eat.
Caleb	Correct.

Bernie	They eat shit.
Caleb	Right.
Bernie	They eat fish. They ate all the fish. They eat animals. They ate all the animals.
Caleb	Good. You did good.
Bernie	What did I do?
Caleb	You did good.
Bernie	To go fast?
Caleb	And to include your mother and brother and sister-in-law.
Bernie	And?
Caleb	One line only.
Bernie	Exactly. And not only that.
Caleb	What else?
Bernie	Usually you have behavior. He drinks, he smokes, he hits, and so on.
Caleb	And?
Bernie	Here we have no behavior.
Caleb	Rule number five.
Bernie	The fifth rule.
Caleb	No sitting, standing, slapping, kissing, drinking, eating or doping.
Bernie	No.
Caleb	No walking, running, hiding, looking, or waiting.
Bernie	Wait.
Caleb	What?
Bernie	Maybe sitting. Maybe standing.
Caleb	Okay.
Bernie	Maybe slapping.
Caleb	Okay.
Bernie	Maybe looking and waiting.

Caleb	Okay.
Bernie	So that's the sixth rule.
Caleb	Fine and good.
Bernie	No behavior.

Rosie and Caleb

Rosie	Hello this is Rosie.
Caleb	Hello, Mom!
Rosie	Hello.
Caleb	Hello, hello.
Rosie	So what's up with you guys?
Caleb	Marriage and school and school and marriage. What else? And you?
Rosie	Me, I'm in Rio, I'm experiencing life for others.
Caleb	That's what you did here, am I wrong?
Rosie	Wrong.
Caleb	How am I wrong?
Rosie	There, I did my duty. Here I serve.
Caleb	What can I say?
Rosie	Don't say anything.
Caleb	You're all right?
Rosie	I'm perfect.
Caleb	Perfect already?
Rosie	Certain things are the same, I'll have to admit.
Caleb	Tell, admit.
Rosie	It's the human body, it's just the same, only worse. That's why I left the states.
Caleb	Say again?

Rosie	Flesh and blood idiots. Teeth and tongues and toilets.
Caleb	You thought you could get away from that?
Rosie	No, only my own genes.
Caleb	You brought them with you.
Rosie	The family and you.
Caleb	I have the same or different genes.
Rosie	I knew you like the back of my hand.
Caleb	What else is new?
Rosie	I'm sick of the back of my hand.
Caleb	You're sick of me.
Rosie	I'm sick of you.
Caleb	I'll hang up now if you don't mind.
Rosie	How can you blame me?
Caleb	I don't blame you.
Rosie	Even you don't like being you.
Caleb	Who does?
Rosie	I do.
Caleb	You do?
Rosie	Definitely, though not all the time.
Caleb	Nobody does anything all the time.
Rosie	We're talking about states.
Caleb	That reminds me.
Rosie	What?
Caleb	Never mind.
Rosie	There is no same state for long.
Caleb	That's what I mean.
Rosie	You can't do anything all the time.
Caleb	That's what I said.
Rosie	So what reminds you of?
Caleb	Of?

Rosie	Never mind.
Caleb	I know—a same state solution.
Rosie	That's ridiculous. That's absurd.
Caleb	One state for Arabs and Jews.
Rosie	Forget about it.
Caleb	It's Bernie's idea.
Rosie	Don't blame Bernie.
Caleb	Hang up, why don't you?
Rosie	One state for Jews only.
Caleb	Hang up.
Rosie	The others can go ahead and die.
Caleb	I'll hang up now.
Rosie	No, I think I will.
Caleb	Go ahead. Go.
Rosie	Bye.
Caleb	I'll call you.
Rosie	Call. See if I care.

Chrystal and David

David	The other rule is, you don't say the name of G-d. You say G-d with a dash.
Chrystal	God has a name?
David	In Judaism He has a name.
Chrystal	This must only be for the gentiles.
David	Excuse me?
Chrystal	His name.
David	No, never mind.
Chrystal	I mean the dash.

David	You're not supposed to say the name.
Chrystal	That's fine.
David	That's all I mean.
Chrystal	Fine and good.
David	That's the seventh rule. And no interpretation.
Chrystal	No interpretation of the seventh rule is the eighth rule?
David	No interpretation and no behavior.
Chrystal	No interpretation of behavior? (We're talking performance here.)
David	No interpretation OR behavior.
Chrystal	That's eight or nine rules we have already.
David	Check out Leviticus.
Chrystal	Tell them what we're talking about.
David	I don't know if I should.
Chrystal	Tell them or they won't know. (We're talking about acting.)
David	(We're talking about acting.)
Chrystal	It's because people have limitations.
David	It's beyond limitations.
Chrystal	What do you mean?
David	You should talk to my Grandmother.
Chrystal	I have talked to your Grandmother.
David	They're like incomplete beings, cells in a larger structure.
Chrystal	What is?
David	I take that back.
Chrystal	You can't take it back.
David	Why can't I take it back?
Chrystal	Because you already said it.
David	You mean it's written?
Chrystal	It's written down in the Book of Life.
David	Amazing, Chrystal.

Chrystal	It's like with predestination.
David	What is?
Chrystal	People say that after it's already happened.
David	Maybe you should explain.
Chrystal	(People say it had to happen after it already happened. So, of course.)
David	I don't know if they got that.
Chrystal	I talked to your mother, too.
David	When was this?
Chrystal	She used to sit in the mall while I shopped.
David	(What can you expect from such a creature?)
Chrystal	She'd sit on the edge of the bench in her dark glasses, eyes half-closed.
David	She watched the creatures.
Chrystal	She watched and she despaired.
David	She knew what they were thinking. She could hear their greed.
Chrystal	She'd see a kippa and want to throw something.
David	"Don't be holy in front of me," she'd say.
Chrystal	"I know you," she'd say.
David	"You're in a state of self-righteousness."
Chrystal	On the other hand, she could smell an anti-Semite at a hundred yards.
David	You don't have to go far in a mall.
Chrystal	"I'm not interested in buying anything," she'd say. "It's all cheap shit."
David	Isn't that depression? Isn't that classical depression?
Chrystal	I think it is, actually.
David	I think it is.
Chrystal	What is this larger structure?

David	I believe it's life on earth.
Chrystal	"Either vermin or angels."
David	What angels?
Chrystal	Your mother would say.
David	What's the difference?
Chrystal	Angels take care, vermin eat and then they eat again.
David	It's all about reproduction, my mother said, and fertilizer.
Chrystal	Right. And all kids think they have a right to live.
David	My brother won't come out of his room.
Chrystal	He wants his Mama.
David	She left before he locked himself up.
Chrystal	She could see it coming. Now what?
David	Get Grandma Rosie to come home.
Chrystal	You do it.
David	Okay, I'll do it.
Chrystal	Call her.
David	Okay.
Chrystal	On her cell.
David	I'll do it.
Chrystal	Do it now.
David	Okay, in a minute.

Moments later.

David	Hello, Grandma.
Rosie	Who is this?
David	You know me, Grandma.
Rosie	So say your name why don't you, what could it hurt?
David	It's David.
Rosie	I know why you called.

David	Tell me why I called.
Rosie	You called for your father.
David	No.
Rosie	How is your father?
David	You should call him.
Rosie	I'll call him.
David	Call him.
Chrystal	Hello?
Rosie	Who's this?
Chrystal	This is Chrystal.
Rosie	What happened to the other one?
Chrystal	The other one?
Rosie	On the phone. He was a man, I believe.
Chrystal	That was David.
Rosie	David?
Chrystal	My husband.
Rosie	You called for your husband?
Chrystal	I have to admit.
Rosie	Where is he? He's hanging by the phone?
Chrystal	He's hanging by the phone.
Rosie	Say hello and tell him to take three steps back.
Chrystal	Hello and three steps back.

DAVID takes three steps back.

	Okay, he did it.
Rosie	So what's the matter?
Chrystal	Bernie won't come out of his room.
Rosie	How do you know?

Chrystal	We look at his room. The door is closed. He won't come out.
Rosie	Oh.
Chrystal	This isn't the first time.
Rosie	Oh. He's not going to school?
Chrystal	And it won't be the last.
Rosie	I see.
Chrystal	You're not worried?
Rosie	Why should I worry?
Chrystal	It could be a sign of mental illness.
Rosie	Are you crazy?
Chrystal	Not me, him.
Rosie	The whole planet is nuts and you bring up Bernie?
Chrystal	You have a point.
Rosie	The earth is having a fit, a fever and a conniption. Guess why?
Chrystal	It's because of us.
Rosie	Congratulations.
Chrystal	That's why Bernie won't come out of his room.
Rosie	Why should he?
Chrystal	And you won't come home.
Rosie	I'm in Rio. It's too far to travel.
Chrystal	You're not in Rio.
Rosie	Says who?
Chrystal	A bird told me.
Rosie	Fuck the bird.
Chrystal	Come on, Rosie.
Rosie	Why should I?
Chrystal	You're needed. We need you here.
Rosie	That's nice.

Chrystal	Seriously.
Rosie	Here I'm working with the poor. They have some common sense. They know who their enemies are. By you, they believe anything and get it all mixed up with God. God forbid.
Chrystal	It's true. Here I'm attending to complete strangers.
Rosie	That's what I heard. They don't know which end is up, most of them.
Chrystal	I know, believe me.
Rosie	I believe you, I believe you.
Chrystal	But I hear it's just as bad in Rio.
Rosie	You heard what?
Chrystal	I heard it's crazy in Rio.
Rosie	Crazier than Brooklyn?
Chrystal	Yeah.
Rosie	I think so, too.
Chrystal	Well, there you go.
Rosie	I don't think so. I think I'll stay.
Chrystal	You might as well be here.
Rosie	No, thanks. I don't go anywhere and it's a bad situation.
Chrystal	We're lucky.
Rosie	We're lucky we're not eating each other yet.
Chrystal	That's what I mean.
Rosie	No, it isn't.
Chrystal	There's earthquakes, tsunamis, torpedos—I mean, tornadoes—fires, and hurricanes.
Rosie	Of course. That's what it means for the earth to have a fit and a conniption.
Chrystal	Of course.
Rosie	But don't explain too much.

Chrystal	I won't.
Rosie	The earth has bugs and we're the bugs.
Chrystal	I hear you.
Rosie	My own mother used to say.
Chrystal	I'll call again soon.
Rosie	Good.
David	I'll talk to her. Let me talk to her.
Chrystal	David wants to talk to you.
Rosie	Who?
Chrystal	David. Your grandson.
Rosie	Put him on the phone.
David	Hi, Grandma.
Rosie	Hi, honey. I heard there's insanity going around.
David	You heard right.
Rosie	Kill them all and then kill yourself.
David	Excuse me?
Rosie	I said, kill them all and then kill yourself.
David	That's what I thought you said.
Rosie	It's the only solution. I couldn't stop shooting. People have yellow plaque on their brains. And fungi on their toes. And tumors in their lungs. I could go on and on.
Chrystal	Get off the phone.
David	But I have to get off, Grandma.
Rosie	I got the picture.
Chrystal	I want to talk to her.
David	I think you got the picture, Rose. Here's Chrystal.
Rosie	Thank you, Chrystal!
Chrystal	You're welcome!
Rosie	Good bye and good luck!
Chrystal	You too!

Rosie	It's a pleasure!
Chrystal	Me, too!
David	What did you want to say to her?
Chrystal	Just a minute.
David	Say it already!
Rosie	Who is yelling there?
Chrystal	Your grandson, David.
Rosie	Tell him to shut up.
Chrystal	Shut up. Okay where was I?
Rosie	I'm in Rio and you're in Brooklyn. So far so good.
Chrystal	I've been meaning to tell you.
Rosie	Yes?
Chrystal	When you go to the mall, who takes you to the mall?
Rosie	The mall?
Chrystal	The mall.
Rosie	No one.
Chrystal	No one?
Rosie	No one takes me. Anymore.
Chrystal	Okay, if by any chance they do take you, remember.
Rosie	What?
Chrystal	You have to pay.
Rosie	No, I don't.
Chrystal	Why not?
Rosie	They are capitalist pigs and they owe us our very lives, that's why.
Chrystal	Okay, I'm sorry I brought it up.
Rosie	Put your son back on.
Chrystal	He's your grandson, Rose.
Rosie	Put him on.
Chrystal	He's my husband.

Rosie	So put him on already.
David	Hello.
Rosie	Listen, have a baby. You remember how to do that?
David	Sure, Grandma.
Rosie	Otherwise, keep your mouth shut.
David	Good bye, Grandma.
Rosie	Good bye.

David and Chrystal

David	You call that a conversation?
Chrystal	Yes, what do you call it?
David	There are no words.
Chrystal	I thought it was a wonderful conversation.
David	It's not rational.
Chrystal	Since when are you so rational? You're an anxiety neurotic.
David	What does that mean, exactly?
Chrystal	It means you're in a state of anxiety. Did you take your pill?
David	I'll take it now.
Chrystal	Good. You'll calm down and feel normal.
David	What about Rosie?
Chrystal	She's not gonna calm, I mean come.
David	Why not, I wonder?
Chrystal	Come on David, she's in Rio, it's too far.
David	The fanatical Marxist.
Chrystal	At least we know where the clothes are.

David	Where are they?
Chrystal	Where I don't know.
David	You just said you know.
Chrystal	I mean in Rio. How did they know it's this family?
David	My father's card.
Chrystal	Your father has a card?
David	That's all I can think of. My father has a card.
Chrystal	And for your information, David, I pay for my own clothes.
David	With your own card, I presume.
Chrystal	Correct.
David	That's why this country is up to its eyebrows in debt.
Chrystal	It wasn't me, David.
David	I'm not saying it was just you, obviously. I have a card.
Chrystal	You have a card?
David	Of course I have a card. And you have a card.
Chrystal	Think of this: No more money. No more goods. No more nothing.
David	That was a thought?
Chrystal	That was the beginning and ending of a thought. No more money, ending with no more nothing.
David	What's in the middle?
Chrystal	The middle is to make money on money is extreme capitalism.
David	I'm not even going to comment on that.
Chrystal	Okay.
David	That's what I do, obviously. I'm in the top one percent and so are you.
Chrystal	I'm so happy I can't stand it.
David	Good.

Chrystal	Meanwhile, your brother Bernie has packed it in.
David	He's on line.
Chrystal	What does that mean?
David	The chickens come home to roost.
Chrystal	They have to go somewhere.
David	They're running around in his head.
Chrystal	I thought you were a nice guy, David.
David	I am.
Chrystal	What happened?
David	Everything's out of control.
Chrystal	Meaning?
David	People can't remember and can't think straight.
Chrystal	They never could.
David	It's gotten worse.
Chrystal	It's always been the same.
David	You have to have educated people in a democracy, not consumist idiots who can't spell.
Chrystal	That's not a word, consumist.
David	Consumer, okay?
Chrystal	It's true. People don't know much, but they never did.
David	Why not?
Chrystal	They're animals.
David	So we let them vote?
Chrystal	Idiots will take us to war and take our money, too.
David	Thank God we live in a democracy, Chrystal.
Chrystal	Where the idiots aren't taking us to war?
David	I can't argue with that, honey.
Chrystal	So this conversation is nearly over.
David	It is as far as I'm concerned.
Chrystal	Wait for a tornado, David.

David	What does that mean, wait for a tornado.
Chrystal	Wait for a tornado.
David	What does it mean?
Chrystal	To sweep you into the sky.
David	Sweep?
Chrystal	Vanish.
David	Okay, Chrystal.
Chrystal	Into the sky.
David	Thanks.
Chrystal	In the wind. A big wind.
David	Thanks a lot.
Chrystal	Don't insult me.
David	What is going to be the answer to this situation?
Chrystal	I don't know. Who made the wind?
David	Nature made the wind.
Chrystal	Nature made the wind and we made the velocity.
David	I don't disagree with you.
Chrystal	You don't?
David	No.
Chrystal	The Hopi had it right.
David	The Hopi had it right.
Chrystal	So it doesn't matter—Rosie in Rio, Bernie in his room.

Caleb and Bernie

Caleb	So what are you doing in there all day and all night?
Bernie	I'm connected.
Caleb	To what are you connected?

Bernie	I got computer software variations, video games, TV, radio, plus an iPod and a cellphone. I can do everything from here that you could do from anywhere else. There's no reason at all for me to leave this room except to burn down the neighborhood.
Caleb	Excuse me?
Bernie	Just a thought, Dad.
Caleb	That's the thing, you're thinking too much.
Bernie	I'm not thinking. I'm planning, I'm looking, I'm listening, I'm figuring it out.
Caleb	That's not thinking?
Bernie	Call it whatever you want.
Caleb	Maybe you should do some real thinking.
Bernie	You're contradicting yourself again, Dad. *Otra vez.*
Caleb	You can see that a normal human being doesn't stay in his room all the time. Only prisoners do that. On death row.
Bernie	That was good, Dad.
Caleb	You can't stay in your room all the time. That's final. You have to go to school. You have to go out and play. You have to help your Dad.
Bernie	I'll help my Dad from here. The rest you can forget about.
Caleb	How do you figure that?
Bernie	By phone and by e-mail and so on.
Caleb	I'll call the police.
Bernie	Go ahead. I'll stay in jail.
Caleb	I'll call an ambulance.
Bernie	I'll stay in the hospital.
Caleb	You can't stay in the hospital.
Bernie	Why not?
Caleb	There's nothing wrong with you.

Bernie	I see and hear Coyote, often.
Caleb	Except in the head.
Bernie	It's what they call a mitzvah, Dad. Only the sublimely gifted can see Coyote.
Caleb	You don't say?
Bernie	I just said.
Caleb	I'm your father.
Bernie	There's nothing wrong with that.
Caleb	That's not what I meant.
Bernie	What did you mean?
Caleb	You have to do what I tell you, and if you don't—
Bernie	What?
Caleb	I'll kick the shit out of you.
Bernie	Sure, you will.
Caleb	You heard me!
Bernie	You haven't raised your voice in anger in fifty years. Now you'll start? I don't think so.
Caleb	You never know. But you better listen to me.
Bernie	Or?
Caleb	I'll kick the shit out of you and I'll take away your toys, that's what! I'm your father! *(Stands)*
Bernie	Where are you going?
Caleb	I'm not going.
Bernie	Then why are you standing near the door?
Caleb	I'll sit down again, because I'm not done.
Bernie	Sit down, why don't you?
Caleb	I have more to say here. I have a tire iron.
Bernie	You have a tire iron?
Caleb	I have a tire iron.
Bernie	Everybody has a tire iron. In their car.

Caleb	I keep it near me at all times. *(Reveals a tire iron, the only actual prop, and swings it like a club)*
Bernie	Dad, can we take a break?
Caleb	Sure we can take a break.
Bernie	Go out and come back later.
Caleb	Okay, let's say I did that and now I'm back, we'll take a pause and start over. *(Pause)* Of course, it's all quite mysterious. She drowned, you know, your mother. Sarah. She drowned.
Bernie	I know.
Caleb	It's a good way to go. We'd talked about it often. You swim out into the ocean until you get tired and then you keep on swimming, and swimming, and then it's too far, you've gone too far and you can't make it back, and you're so tired, it's easy to let it go, so you let go.
Bernie	I used to dream about that.
Caleb	What was the dream?
Bernie	I can't remember exactly. Only, I couldn't save her, mainly.
Caleb	Let's take another break.
Bernie	Okay. *(Pause)* The tire iron, Dad?
Caleb	I'd just like to point out, I don't think it's a conscious intention, of course, it's more a subconscious intention, which is much more important and consequential. I'll tell you one thing that happened. I wanted to go around armed. I mean, I wanted to arm myself. The idea began occurring in my mind—while dozing, or waking up in the morning, the sense of wanting to be armed with a stick or a club, even a gun. I ended up using a tire iron. I keep it near me at all times. I know that if I'm attacked,

	I'm going to use it, I'm going to beat my attacker to a bloody pulp. *(Pause)*
Bernie	Should we pause?
Caleb	This may have some relevance to your ideas about the Jewish state, but I'll tell you one thing: I will always be armed.
Bernie	Thanks, Dad.
Caleb	I'm leaving now. I can't stay in this one room so long. And you can't, either.

Bernie

Coyote leers at the audience. He is a Hopi Black Arabian Jew.

You have turned everything to shit, he says,
And you blame it all on me!
All I ever wanted to do was eat and fuck,
Just like you, you piece of walking excrement,
You fertilizing fuckhead, you TV flacko,
You jumbo mumbo fantasy believer,
You helpless scab-scratcher, you aging hipster,
You corpse-breathing writer of songs,
The hell with you!

Caleb and Rosie

Caleb	Bernie won't come out of his room.

Rosie	Who can blame him? America is ugly and mean.
Caleb	Who's talking about America?
Rosie	It's full of devils and I'm never coming back.
Caleb	Devils? You believe in devils?
Rosie	Of course I believe in devils and demons and God knows what.
Caleb	Only America is ugly and mean?
Rosie	No. The whole world is ugly and mean.
Caleb	You believe in Coyotes?
Rosie	I don't believe in Coyotes. Coyotes are dogs. Dogs are dogs.
Caleb	Bernie has a friend who is a Coyote. *(Silence)* Okay. Did you hear what I said?
Rosie	When?
Caleb	A minute ago.
Rosie	What?
Caleb	Bernie won't come out of his room.
Rosie	So what? Maybe he needs a break from people.
Caleb	That's what he says.
Rosie	Maybe it's true.
Caleb	What if he comes out of there with a gun or a knife?
Rosie	Why would he do that?
Caleb	I don't know. I told him I had a tire iron, which I do.
Rosie	That's good.
Caleb	I don't know if it's good.
Rosie	Then why are you asking?

CALEB *sighs.*

What's the matter?

Caleb	Nothing. *(Silence)* I do have one. *(Silence)* When Sarah died I had a violent paranoid streak.
Rosie	I'm sorry to hear that, but it's entirely your own fault.

CALEB *sighs.*

	What's the matter now?
Caleb	Nothing, Mom.
Rosie	People have forgotten their ideals, their responsibilities to the working class.
Caleb	I agree with that.
Rosie	Good.
Caleb	People just want to buy things. Made in China, of course.
Rosie	You could send them to Harvard, whatever, the London School of Economics, they're still Chinese.
Caleb	I don't know if I got that, Mom.
Rosie	What is it with the Coyotes?
Caleb	He's a figure.
Rosie	I thought he was an animal.
Caleb	He's a legendary figure.
Rosie	Like Stalin, the Man of Steel.
Caleb	Not really.
Rosie	Me, I live in Rio, where the animals are animals and there are no men.
Caleb	He'll come out of there and open fire or start a fire.
Rosie	Stalin?
Caleb	No, Bernie. *(Sigh)*
Rosie	Where do the dogs come into this?
Caleb	Coyotes. He has a friend named Coyote.
Rosie	He talks to his friend Coyote?

Caleb	So he says.
Rosie	That can't be all bad. (Only divine intervention can help us now.)
Caleb	He'll burn the place down.

VOICE OF COYOTE: *A fire will go around the earth. The earth's crust will burn to a cinder.*

Rosie	And then what? What? What? What?

VOICE OF COYOTE: *The earth will burn. The atmosphere will evaporate. Nothing will live. Including Brazil, where the water is going fast and the trees are burning. And these assholes continue lying and leering.*

Rosie	All right, I'll talk to him, whatshisname.
Caleb	Bernie.
Rosie	I'll talk to him. And his friend, too.
Caleb	Coyote.
Rosie	I'll talk to him, too.
Caleb	You can't see him.
Rosie	Good. It's just as well.

Rosie and Bernie, and Caleb

Rosie	Only divine intervention can help us now.
Bernie	Should I pray?
Rosie	Pray.

Bernie	I don't know how to pray.
Rosie	Get down on your knees and get ready to die.
Bernie	Is that prayer, Rose?
Rosie	That's all I know. Don't call me Rose.
Bernie	That's not prayer.
Rosie	It's either that, or join the Party.
Bernie	The Communist Party?
Rosie	You heard me.
Bernie	All right. I'll do that.
Rosie	Go for a walk.
Bernie	A walk?
Rosie	I said go for a walk.
Bernie	No.
Rosie	No?
Bernie	I'll tell you what, Grandma.
Rosie	What?
Bernie	I see devils.
Rosie	Devils? Who told you that?
Bernie	They look like American people, but they're not.
Rosie	I understand. (Someone told him.)
Bernie	They're stupid and mean.
Rosie	That's not devilish. That's us.
Bernie	Well, they're trying to trick you, so they can go to the store.
Rosie	I see.
Bernie	They want to buy stuff.
Rosie	Well, you seem friendly enough, and young.
Bernie	It's Bernie.
Rosie	And I know you'll do everything you can to help the unfortunate, which is all of us.

Enter CALEB

Bernie	You don't recognize me, Grandma, but I love you.
Rosie	Yes, I can feel that you do. Likewise, I'm sure.
Caleb	Hi.
Bernie	Here's my Dad.
Rosie	Yes, I feel like I know you as well and that you are a very good person. You probably take good care of the people around you.
Caleb	Thank you. This is Bernie, remember, who stays in his room?
Rosie	(Yes, and this must be his room.) Bernie, I heard you stay in your room a lot.
Bernie	I do. All the time, actually.
Rosie	Why?
Bernie	I have everything I need there.
Caleb	Electronics.
Rosie	Elect what?
Caleb	He has a lot of equipment in his room.
Rosie	What if he has to go to the bathroom?
Caleb	He has his own bathroom.
Rosie	Don't you need to go to school?
Bernie	No.
Rosie	You seem young.
Caleb	He has contacts.
Rosie	Contacts?
Bernie	Certain forces of nature, as represented by the Hopi Prophecy, and a legendary figure named Coyote.
Rosie	The happy what?

Bernie	It's hard to explain.
Rosie	Of course, it is. I had a visitor recently who had a lot of equipment.
Caleb	Cameras.
Rosie	She had come a long way to see me.
Bernie	All the way to Brazil. *(Laughs)*
Rosie	What's funny about that?
Bernie	I'm sorry.
Caleb	That was Mrs. Jonah, Mom, an old friend of yours.
Rosie	Yes, I recognized certain qualities in her.
Caleb	She's making a documentary, about survivors.
Rosie	Oh, yes, I am a survivor. I don't know if that was good or bad, and you don't either. Thank you both for coming.
Caleb	I'll take you home, Mom.
Rosie	You're very nice. I have a lot of work to do at the moment. Soon as I get there. To prepare.
Bernie	To prepare?
Rosie	You know, flyers, meetings, e-mails, the whole gamut. Organization is the key. Try to remember that.
Caleb	Let's go, Mom.
Rosie	Bye, bye.

Rosie

(Here in Rio. They don't look at you in the eye. They look at the sidewalk. They jiggle their money. They're thinking bad things about themselves or others. They want to have a good time. They like to watch television and go to a ballgame. They're interested in sex. That is, for fun, more than reproduction. They drive their cars into each other and enjoy the noise. They want to survive. They fear their own nonexistence. I wanted to explain about the Jewish Museum, how my mind was changed at that time, and I felt happy for the Jews, how we had not been slaughtered in vain, how History was alive in some way. It was seeing the pictures of the children, and the books, and the wisdom of the Fathers. I know there are those who don't believe me and don't want to hear about it. I know from my own experience. The Germans, they don't want to hear about it. Myself, I said I would never go to Germany. But then, in my old age, I saw with my own eyes how my mind could be changed. My own mind.)

Bernie and David

David   You were saying, what happened in the dream?

Bernie   I wasn't doing anything or saying anything.

David   Try.

Bernie   I'll try.

David   And don't look at the audience. So, Bernie.

Bernie   Yes?

David   They don't realize they're alive, they think they're going automatically to heaven.

Bernie   Is that right?

David   That's what you've been saying.

Bernie   I was only asking, Is that true of them?

David	I don't know. How would I know?
Bernie	You're not wrong. But I don't think you're right, either.
David	Forget it. Just don't look at them.
Bernie	I'm not looking. *(Looks)*
David	Don't let them see you do that. Look at me.
Bernie	Okay.
David	Look at me.
Bernie	I'm looking. *(Pause)* I have a question.
David	Go ahead.
Bernie	What do you mean by heaven?
David	According to the gentiles, it's where our Father lives.
Bernie	Dad?
David	No, Bernie, I think they mean God.
Bernie	What about us?
David	Us?
Bernie	Do we go to heaven?
David	For us it's not so automatic.
Bernie	What do we have to do?
David	We have to be nice. On Yom Kippur we pay our dues.
Bernie	I don't get it.
David	Me, neither.
Bernie	You're supposed to be a teacher.
David	I don't teach theology.
Bernie	But what the fuck is heaven? (Excuse my language.) It's absurd.
David	That's what I'm saying.
Bernie	And then you got these other ones making bombs to blow people up.
David	That's right.
Bernie	They go to heaven?

David	I don't know, Bernie. You figure it out.
Bernie	That's what Dad said.
David	He doesn't know either.
Bernie	He doesn't remember my name half the time.
David	I know.
Bernie	I'm his son. He calls me you.
David	He might go to heaven because he doesn't know which way to turn.
Bernie	That's funny. But this is serious.
David	Is that why you stay in your room?
Bernie	People are blowing themselves up with bombs.
David	Exactly, meat for the worms. You didn't answer me.
Bernie	What was the question?
David	Can you tell me what she said?
Bernie	Who?
David	Mom. Can you tell me what she said?
Bernie	Rosie?
David	No, Mom. Come on, Bernie. You told Dad you had a dream about Mom.
Bernie	I did.
David	Tell me what she said in the dream.
Bernie	She said the Indians had it right.
David	What did they have right?
Bernie	They had a lot of things right, David.
David	What did she say?
Bernie	"They didn't bury their dead, because they would contaminate the earth."
David	And?
Bernie	"They didn't burn their dead because they would contaminate the air."

David	So what did they do?
Bernie	They put them on scaffolds so the vultures could eat them.
David	Oh. Great. What did you say?
Bernie	I was dreaming.
David	Mom said things.
Bernie	The dreamer doesn't say things. My main idea was we should have one country, Palestine. But I didn't speak it.
David	I see. And what did she say?
Bernie	She said, "They won't have water or air." One country with Arabs and Jews together. I thought, "What could be wrong?" She said, "Don't burn the oxygen out of the air."
David	But what does that mean?
Bernie	I don't know. I'm just telling you.
David	Talk some more to your mother, Bernie, who is not here anymore.
Bernie	And you believe me?
David	What?
Bernie	You believe I can talk to our mother in my dreams?
David	I don't know what to believe. Like heaven and hell and spirit worlds and Coyote and the rest of it.
Bernie	Or you're being nice because you might want me to come out of my room.
David	Who said anything about coming out of your room?
Bernie	*(Looks at the audience)* No one.
David	Look this way. Good. I have to go now. I have a wife. Speaking of which, she'll give you a call.
Bernie	Well and good.

Bernie and Chrystal

Bernie	Chrystal?
Chrystal	Yes, yes, yes?
Bernie	It's nice to speak with you.
Chrystal	Hello, Bernie.
Bernie	Hi, Aunt Chrystal.
Chrystal	Oh, that's nice. Hi.
Bernie	Hi.
Chrystal	Actually, I'm your sister-in-law.
Bernie	Exactly.
Chrystal	Nice talking to you.
Bernie	I know.
Chrystal	I was wondering.
Bernie	What?
Chrystal	You want to go to a ballgame?
Bernie	Oh, God, no.
Chrystal	Why not?
Bernie	Too many people and too many cars. And the garbage is a foot deep.
Chrystal	How about a concert?
Bernie	What kind of concert?
Chrystal	Classical?
Bernie	No.
Chrystal	Rock & Roll?
Bernie	No.
Chrystal	Jazz?
Bernie	No.
Chrystal	Punk?
Bernie	No.

Chrystal	What kind of music do you like?
Bernie	The kind I can listen to in my room. Here, I have total freedom of choice.
Chrystal	It's also social. It's also about being with other people. Concerts. Events.
Bernie	I don't want to be with other people, obviously.
Chrystal	Don't you want to be with your Aunt Chrystal?
Bernie	You can visit me.
Chrystal	You can visit me, too.
Bernie	I said it first.
Chrystal	You could come to my school.
Bernie	I don't go to schools.
Chrystal	Why not?
Bernie	They're out of control. You know how it is with like a dreidel?
Chrystal	I'm not sure.
Bernie	Are you Jewish?
Chrystal	You know I'm Jewish.
Bernie	You're a convert.
Chrystal	True. The best kind. Of Jew.
Bernie	So you know what a dreidel is. You spin it and eventually it wobbles. The earth is spinning but not quite at the right rate, so there's a glitch in the rotation. Could you follow that?
Chrystal	I think so.
Bernie	The way you can tell that is in the schools. No one knows how to be because the spin is out of control. So there's no ideal and the hierarchy is out of whack. In these kinds of situations the cosmic forces have to redo the situation from scratch.

Chrystal	That's a fantastic theory.
Bernie	Well, you can believe it or not, it's up to you.
Chrystal	It does make sense.
Bernie	Because everything is connected.
Chrystal	Of course they are.
Bernie	So, you see what I mean?
Chrystal	I think I do, yes.
Bernie	Why I stay away from the schools.
Chrystal	Where did you learn about this, if you don't mind my asking? *(Silence)* Don't tell me if you don't want to.
Bernie	From the Hopi.
Chrystal	Are they Native Americans?
Bernie	They're Indians.
Chrystal	That's what I meant.
Bernie	Yes.
Chrystal	Bernie, you have time for another question?
Bernie	What's the question?
Chrystal	What does this all have to do with fire?
Bernie	Who told you about fire?
Chrystal	Your brother, David.
Bernie	He doesn't know anything about it.
Chrystal	That's why I'm asking you.
Bernie	Fire is oxygen combining with other elements to create heat and light. (And rust.)
Chrystal	Is that why you want to burn things?
Bernie	Who said I wanted to burn things?
Chrystal	I don't know. Somehow I got that idea.
Bernie	There's all kinds of ideas sloshing around in people's heads.
Chrystal	Like what?

Bernie	Like the amount of oxygen is always the same.
Chrystal	Isn't it?
Bernie	No. The higher you go the less there is.
Chrystal	What are you doing all day long?
Bernie	I have everything I need, right here in my room. I study, I watch things, I talk to my friends. I play video games. I'm like any normal teenager.
Chrystal	Bernie, come out of your room and go to a real school.
Bernie	No.
Chrystal	If you're such a normal person, act like a normal person.
Bernie	Okay, I'm not normal.
Chrystal	Yes, you are.
Bernie	No, I'm not.
Chrystal	You have a window?
Bernie	A window?
Chrystal	In your room.
Bernie	Of course.
Chrystal	Good.
Bernie	What are we talking about now?
Chrystal	I don't know. You lost me, or I lost you.
Bernie	Come on over, we'll play something on my digital electronics.
Chrystal	What?
Bernie	You know, music or a speech or an opera.
Chrystal	Okay, Bernie.
Bernie	Anytime.
Chrystal	I will do that.
Bernie	Okay, I'll see ya.
Chrystal	So long.
Bernie	Thanks for calling, Aunt Chrystal.

Caleb and David

Caleb   The sins of the fathers.

David   What does that mean, the sins of the fathers?

Caleb   I'm not sure. It sounds right.

David   The sins of the fathers. Where is that written?

Caleb   I don't know. I never learned where things were written.

David   Somewhere in the Bible.

Caleb   Your grandfather, he came to America in 1905, he never learned a word of English. All his life he was illegal.

David   So?

Caleb   That must mean something. On the other side, Rosie was the only one to come over. She lost everybody. Not a single relative survived.

David   What does it mean?

Caleb   Something is passed.

David   Why Bernie wants to burn things down.

Caleb   Something like that.

David   I don't.

Caleb   You won't procreate.

David   It's not up to me.

Caleb   Still.

David   Still?

Caleb   Something is passed, it has consequences for generations. You have these German kids now, I wouldn't be surprised if they had problems, like autism.

David   You should look it up on the Internet.

Caleb   Maybe I will.

David	Excuse the expression, but the kid is an idiot.
Caleb	You mean Bernie?
David	Yes, the very Bernie who wants to burn things down. I'll say it again, the fuckin' idiot is a fucking idiot.
Caleb	That was brilliant. And you, you won't have children and you walk around with a yarmulke, and you have no idea why you do or what it means.
David	What does it mean?
Caleb	It's so birds don't shit on your stupid head.
David	Thanks, Dad.
Caleb	Don't mention it.

Later.

Caleb	It's like Rosie says. Half-assed so-called human beings shitting on their own world.
David	So what did you expect?
Caleb	I don't believe in anything. I believe in nothing.
David	You repeated yourself.
Caleb	I don't give a shit.
David	Neither do I. They're not rapturing *us* up.
Caleb	So what's the plot?
David	What's the plot?
Caleb	What's the plot?
David	You mean the theory?
Caleb	Yes.
David	The plot is that some Christian people are planning to ratchet up to the heavens and I don't think they're taking us with them.

Caleb	Explain it to me again, how does this affect the state of Israel?
David	The state of Israel is told about in the Bible.
Caleb	This I know already. Where it is spoken about, I don't know.
David	I don't either, but because of the war over there, the time has come for these people to be catching the train to heaven.
Caleb	Oh.
David	Well, it's not a train.
Caleb	What is it?
David	We've reached the limit, Dad, of my understanding.
Caleb	And this is why Bernie wants to burn things down?
David	I don't know why Bernie wants to burn things down, maybe his grandfather never learned English and chased after women. Like you said.
Caleb	And this is why he won't come out of his room?
David	I don't know the answer to that either, except he lost all his relatives on his Grandmother's side by their being shot in the head and suffocated by gas and hung from the rafters and strangled and starved to death, and so on. The unspeakable.
Caleb	So the question is. *(Silence)*
David	What?
Caleb	Who goes first?
David	You mean, like the Marx brothers?
Caleb	No, I mean, yes.
David	You mean the baseball joke, like with Abbott and Costello? Who's on first?
Caleb	No.

David	You mean, which mad person goes violent first and where?
Caleb	Yes. Bingo. And I think it has to be Rosie because of the connection there with the Holocaust, like you mentioned.
David	Wait a minute.
Caleb	Why?
David	I have to catch my breath here.

Moments later.

David	Well, you lost me there, Dad.
Caleb	I was only thinking.
David	Let's pause again please. *(Pause)*
Caleb	That could definitely be Rosie. Each day she goes more into Brazil.
David	I've been meaning to say.
Caleb	Yes, you have. *(Silence)* Yes, you want to say something?
David	Yes, the sad thing is the connection between Chrystal and me.
Caleb	This is true.
David	A loss of faith.
Caleb	Who could blame her?
David	I don't blame her.
Caleb	She's not Jewish.
David	She is Jewish.
Caleb	So you can't blame her.
David	She's more Jewish than I am.
Caleb	This is true. Let's see what happens.
David	This happens. That's why people should stay together.
Caleb	I didn't get that.

David	That's why people should stay together.
Caleb	Why? Because this happens?
David	Yes.
Caleb	I don't get it.
David	That's all that happens.
Caleb	So people should stay together?
David	Yes. Because it's the only thing that happens.
Caleb	Okay, if that's what you think.
David	That's what I think.
Caleb	It doesn't make any sense, but that's fine with me.
David	Good.
Caleb	Hopefully, you will stay together.
David	You didn't.
Caleb	No.
David	What happened?
Caleb	She may have had a brain disorder. Sarah.
David	You don't know?
Caleb	We never found her. Maybe she got raptured.
David	I don't think so.
Caleb	Just a joke. Bad joke. Very bad joke.
David	I'm not laughing.
Caleb	I was a dedicated teacher, like you. Biology, chemistry. Then the respect went out the window and into the streets. I fell into a bad mood of various dimensions. For Sarah, it was a sign of the end of all things to come.
David	That's too much.
Caleb	It was a bit much.
David	I think so.
Caleb	Shut the door, David. I don't know why I said that.
David	It's okay.

Caleb	Leave it open. You were here at the time. You heard the news.
David	It was hard to hear. It's hard to hear to this day.
Caleb	Hard to hear. Then I had to stand there feeling my teeth in my mouth, the back of my tongue coated with bacteria, my feet aching on the floor and a lump of emotion in my chest I could do nothing about. What is that?
David	It's grief. We have no control over grief.
Caleb	That's what I said. I said I have no control. Like Bernie, I was afraid to leave the house.
David	Maybe some people have control.
Caleb	Who?
David	I don't know who. Some people.
Caleb	Maybe they're already dead.
David	I have control.
Caleb	No one has control. Emotion comes up, that's it. Otherwise, no emotion.
David	Maybe that's me, then. Maybe I'm dead.
Caleb	You have no emotion?
David	Chrystal says I have no emotion.
Caleb	You have no emotion so you have plenty of control?
David	That's what she says. So I must be dead.
Caleb	No, no, no.
David	I think I'm dead.
Caleb	You're not dead. She should get pregnant.
David	She can't get pregnant, Chrystal.
Caleb	Excuse me, but do you have intercourse?
David	None of your business, Dad.
Caleb	Excuse me for asking.
David	None of your fucking business.

Bernie and Rosie

Bernie	Grandma?
Rosie	What?
Bernie	I was trying to explain.
Rosie	What?
Bernie	This happens.
Rosie	This happens?
Bernie	Yes.
Rosie	So, what happens?
Bernie	This.
Rosie	Bernie, don't talk to me if that's how you talk.
Bernie	A mega-volcano could erupt and destroy us all.
Rosie	Let it erupt.
Bernie	You're a misanthrope.
Rosie	What's that?
Bernie	You don't like people.
Rosie	Neither do you.
Bernie	Or seventy-five atomic bombs could go off.
Rosie	Why seventy-five?
Bernie	I don't know why. Do you care?
Rosie	No and yes.
Bernie	You can't say no and yes.
Rosie	Yes, I can. I'm in agreement with the Hopi, like you. I saw the end of mankind.
Bernie	In the camps?
Rosie	In the camps, and in your basic human stupidity.
Bernie	Say more.

Rosie	People don't understand anything, least of all each other.
Bernie	So it's a failure.
Rosie	It's a failure. They never will. It's too bad.
Bernie	A few miles down, you come to hot magma.
Rosie	I know. That's what I said.
Bernie	You're a smart grandmother, Grandma.
Rosie	Definitely. I was in a concentration camp when I was twelve. Angels were being prepared there for a life in heaven.
Bernie	Somehow I don't feel like I've explained myself successfully.
Rosie	That would be right, my boy.

Chrystal and David

Chrystal	He plays with matches.
David	Who does?
Chrystal	Don't say who does.
David	Who does?
Chrystal	Your little brother Bernie, for burning.
David	It's Bernard.
Chrystal	He's out of his little mind.
David	He had the highest test score in his class.
Chrystal	What test?
David	I don't know what test. It was a smart test.
Chrystal	So he's so smart he won't come out of his room?
David	He's sensitive. Generations of rabbis came before him.
Chrystal	How do you know?

David	Intelligence is a wonderful thing.
Chrystal	Sure, if the brain is attached to the body.
David	Rabbis were in Poland since the fifteenth century.
Chrystal	That was a few lines back, David.
David	Who cares?
Chrystal	Certainly not me.
David	Rosie's family was in horses.
Chrystal	What were they doing in horses?
David	It's not a town. It's a profession. They bought and sold horses near the city of Pinsk.
Chrystal	Where is that?
David	Ukraine.
Chrystal	Not Poland?
David	That was my father's side.
Chrystal	Ultimately, we're all Jewish.
David	No, we're not. Tell me, What do you like so much about it?
Chrystal	It's simple, lots of rules, 24/7, remember who you are and what you're here for. You don't have to think too much.
David	What do you think about getting together?
Chrystal	How is that related?
David	It's a commandment: Be fruitful and multiply.
Chrystal	I don't think so at the moment.
David	Maybe later?
Chrystal	I don't care if he never comes out.
David	Who is that?
Chrystal	Bernie. Bernard.
David	Did you hear what I said?
Chrystal	Especially not with matches or a lighter.
David	You didn't hear me.
Chrystal	I heard you. The answer is no.

David	Why?
Chrystal	Don't take it personally.
David	How can I not take it personally?
Chrystal	There are too many fucking people in the world already.
David	Kiss me, at least.
Chrystal	I'll kiss you, but that's as far as it goes.
David	Kiss me here.
Chrystal	All right. I'll kiss you there, too.
David	Thank you.
Chrystal	Don't thank me.
David	I take it back.
Chrystal	Don't take it back. Be quiet.

David

(And then I submitted. She said "relax" and I relaxed. I felt the warmth of Mother Earth and the love of a woman. Things were all right for a couple of days after that. Then, to gratify her, I gave up all pork products, and after that, I separated milk from meat, and refused to eat the two together on the same plate, a kosher decision which made Chrystal happier still.)

Caleb and Rosie

Rosie	You start with nothing and you end with nothing and nothing's in between.
Caleb	Motherhood?
Rosie	Maybe motherhood.

Caleb	Some people are just glad to be alive.
Rosie	Don't start.
Caleb	Breathing air.
Rosie	Mazel tov.
Caleb	Not six feet under.
Rosie	More power to them.
Caleb	Alive! Alive! Be happy!
Rosie	It's okay with me.
Caleb	Enjoy the moment!
Rosie	And now it's gone.
Caleb	It's so interesting.
Rosie	What is?
Caleb	The difference in attitude.
Rosie	It could just be IQ.
Caleb	It could.
Rosie	You're my son, but I'm smarter than you.
Caleb	That's what I'm saying.
Rosie	You got cheated on half the genes.
Caleb	I'm not that stupid.
Rosie	Let me ask you something.
Caleb	Ask.
Rosie	Why did you turn her to ashes?
Caleb	Who did I turn to ashes?
Rosie	Sorry. What's her name, your good wife, as you call her?
Caleb	Sarah. She was a good wife.
Rosie	It's against the Jewish religion.
Caleb	What is?
Rosie	To burn people.

Caleb	She wanted to be burned. She thought burning was good. In India they're going up in smoke all over the place. But we never found her, actually.
Rosie	It's not a good idea.
Caleb	It's a totally different religion.
Rosie	I don't care. I'm totally against it.
Caleb	We never found her, Mom, I just told you.
Rosie	Sarah?
Caleb	Yes. We never found her body. So there was nothing to burn.
Rosie	What do you do with the ashes?
Caleb	They're in a box usually.
Rosie	And where do you put the box?
Caleb	The box is kept in a crypt.
Rosie	And where is the crypt?
Caleb	The crypt is in the cemetery.
Rosie	Me, I've thought if over, I want a regular Jewish funeral.
Caleb	You've thought it over about cremation?
Rosie	Yes, but I'm against it. It doesn't seem right in this place.
Caleb	In the camps, of course, they had ashes.
Rosie	That's correct. Former human beings.
Caleb	I'm sorry I said that.
Rosie	Why? It's the truth. What do they do with the ashes here?
Caleb	Some people scatter their ashes.
Rosie	They scatter them?
Caleb	Yes. Over the water. Over the land.
Rosie	Over someone's head maybe.
Caleb	There's an idea.
Rosie	Life is strange and disappointing.
Caleb	People don't like to hear that.

Rosie	I don't like to hear it either.
Caleb	Nobody wants to hear about it.
Rosie	There are plenty of Jews here, believe it or not.
Caleb	Hard to believe.
Rosie	They were here before New York or Charleston.
Caleb	I don't think so.
Rosie	You could look it up. It's all written down.
Caleb	I will. I'll check it out, Mom.
Rosie	Do it before the earth burns up and the oceans boil, David.
Caleb	It's Caleb.
Rosie	Caleb.

Bernie and Caleb

Caleb	Bernie, why don't you come out of your room finally, at last?
Bernie	I don't want to.
Caleb	Why not?
Bernie	I don't want to come out of my room.
Caleb	Come out of there this instant.
Bernie	No.
Caleb	Act like a normal person.
Bernie	I am a normal person. I did this already with Chrystal, Dad. We had a total conversation.
Caleb	So what? This is your father talking. Act like a 13-year-old.
Bernie	I am a 13-year-old. You didn't hear what I said.
Caleb	So come out of your room.

Bernie	No.
Caleb	Bernie, this is really hard for me.
Bernie	I'm sorry.
Caleb	I miss you.
Bernie	I miss you, too, Dad.
Caleb	Then come out and be with me once in a while. We'll go to a game, we'll go to the movies. We'll do things.
Bernie	Maybe later.
Caleb	When later?
Bernie	I don't know.
Caleb	You know what it's like for me?
Bernie	No.
Caleb	Do you want to know?
Bernie	No and yes.
Caleb	It's lonely. I don't have anyone to talk to. I spend days and nights by myself.
Bernie	I'm sorry, Dad.
Caleb	I'm sick of myself. Aren't you?
Bernie	No. I have a lot to do. I talk to people all the time.
Caleb	I don't.
Bernie	You should, Dad.
Caleb	I should, but I don't. I have no one to talk to.
Bernie	David?
Caleb	He's a married man. He has no time for me.
Bernie	Your mother?
Caleb	That's a riddle, not a conversation. She thinks I'm David.
Bernie	Join a club, Dad, or go back to work.
Caleb	I suppose I could do that.
Bernie	Get married again.

Caleb	To who?
Bernie	Get out and meet someone.
Caleb	I don't know how to do that anymore. I think about the next thing with a woman and I lose interest.
Bernie	What next thing?
Caleb	The next thing to say, the next thing to do. The whole thing is a pain in the ass. On the other hand, I'm by myself too much. I'm afraid I'll start talking to myself.
Bernie	I'm sorry. It's not my fault. Don't start talking to yourself.
Caleb	I see myself doing it.
Bernie	Call someone on the phone.
Caleb	Like I just did?
Bernie	Yeah.
Caleb	Excuse me, but I don't understand. Do you?
Bernie	What?
Caleb	Call, Bernie.
Bernie	You took away my cellphone, remember?
Caleb	Yes, of course.
Bernie	So I only use the walkie-talkie. Only relatives.
Caleb	That's right.
Bernie	People. I don't like them and I'm afraid of them.
Caleb	I thought you said—
Bernie	I stick to videos.
Caleb	You watch TV?
Bernie	No.
Caleb	You don't watch TV?
Bernie	No.
Caleb	Because it's the last thing I want you to be doing in there.
Bernie	It's all lies, Dad. Lies and people selling you shit.
Caleb	That's what I'm saying.

Bernie	And bad acting. Like I can't stand another minute.
Caleb	So come out and be with people.
Bernie	It's all over with people, Dad.
Caleb	Can't be, son.
Bernie	Not like they have TVs in their heads, but something similar.
Caleb	I didn't follow that.
Bernie	Anyway, it's not that. It's the violence.
Caleb	All people?
Bernie	Humans. All.
Caleb	All?
Bernie	Yes, but I make an exception for the relatives.
Caleb	Well, thank God for that.
Bernie	If they do the walkie-talkie thing, only.
Caleb	Why?
Bernie	Why?
Caleb	Why?
Bernie	Because of the Hopi.
Caleb	Leave the Hopi out of this.
Bernie	Because of the people.
Caleb	Why? Explain it to me, please.
Bernie	Because you don't know what they'll do next. You don't know and they don't know. So how can you trust them, how can you like them? Their only predictability is biological. They have to eat, sleep, shit, and reproduce. Otherwise, they'll kill each other at the drop of a hat. Or if you bend over to tie your shoelaces. Or if you lean against a building. Or if you go for a walk with your dog. They'll kill you with a car bomb if you're in the vicinity, so my advice to you is to stay out of the vicinity.

Caleb	So what can we do?
Bernie	Stay out of the vicinity. They'll kill you by air or by sea, you won't know which. And not only that, their minds are not attached to their tongues, their minds are attached to their sex organs or to their intestines. That's where their minds are. So it's a mistake to talk to them. I only talk to my immediate family—like you, Dad—and I try to keep it to a minimum. They'll throw up on you, too.
Caleb	They?
Bernie	Yes. And I talk to Coyote. The people have no control over their functions, which makes them unpredictable, like I say, which makes them mad. So they want to destroy Earthmother. They just want to piss on her or pour poison into her veins. That's their attitude. Just ask anybody. Who comes first? Them. They come first. They come first over Earthmother.
Caleb	You're reading too much Hopi Indian material, Bernard.
Bernie	No, I'm not. It's not just the Hopi.
Caleb	Yes, it is. That's why you talk like that. That's why you won't come out of your room.
Bernie	Look around you, Dad. Some of them think they're going to heaven. They're rotting corpses and they think they're going to heaven. They're rotting while they're alive and they think they're going to heaven, and they throw their garbage into the street. They throw their garbage into the street and their shit they throw into the water, into the rain.
Caleb	Okay, that's enough.
Bernie	That's why I'm afraid of them and I don't like them. *(Silence)* You asked me, Dad.
Caleb	And you?

Bernie	Me, too. I don't like me, either. I'm just like them and just like you.
Caleb	Oh.
Bernie	Full of shit and false ideas.
Caleb	I see.
Bernie	So if I ever get out of here I'll burn the place down.
Caleb	Stay here, then.
Bernie	I'm not ready right now to go out there and start burning it down.
Caleb	Good.
Bernie	Destroying the safe places and the armaments they all use.
Caleb	Okay.
Bernie	Not just yet.
Caleb	I wish your mother was here.
Bernie	I don't.
Caleb	You don't?
Bernie	No, the earth is not the place to be these days.
Caleb	Your grandmother then.
Bernie	The days are numbered in Brazil, too, Dad.
Caleb	She's not really in Brazil.
Bernie	She is in her mind.
Caleb	Don't do anything until I talk to your grandmother.
Bernie	What does that have to do with anything?
Caleb	Just don't do anything until I talk to somebody.
Bernie	Talk to somebody, Dad.
Caleb	Please don't do anything weird.
Bernie	You too, Dad.
Caleb	Come out of there.
Bernie	Don't start talking to yourself.

Caleb	This is your father talking.
Bernie	She can't remember anyway, Grandma.
Caleb	You heard me, Bernard. Bernard?
Bernie	What?
Caleb	What's that smell?
Bernie	It's the TV burning.
Caleb	Bernard!
Bernie	What?
Caleb	Just pull the plug! Pull the plug!
Bernie	Okay!
Caleb	Pull the plug! Pull the plug or I'll call the police!
Bernie	I pulled the plug! It's not burning!
Caleb	Put the fire out and pull the plug!
Bernie	I did!
Caleb	Or I'll call the fire department, the police, and an ambulance!
Bernie	I did, Dad!
Caleb	Is the fire out?
Bernie	It's out.
Caleb	Thank God. Now, give it to me, please. No more TV.

Rosie and Caleb

Caleb	Rosie. It's me. Caleb.
Rosie	I know. Don't call me Rosie.
Caleb	I'm sorry.
Rosie	I'm your mother.
Caleb	My son Bernie is in his room.
Rosie	I heard.

Caleb	He doesn't come out.
Rosie	Right.
Caleb	He set fire to his television set.
Rosie	How can you do that?
Caleb	I don't know how.
Rosie	It's dangerous.
Caleb	This is your grandson we're talking about.
Rosie	Not a smart idea.
Caleb	No. So I took it away from him.
Rosie	Good.
Caleb	I told him I would talk to you.
Rosie	Why?
Caleb	I don't know why.
Rosie	What can I do?
Caleb	Talk to him. He talks to his relatives.
Rosie	Think about it.
Caleb	What does that mean, "think about it."
Rosie	I don't know. It must mean something.
Caleb	It's completely meaningless.
Rosie	Have it your way.
Caleb	I think I'll change the subject now.
Rosie	See if I care.
Caleb	David asks me to have a meeting with Chrystal.
Rosie	David? Chrystal?
Caleb	That's your other grandson and his wife.
Rosie	About what?
Caleb	About having a child.
Rosie	Nice. And?
Caleb	I avoided the meeting. I pretended I didn't hear him.
Rosie	Why?

Caleb	I have my own problems.
Rosie	You can't interfere.
Caleb	Exactly.
Rosie	On the other hand, he's your son.
Caleb	I thought he meant something else, David. I said that. And then I said, of course.
Rosie	You lied.
Caleb	I half-lied, because I was actually confused. I thought I should.
Rosie	But you didn't want to.
Caleb	Right. I wanted to go home and watch the news and deal with Bernie.
Rosie	Not deal with Bernie.
Caleb	And not deal with Bernie. I was divided in two.
Rosie	I have had that. Experience.
Caleb	All I could do was lie.
Rosie	You tend to do that.
Caleb	There was two of me, meanwhile I pretended there was a third one.
Rosie	Who couldn't hear?
Caleb	Right, confused by early Alzheimer's.
Rosie	And you liked the power of being asked, the attention?
Caleb	Right.
Rosie	So you were tempted in the first place?
Caleb	Yes, but I didn't want to seem too eager. Being asked for help.
Rosie	The helpful Dad.
Caleb	Yes. Even though my heart was pounding. I lied.
Rosie	What did you say?

Caleb	I said Bernie was waiting for me at home.
Rosie	They had invited you for dinner?
Caleb	Yeah. I said, let's have coffee another time, because coffee is less serious.
Rosie	But they had invited you for dinner?
Caleb	Yes.
Rosie	Now what?
Caleb	I'll talk to Chrystal.
Rosie	What will you say?
Caleb	I'll say nobody knows, and nobody will ever know.
Rosie	What?
Caleb	Anything.
Rosie	Anything?
Caleb	Neither the future nor the past. Meanwhile, there's Bernie to consider.
Rosie	You remember Rabbi Nachman?
Caleb	Of course.
Rosie	He also never came out of his room.
Caleb	There's no comparison, the kid is an idiot. *(Silence)* I'm sorry.
Rosie	What do you want from me?
Caleb	Talk to him. Get him out of his room.
Rosie	I'll talk to Bernie, you talk to Chyrstal.
Caleb	It's a deal.
Rosie	Not that it will do any good.
Caleb	Why do you say that?
Rosie	We have passed the point of no return, David.
Caleb	Caleb.
Rosie	What's the matter with you?
Caleb	Nothing.

Rosie	And the other one?
Caleb	Bernard?
Rosie	He shouldn't play with those things.
Caleb	The TV?
Rosie	Right.
Caleb	I agree, Mom. I took it away.

Rosie and Chrystal

Rosie	This is Rosie, who is this?
Chrystal	Chrystal. You dialed my number.
Rosie	Are you all right?
Chrystal	What do you mean by that?
Rosie	Are you all right?
Chrystal	No. At the moment I feel more wrong than right.
Rosie	What did you do wrong?
Chrystal	It doesn't matter what.
Rosie	It's Kafkaesque. You feel it's your duty.
Chrystal	My duty?
Rosie	To be wrong. It's something in the Ashkenazi genes.
Chrystal	It can't be, I'm a convert.
Rosie	Then you got it from David.
Chrystal	Okay, Rose, maybe I did.
Rosie	That's the only explanation I can think of.
Chrystal	Bernie thinks it's because we declared war on nature.
Rosie	Not us! That wasn't us! That was the gentiles!
Chrystal	God talked to Abraham.
Rosie	Bernie said that?
Chrystal	Yes. God talked to Abraham, from outside life.

Rosie	What was he supposed to do?
Chrystal	He did the best he could.
Rosie	Abraham or Bernie?
Chrystal	Both.
Rosie	Bernie could be confused.
Chrystal	He listens to the Hopi.
Rosie	They talk to him?
Chrystal	Like God talked to Abraham.
Rosie	Oh, I can't believe that.
Chrystal	It's the end of the Fourth World.
Rosie	Why Bernie?
Chrystal	I agree with the Indians. They didn't get enough credit. They took care.
Rosie	You didn't answer the question.
Chrystal	I don't know why Bernie.
Rosie	Maybe he's imagining things.
Chrystal	It's like the Tibetans and the Dalai Lama.
Rosie	What is?
Chrystal	Why Bernie is chosen.
Rosie	He's Jewish for God's sake!
Chrystal	His parents separated, or his mother drowned, he broke in two, and now a third party joined in.
Rosie	Who is that?
Chrystal	A Coyote. Mr. Coyote.
Rosie	Indeed. He talks to a dog?
Chrystal	He's not exactly a dog.
Rosie	The dog talks back to him?
Chrystal	He says a mega-volcano is about to erupt.
Rosie	Where?
Chrystal	Somewhere in Asia.

Rosie	When?
Chrystal	Soon.
Rosie	Great.
Chrystal	Sulphuric acid will take the place of oxygen in the air.
Rosie	Great talking to you.
Chrystal	So what should we do?
Rosie	Talk to Mr. Coyote?
Chrystal	He's not a person.
Rosie	Of course he's not a person!
Chrystal	He's a spirit. He lives in the Spirit World.
Rosie	So how do you talk to him? Walkie-talkie?
Chrystal	Bernie talks to him.
Rosie	I'll call him.
Chrystal	Coyote?
Rosie	No, Bernie, obviously, Sarah.
Chrystal	It's Chrystal, Rose.
Rosie	Obviously.
Chrystal	You have to call Caleb, who gets him on the phone, or go over there yourself.
Rosie	I'll go.

Bernie and Rosie

Rosie	Hello, Bernie.
Bernie	Hi, Rose.
Rosie	Don't call me Rose. I'm your grandmother.
Bernie	Grandma.
Rosie	You're mad at your mother because she went to hell?
Bernie	Wouldn't you?

Rosie	Hell is a state of mind, like Rosie in Rio.
Bernie	You're talking about yourself in the third person.
Rosie	So what? This bothers you?
Bernie	Not really.
Rosie	That's the trouble with the Ashkenazi.
Bernie	What?
Rosie	They're bothered by something they can't put their finger on it.
Bernie	I know what it is.
Rosie	That's why I wanted to talk to you. *(Silence)* So tell me already.
Bernie	It's because God talked to Abraham.
Rosie	How do you know this?
Bernie	It's in the Bible.
Rosie	Noah's ark is also in the Bible!
Bernie	So?
Rosie	You believe that, too?
Bernie	It depends on how you look at it.
Rosie	Let's get back to the original question.
Bernie	Why God talked to Abraham?
Rosie	No, why you're mad at your mother.
Bernie	I'm not mad.
Rosie	What are you?
Bernie	I'm sad.
Rosie	I'm sorry. *(Silence)*
Bernie	Why did you do it?
Rosie	What?
Bernie	Go to Brazil.
Rosie	I wanted a second chance. I didn't realize.
Bernie	What?

Rosie	I had no more chances. *(Pause)* Brazil is going fast.
Bernie	Why is that?
Rosie	Nobody has their own money. Everyone has other people's money.
Bernie	I see.
Rosie	So anyway. Who is this Coyote?
Bernie	He's not a person.
Rosie	What is he?
Bernie	He is what's left over when the world is destroyed.
Rosie	Where will he live?
Bernie	In the wind. In the waterfall. He's also known as Trickster.
Rosie	What will he do?
Bernie	He'll trick one of the cosmic heavyweights to send an arrow down here.
Rosie	A what?
Bernie	An arrow. It'll stick in the ground and bring new life.
Rosie	I see.
Bernie	He'll challenge one of the gods to a bow and arrow context.
Rosie	You mean contest.
Bernie	Contest. And Earthmother will get one in the butt.
Rosie	Okay, Bernie. I miss you.
Bernie	Come home then.
Rosie	I'm thinking about it.
Bernie	I'll have Coyote give you a call.
Rosie	I don't know about that.
Bernie	It won't be like a regular phone call, Rose.
Rosie	Okay.
Bernie	It'll be like a balloon or something, or a kite, or a cloud.

Rosie	Okay.
Bernie	Or a shine in the sky.
Rosie	Okay, Bern.
Bernie	So watch the sky.
Rosie	I will. I'll watch the sky.
Bernie	Look up once in a while, like every hour of every day.
Rosie	Okay, son.
Bernie	And you'll see something. Something weird and interesting.
Rosie	I guess I've given up.
Bernie	What?
Rosie	Getting you out of your room.
Bernie	Don't worry, Grandma. You'll be the first to know.

David and Chrystal

David	They say the earth has died three times already. Once by ice, once by flood.
Chrystal	Who says?
David	The Hopi. I forget the other, maybe dust. Volcanoes and earthquakes.
Chrystal	Bernie's into fire.
David	Yeah, he's into fire. And you? What are you into?
Chrystal	I think we'll suffocate for lack of oxygen.
David	Oh for God's sake.
Chrystal	That's a good one. For God's sake. The magma is not far down.
David	What do you mean?
Chrystal	The magma of the earth, molten iron. It's not that far below the crust.

David	Why suffocate?
Chrystal	The oxygen is draining away. Fire can do it. Heat. Sulphur.
David	You're unbelievably pessimistic.
Chrystal	I have a head on my shoulders and something between the ears.
David	I get it.
Chrystal	You don't have to be a genius to see what's coming, just average intelligence.
David	It's not that I disagree.
Chrystal	Of course not. You're not stupid.
David	We could get hit by a meteor.
Chrystal	If you throw shit into the water it becomes shitty water.
David	We could lose our fertility.
Chrystal	Same with the air.
David	Do you have no hope?
Chrystal	None. You take me for an idiot?
David	No, I'm sorry.
Chrystal	And I won't perform a sex act.
David	Why not?
Chrystal	It's feeding the beast.
David	It's new life, Chrystal.
Chrystal	It's creepy. And what'll it eat?
David	Milk.
Chrystal	I'll have no milk. It'll be contaminated by things like chromium and rust.
David	Then I won't go on living.
Chrystal	Radioactive dust.
David	Did you hear me?
Chrystal	Neither will I, David.
David	What should we do?

| Chrystal | We don't need to do anything. Just wait. And be kind. And I'm glad you're kosher finally. |

David and Chrystal, and Caleb

David	It's my father on the phone.
Chrystal	What's he want?
David	I don't know. Ask him.
Chrystal	He wants to put his two cents in.
David	She says you want to put your two cents in.
Chrystal	Tell him I talked to his mother.
David	She said she talked with your mother. Here you talk to him.
Chrystal	Caleb?
Caleb	This is not a movie. The Messiah is not coming.
Chrystal	Who said the Messiah is coming?
Caleb	Not you. Excuse me.
Chrystal	I wouldn't know the Messiah if he was you or David or Bernie.
Caleb	None of the above.
Chrystal	He's not coming, Caleb.
Caleb	How do you know?
Chrystal	Keep an eye on your younger son. He's a pyromaniac.
Caleb	I never said he was coming in the first place.
Chrystal	Bernie or the Messiah?
Caleb	The Messiah. Bernie is home with his books and his DVDs and his iPod.
Chrystal	What does it mean, Caleb?

Caleb	What does what mean?
Chrystal	To keep on dying, generation by generation.
Caleb	You mean to keep on living?
Chrystal	Living and dying.
Caleb	It passes the blood.
Chrystal	The blood is immortal?
Caleb	Yes.
Chrystal	Excuse me, but I don't think so.
Caleb	Our blood is us, our ancestors and our future.
Chrystal	No longer, Caleb. Do you know why? Too much carbon in the air.
Caleb	Not exactly.
Chrystal	They thought they could just suck it up, between the magma and the crust.
David	(What was that?)
Chrystal	Suck up the oil and burn it, cook the atmosphere. But the magma is boiling.
David	(I don't think he heard you.)
Chrystal	The magma is boiling, Caleb, meaning earthquake and volcano.
Caleb	Then what?
David	(Storm and flood. Hurricane and cyclone. Tsunami.)
Chrystal	That's right, David. Caleb, are you there? Well, the line is dead.
David	There's a dead zone there on his balcony.
Chrystal	Yes, you're right. I'll call him back later.

Bernie and Caleb

Bernie	The Hopi will go into underground caves, Dad.
Caleb	Is that where you're going?
Bernie	They have magical pictures of bison and antelope and little horses.
Caleb	Well, that won't save them.
Bernie	We are creatures which makes sunlight into intelligence.
Caleb	How do you know?
Bernie	We're like sensitive wires.
Caleb	Who told you this?
Bernie	Coyote. But when the oxygen is gone, they'll go down, down into the ground.
Caleb	The Hopi?
Bernie	They'll come up again with eyes the size of beachballs.
Caleb	You're out of your mind.
Bernie	No bodies hardly at all. And they'll eat the sulphur.
Caleb	Am I responsible for this atrocity?
Bernie	You and everybody else.
Caleb	God help us. You especially.
Bernie	Pray, Dad, or praise. Whatever that is. Praise and praise.
Caleb	I'll go to the Wall and bow.
Bernie	Too late. Go to a cave and hide your face. Put on a holy garment.
Caleb	You come with me.
Bernie	No.
Caleb	Where are you going?
Bernie	I'm going with Coyote to the Land of the Dead.
Caleb	Where is that? *(A pause)* Bernie!
Bernie	What?

Caleb	Where is that?
Bernie	I don't know. Brazil, maybe.
Caleb	Oh, for God's sake!
Bernie	It's for Earthmother, Daddy, for Earthmother.

Rosie and Caleb

Rosie	Rosie, your mother.
Caleb	Caleb.
Rosie	I know.
Caleb	Bernie's not in his room.
Rosie	Uh, oh.
Caleb	Who knows where he is or what he's doing.
Rosie	He's setting fires is what he's doing, the fucking arsonist.
Caleb	Who knows?
Rosie	Good God, they'll blame the Jews for everything.
Caleb	There'll be no everything.
Rosie	There'll be no Jews.
Caleb	There'll be no nobody.
Rosie	When the Jews are gone, what's left?
Caleb	The earth itself will die. It says so in the Talmud.
Rosie	Where in the Talmud?
Caleb	I forget now. It's carbon. When there's too much carbon you can't breathe.
Rosie	I see.
Caleb	So we'll say good-bye.
Rosie	Good-bye.
Caleb	Bye, Mom.
Rosie	Bye, bye, Baby.

Caleb   Bye.

Bernie

(Coyote looks at the audience. They resist the impulse
to applaud. What does this have to do with the fate of
the Jews, they wonder. The Jews are us, says Coyote,
calmly, we are all Arabs. Pause. Well, it's all right if you
don't think so. Me and my Hopi friends are not Arabs
and you are all shit and not too bright. How's that? No,
insults don't seem to work either. Anyway, I'm escorting
the Hopi to their special caverns set aside for them by
Earthmother. We'll clean things up eventually and we'll
start over. Meanwhile, we thought we'd take a few
righteous Jews with us to the center of the Earth. Those of
you who qualify, and want to come, follow me. Oh. The
gentleman over there asked how you qualify. Well, you
have to be an American, of course, and have harbored no
resentments for the last 90 seconds. Okay? Let's go.)

The End

The Inside Job

by Guy Zimmerman

An earlier version of The Inside Job *was produced by Padua Playwrights at 2100 Square Foot Theater, Los Angeles in November, 2003 under the direction of Guy Zimmerman, and with the following cast:*

Max *Barry Del Sherman*
Victoria *Jessica Margaret Dean*
Heidi *Holly Ramos*

Characters

Max—*40s, a disgraced corporate manager.*
Victoria—*40s, a socialite.*
Heidi—*20s, an espresso vendor.*
Claude—*20s, Heidi's brother, a former revolutionary.*

Setting

The bare, dark living room of a suburban condo. A bar is UPSTAGE. *Exits* STAGE LEFT *and* STAGE RIGHT. DOWNSTAGE *(imagined), a large picture window. A straight-backed chair, a single barstool, and a standing lamp are the only furnishings.*

Scene 1

Late afternoon. MAX in the doorway. HEIDI
downstage, inspecting the room. In shadow stage left,
seated in the straight-backed chair, is VICTORIA.
The lamp is off, so all we see are her legs and feet.
As he speaks, MAX moves to the bar and mixes
himself a Scotch on the rocks.

Max   I went to Rutgers in New Jersey
To me it was always just a dog shit school
Rutgers the whole city too
New Brunswick
Was just dog shit I grew up in the projects there
My mother was a lesbian
She came out when I was nine
Money is all I ever wanted more and more and more
My older brother and I set up a table
At the flea market we sold rocks
He had heart surgery when I was six
Big red scar like a zipper down his chest
I could always stop him dead
With one knuckle on that scar
I kept fighting fish
Siamese fighting fish were my passion
Beautiful gorgeous creatures majestic
With long colored gauze-like fins
They would tear each other to ribbons
The-fish-with-no-name was my all-time champ
He defeated dozens and consumed them

When he died I buried him in the hillside out back

Can I get you some red wine?

Heidi Can't stay long no

Max I remember you from the Church

You were always so alternative

With your little espresso cart

Heidi Sold that espresso cart

Max Aw

I liked the espresso cart

Heidi Like I told you in the car

Changed my line of work

Max What is it now

Your line of work?

Heidi Personal assistant

Wealthy man

Right now he needs a hideaway

To stash a certain what you might call mistress

That's why I agreed to get in your car

Come check out your condo

Max We used to joke about you in the men's room

To be honest

The men's room in the mega-Church

Terrible the things men say when women aren't around

That was my one good year yes

The year I met you was my one good year

I refer to it as my one good year

Because that's exactly what it was

Other years have been intermittently good

But that year was solid good

All year long Heidi the tumblers

Were just falling into place
Money my God I had money
And with that money came everything else
Doors everywhere opening wide
Money I love money the thought of money
Knowing I have it and am removed from want
I am not alone in this of course
All you need in this world is money
And if you don't have money that's it
Doesn't matter what else you have
The love of beautiful women, a lavish home
Look for them in your rearview mirror
Lose all your money like I did
It's a tightness in your chest
Not having money
And you will contemplate many things
Heidi
To relieve that pressure in your chest

Heidi   Hey, Max.

Max   Tell me
Go on
Don't be afraid

Heidi   Well I notice you don't have much
By way of furnishing

Max   No no furniture but for that chair
And the lamp
The rest I put outside
Sold my horse set my dog free
Drove up to Pismo set him free on the beach
I keep the bar well-stocked of course

A brief pause.

You may not like me much

You may not find me that interesting

But I am one of the guys

Heidi

One of the guys who make things how they are

In America

A pause. LIGHTS *shift.* MUSIC.

*

Scene 2

Moments later. MAX *at the bar, mixing another drink.*
HEIDI *across from him.*

Max   Let me tell you something, Heidi

You haven't lived until you've lost billions

Of other people's money

Widows out on the street, etc.

Pensioners

No no, don't say a thing

I don't want to be absolved

I don't want to explain anything away

How can I put this

I see that I am not clear

That the world is somehow much different

It makes me feel a little sick inside

I don't want to die an idiot
Do you see?
With my head in a sack
I was once a man of means
Do you know what I used to do?
I'd stay up late-late-late eating ice cream from the carton
I'd watch sports on the mini-TV
In the little breakfast nook of my immaculate mansion
Just like a regular Joe I'd watch the little TV
In the tiny nook eating ice cream right out of the carton
As if there weren't beneath my feet a cellar
Containing rack after rack of priceless wine

Heidi   Max?

Max   Yeah?

Heidi   Why did you bring me here?

Max   Oh

MAX crosses and turns on the lamp beside the chair, revealing VICTORIA, staring forward, impassive, wearing a dressing gown.

Max   To meet my wife

MUSIC. LIGHTS shift.

*

Scene 3

MAX beside VICTORIA. HEIDI at the front window looking back at VICTORIA, who sits motionless, as before.

Max
The beautiful Victoria
She's taken a vow of silence
At least that's what I think it is
A vow of silence
And I hate silence this guy up the hill Renner
Is having a party tonight
An important party given by Renner
We weren't invited but I want to go anyway
I want to crash Renner's party
And I want Vic on my arm
She's at her best in a social setting Victoria
As opposed to me
I've always been terrified of people
Why not admit it
But tonight is important
The one who attends this party will be saved
The others will be hung
I do not want to be hung
She must break her silence
I've explained this to her ad nauseum
When faced with the choice I would rather hang than
be hung
She must speak she must be charming
She must enter on my arm with her head held high
She's upset who wouldn't be

Our long slide the company falling apart
My name on all the front pages
Coupled with words like "fraud" and "criminal
investigation"
I'm not one of those patrician types, okay
I did not attend Princeton or Yale
Everything I've pulled off in this life...
Well I was more ruthless
And I will not take the fall
Not alone at least
Yes I testified
Testified before the subcommittee
Why not
And our neighbors evicted and disowned us
Up there in the exclusive Oaks
That thought just came to me
We've been evicted from the Oaks
Two months now of total silence from Victoria
Sex we still have sex believe it or not it's pretty good
She mentioned you, Victoria did
With her last words she said "Heidi"
"After Church I went to see Heidi" she said
And that was it not another word
So I guess where she knows you from is the Church
"I went to see Heidi" she says
Sure I've been going down there every week
Waiting in the pews St. Luke's
Asking the congregants about you
Those still willing to speak to me
They wonder why you don't come around anymore

They say you had a gift

They say you could see things others can't see

That you had the gift of healing

HEIDI turns away. MAX moves in behind her.

Heidi	I just sold coffee in the parking lot
Max	They say you'd stand outside
	Preach your own special gospel
Heidi	Coffee and rolls before you pray
Max	When you were a girl you were a congregant yourself
	They say
	Your mother father the whole family
	You were one of those Mega-Church families
	I've read about
	Your whole lives revolving around the ministry of Christ
	Some crap like that
	They say you used to sing in the choir
Heidi	My voice went bad
Max	They say you've been to the other side
	Something happened to you
	To your family too
	In Guatemala
	Where you went on some Church tour that turned sour
	I hate Church tours the very thought of Church tours
	Where you were do-gooders
	Do-gooders full of good-doing zeal
	Helping the poor is what they say
	And something terrible happened
	You witnessed unspeakable acts

	And almost died
Heidi	Yes, I actually died
	They brought my brother to the morgue
	I felt his tears on my face
Max	And that woke you up, huh
	How great is that
	Your brother's tears on your face
Heidi	Later he died too I was told
Max	The tears the tears the tears
Heidi	I talk out loud to him sometimes
	To my missing brother
	Just say whatever comes into my head
	It has a certain rhythm people associate
	With prophetic speech
	So they think what I say will come true
	And try to make sense of what I say
	He disappeared from the beach
	In Guatemala my brother
	The day I got shot in the head
	A group of men dragging him away
	Toward a pickup truck
Max	That's what they do to trouble makers in Guatemala
	Guatemala Latin America in general
	That used to be my market sector
	Poor poor poor beautiful churches
	Colorful, primitive marketplaces
	And everywhere packs of hungry children
	Young boys dirt poor
	Just so poor it's unbelievable
	How anyone could have so little?

A pair of shoes and that's all you have
Do you know what I used to do?
I'd hold up a five-dollar bill
Hold it high in the air
In the dirt of the gutter I'd have them battle it out
To see who was the strongest, the most vicious
And when the winner took the five bucks from my hand
I'd have him arrested for theft
Ha! Was that me?
Yes apparently that was me
Death Christ what was that like?
On second thought I don't want to know
It'll freak me right out
Why is it I can't shut up around you?
Is it because you're really almost no one
I mean in the eyes of society no one
A negative person almost
And you suck the words right out of me
Is that why I go on and on
This rush of words
And no way to stop
Is it possible to talk oneself to death?
I could spool myself right out on the floor
In a heap of words
What happens if I hold my breath?

*MAX holds his breath. HEIDI approaches VICTORIA,
tentative.*

Heidi   I'll tell you one thing about your wife

	She's a beautiful organist
Max	*(Exhaling)* Makes her feel lighthearted church music
Heidi	Long after I sold my cart
	I'd still go to that Church
	I just liked to hear her play
Max	She goes there
	Plays a little organ

HEIDI leans in close, examining VICTORIA'S face.

Heidi	You know Max
	Last time I was there
	They weren't very nice to her
Max	Those Church-goers
	They're pissed off at me
	They punish poor Vic
Heidi	They made fun of her hat
Max	The one with the feather?
Heidi	And the shriveled berries
Max	I gave her that hat
Heidi	A child spat
	They all looked away
Max	I gave her that hat on our anniversary
	The sales girl said it was jaunty
Heidi	I found her hiding in the balcony
	Tears rolled down her cheeks and splashed
	On the organ pipes
	I took her to my place for a cup of mint tea
Max	I see
	To your house

Heidi	My apartment, my flat, my room
	Not far from the Church
Max	You live near the Church, right
Heidi	Spring Street right nearby
Max	That's a truly scummy neighborhood
	Congratulations

HEIDI turns to look at MAX. He looks away. MUSIC. LIGHTS shift.

*

Scene 4

HEIDI at the front window, looking out. MAX beside VICTORIA.

Heidi	Yesterday in my scummy little flat I changed the curtains
	They used to be orange
	I changed them all to green
	Against the wall are my shoe boxes, four of them
	There's a sink by the window
	And a towel
	A little alcove where I hang my dresses
	The street is two stories down
	I hear men talking different languages
	Spanish a lot and the kind of English black men speak
	Their voices mixing with the traffic
	It's as if I'm waiting for something...

Max	We had tea your wife and we talked
	She tried on my brother's bracelet
	(Indicating Victoria's left arm)
	This bracelet right here?
	When was that around eighteen months back?
	Eighteen months ago is when she clammed up
	Is that when that was?
	See, my instincts about you were right on target
	Back when I'd see you pushing your little cart through
	the parking lot
	Peddling cups of café au lait
	You were radioactive with a single message: trouble

Max moves up behind Heidi. A sexual vibe.

Heidi	Is that why you fondled my ass
	At the Christmas pageant?
Max	No
	I don't recall ass-fondling
	At that Christmas pageant no no
	Ass fondling
	Was not a part of my modus operandi
	During my one good year I was very clear
	About the dangers of ass-fondling at all times

Max moves his hand along Heidi's hip.

Heidi	You said you adored me and no one could know
	The reason I remember it so well
	Is because back then

I had never been adored

HEIDI leans her head back into MAX's chest.

Max How about now?
Anyone adore you right now?
Heidi I met someone yes
An older gent he's got a black black heart

MAX moves away.

But he can really see me you know
I'm the type of person I like to disappear
He's very different than you
Never speaks not a word
And yet everyone's running around taking care of
his needs
And he's so filthy rich I break out in hives
Drove me crazy couldn't live with it
Can't be that kind of woman
Revolves around a man I mean
Look at me here I am
Up for an adventure
Max Tell me what you did to my wife
Heidi
And no bullshit either
It's time for plan B but there is no plan B
My wife has stopped talking
And there's an important party
A party given by Renner

What did you say to stop her from speaking
Or did you poison her with bad thoughts
Fill her head with some counter-cultural crap
Speak to her now so I know
What you said to cause this

Heidi   We talked about people
I don't know
How they are
Life
I'm sorry things aren't working out for you
I met your wife I felt bad for her
This is a little bit frightening to be brought here
To be honest when you're so upset

Max   Sure, you're buying your tortilla chips

Heidi   Minding my own business at the 7-Eleven

Max   I had the feeling you came looking for me
It's the way you smiled when you saw me walk in
And now look at you
I don't deserve this, you say to yourself
To be harangued by this jabbering ape
No I deserve to be engaged in a lighthearted manner
I deserve to be entertained and
Listen to me
I presided over one of the greatest financial debacles
In world history!

Pause.

Heidi   I think I better go

Max   *(Crossing to the bar)*

498

Go there's the door
Go

Pause.

Heidi   At the Church
What they'd say
If you want to change your life
More... inner openness
You should you know
Pray

Max   I'm no Christian
Lady

Heidi   Well, you're nothing else either

Max   Listen
I was once a member of the Dozen
That's what we called ourselves, the Dozen
The fraternity at Rutgers we really
Had the world by the short hairs and we
Well, things could get out of hand
How they do
At those parties
(Crossing to the window)
Did I explain about the guy up the hill?
Renner he's having the party tonight
Oh sure he went to Rutgers
We go way back Renner and me
We hated him all of us hated Renner
At breakfast one day we made him swallow a cue ball
Rancid worried soup of a man

They had to operate
Eventually he was so traumatized he left the country
Actually we sent him away
Stuffed him full of cash, put him on a plane to Columbia
He never came back
We sent him down there to purchase cocaine
Hard to believe
Those were wild times
In the business schools of America
Renner never returned he got arrested
And then last year I find him down there
On one of my forays south
As called for by my Latin American strategy
My famous Latin American strategy
Which was designed to salvage the company
But which in point of fact scuttled the company
You can't partner with those people Heidi
Killers all of them killers
And worse than killers, embezzlers
I'm strolling across the Zócalo here comes Renner
Looking tanned and healthy big smile
I thought it was a coincidence
It was no coincidence
Here he comes across the Zócalo
He doesn't even talk like himself

Heidi   Maybe it's that cue ball

Max   Ha funny
He's been living down there
He's made a career
Out of who knows what death squads

I brought him north on the company jet

He was on the run from something evil

Let him stay in the house no questions asked

A strange paralysis takes hold of me

In the presence of Renner

And then I sold it to him my own house

Drug money I have no doubt is what he paid me

I needed cash what the hell to pay my legal bills

All this accounting shit came down they froze my assets

Now he's throwing parties in my house

He doesn't even talk like himself

He sounds like a Texan

Yonder he says over yonder

Cue ball like this you could see it go down

He was a complete loser when I met him

Renner

On financial aid a slacker oh he was ambitious

I've been to the house he grew up in

He needed a ride back to Rutgers

I figured I'd drop him off a couple blocks from campus

So no one would notice my kindness to Renner

Which would at once be construed as a fatal weakness

They lived in the pine barrens

Didn't even have wallpaper

I drove up to this shack this outhouse

Met his mother his sister terrible washed out gray

My heart went out to the guy

Very briefly

Their fridge wasn't even working

This smell of stale cheese

Something ratlike about that house
Now he talks like a regular ranchero
How is it done?
How does one pray?

Heidi   You want to know how to pray?

Max   There are gates in America now
Heidi there are gates
And we are outside of the gates
Victoria and I
We are literally outside the gates
Yes, I want to pray
The technicalities
Right here right now

Heidi   From what I recall
You get down on your knees

Max   Demonstrate
Go on
Show me

HEIDI ponders for a moment. Choosing a spot on the floor, she kneels. MAX remains standing.

Heidi   I guess you hold your hands like this

HEIDI folds her hands. MAX watches, standing over her.

Max   Then what?

Heidi   Well I dunno
I guess you say what you want

	Ask for guidance
Max	*(Gesturing out)*
	But there's no one there
	No one and nothing
Heidi	This is your belief?
Max	It's not a belief, okay
	It's a scientific
	Observation
Heidi	Then pray to that nothing

(HEIDI closes her eyes, in prayer. MAX turns away in disgust. LIGHTS shift.)

*

Scene 5

MAX stands beside HEIDI, hands folded now in prayer. After a beat he opens his eyes and lowers his hands. He looks down at HEIDI.

Max	I don't feel any better, okay?
	When you pray to nothing what can you expect
	I guess is your point
	And this qualifies I suppose as a spiritual lesson
	This is what I hate about religion
	You suddenly find it impossible to think straight
	Okay fine I'll play along you want to fantasize
	Fine we'll pretend someone's there

Come on you can help
We'll pretend I have invoked the forces
That determine how things are
We'll make believe
I have won them over
With a display of humility et cetera
And of modesty and moral righteousness
And let's pretend they have sent an emissary
An angel and that angel is you
Heidi the angel

HEIDI jumps to her feet.

Heidi	Don't do that
Max	Why not?
Heidi	It's dangerous
	To turn someone into an angel
Max	Too late it's done
	For the duration of the evening
	You will be divinely in sync with the forces
	Blah blah blah

Pause.

Heidi	*(Smiling)* Always wanted to be an angel
	All that clarity
Max	You have it now
	Speak
	Trust yourself
	Offer guidance

Make it up as you go along
Like a jazz improv demonstrate
Say anything or I will die on the spot
My life will whither before your eyes
Save me
Save my life
Tell me what I need to know

Pause.

Heidi   Well for starters
I could tell you what I said to your wife
As I put the bracelet on her wrist
See I remembered you from the Christmas pageant
When you fondled my ass

Max   You were awful to me at that Christmas pageant

Heidi   I knew you had a wife and there she was
Crying all over the organ pipes
She came over for mint tea
We were talking about Guatemala
They have no laws down there
I said
As I pulled her hand through the silver hoop
No mechanism
By which to adjudicate disputes
Save violence I explained
No laws so that
The inevitable conflicts of the workaday world
Even minor disagreements
Lead directly to murder I said

Even the wrong kind of glance
The wrong sheen in the eye
A smirk I told your wife
Lead directly to murder
And before long the most violent
Rise I said
And are worshipped adored
And it's hell to live in that sort of world
Where you can be murdered at any moment
And those you love can in an instant be murdered
I said
As I pulled her hand through the silver hoop
And then I told her
"Victoria," I said
"There is someone I want you to meet"
I said as I let her arm drop
With my brother's bracelet now around it

Max Who?!
Who did you want my wife to meet?!

Smiling, HEIDI takes the bracelet off VICTORIA'S wrist.
Immediately, VICTORIA speaks.

Victoria Oh, leave her alone, Max
She's tired and hungry
Let's find out what she wants before we torment her
Come in
Make yourself comfortable
Normally I would offer you wine
An aperitif

I would hang your coat in the closet by the door
She could be anyone, Max
I've made up the bed in the back room
She'll stay the night she'll stay forever
But is that dangerous?
Perhaps she's a thief are you a thief?
What did you come here to steal?
We have nothing left look around you
A chair, a lamp, there is nothing here
We have some memories a few memories
Of a few blissful moments long gone now
You won't find any blissful moments hanging around
Go ahead look and those blissful moments
They cost us plenty didn't they Max?
Oh yes we paid in blood
We came down hard take what you want
Anything you can find
Leave nothing behind you when you go

She stands and crosses to the bar to stand beside MAX.

It's different for us see
Different to give up
Than to never have you start at the bottom
You've got nowhere to fall
Take you for example
This may sound harsh
But your father was what a gardener?
A seller of fruit? Mangoes? A seller of mangoes?
Saving his nickels so you can go to school

	Learn to habla Ingles?
Heidi	No
	I don't really speak Spanish too well
	Victoria
	You mistake me for somebody else

HEIDI sits in VICTORIA's chair.

Victoria	Oh no
	Of course I know who you are
	In the Zócalo on a Sunday in Tegucigalpa
	By the white fountain where the old men
	Set up their easels
	We used to go there in the mornings
	When the air was still cool
	And in your little baby's language you would tell me
	Your troubles and I realized one day
	I can help this girl give her food at least from my breasts
	Which all of a sudden overflowed with nourishing milk
	I could help you and that is exactly what I did
	I'd bring you home to our villa
	I'd wash your tiny arms your feet
	I'd bring you home
	Which was my first mistake
Heidi	No, I met you at St. Luke's

Pause.

| **Victoria** | You aren't the girl we adored so much in Tegucigalpa? |
| **Heidi** | I found you in the balcony of St. Luke's |

	Playing Handel
	You came to my place
	You told me a dream
Victoria	Oh yes I remember for years
	My sleep had been troubled by a dream
	A dream in which our lives were troubled
	Our children lost to us, forgotten
	Back then the two of us were filthy with time
	We had all the world in time on our hands
	This terrible dream in which I couldn't remember
	All I had lost
	With uncertainty everywhere
	He and I... our marriage... everything suddenly in doubt
	We had a family once
	Didn't we Max?
Max	We're in no position to afford a family
	Or even the memory of a family
	To have a family is to hand a dagger
	To your enemies
Victoria	I'll never abandon you again
	Heidi
	Not as long as I live
Max	Well, she said
	It's time for me to go and meet Heidi
	And those were the last words she spoke
	Until just now
Victoria	Yes for the past eighteen months I've been sitting here
	Paralyzed by my own exquisite beauty
	I'll tell you what happened
	Someone paid me a compliment is what happened

It was such a remarkable compliment
I fell into a trance
We've never been to Guatemala, no
But the sand by the water's edge was stained with our
child's blood
(Crossing to HEIDI)
Well
Can I get you some refresco?
Una jojoba?
Un jugo de naranja?

HEIDI stands and moves front.

Heidi Can't stay long no

Victoria Yes the bodies of our children lay bleeding on the sand
    And of course I can never forget it and at the same time
    I can never really remember it either
    Never look directly at it
    Or remember directly that girl we lost
    That little girl born to me
    I was so hurt so betrayed when she stole from us
    And I'm not sorry about what happened to her
    Not at all sorry
    I never think of it
    Can scarcely remember it
    That was before we knew
    How to tell light from dark

Gazing at HEIDI, VICTORIA falls quiet. MUSIC.
LIGHTS shift.

*

Scene 6

Moments later, MAX at the bar mixing a drink. Heidi across from him. VICTORIA seated again, silent.

Max

We Americans, I'll tell you something
We don't understand other people
The citizens of other countries
Might as well be from Mars
We don't understand other people
And our second problem is
We don't understand ourselves
This guy Renner for example
I'll tell you what he wants
He wants me homeless
That's what he's after
I know how his mind works
He won't leave until he sees me face first on the ground
He wants me homeless and despised
He wants me naked in the ditch
Howling as the rain comes down
He lives for the thought of me
Crawling through mud look at me
Look at my back look at it bending
This is what his hatred has done
The weight of his anger his rage
And why? Why is he angry?

He's angry because he has wronged me
Human psychology—ha!
Once he took one thing, he had to take everything
He was destitute, on the run
It's not as if I took advantage
Of his helpless condition
No I was generous
And this is what I must be punished for!
I'm in trouble he told me
I need to leave Guatemala he said
Straight off he said in his Texan accent
For one moment in my life
I gave in to a generous impulse
I smuggled him out via company jet
And for this I must pay
With my life I must pay for my one
Generous impulse
He wants me naked howling at the moon
Homeless homeless homeless
Hey Vic, I just had a terrific thought
We'll bring this girl to the party Heidi
We'll say she's our daughter home from college
It'll placate him completely
Renner
He'll think we're offering her up
Home for the summer from Smith College
Some crap like that what do you think?

Victoria   Our daughter?
No no that's impossible
I would find that traumatic

Max But

It's an important party given by Renner

Important to my future

A fund-raiser for his pet candidate what's-his-name

Soft money

The vice president himself will be in attendance

So I'm told

And I want to meet the vice president

I know some things

I have certain documents tucked away

Never mind about that

And all they need do is quickly *unfreeze* my assets

I ask for nothing but what is already mine

I've explained all this to Victoria ad nauseum

I know certain facts about certain policies

At home and abroad the tentacles

Of what I know spread wide

The vice president will be there

Victoria is on a first-name basis with his wife

They read bad novels together and talk about tax relief

By the shrimp cocktail

I'll zip up I'll say a word

Into the vice president's ear a single word

Heidi You know what he told me once?

Intelligence in foreign affairs is not the sign

Of a great power, he told me

MAX turns, stares at HEIDI.

Max Intelligence not the sign of a great power...?

Heidi	*Stupidity* in foreign affairs
	Is the sign of a great power
	He said

Pause.

Max	I certainly hope and pray
	You aren't
	By any means talking about
	Renner
Heidi	Only the truly powerful can afford to be stupid
	He said
Max	This is Renner talking
	I know the sound his mind makes
	When it works
Heidi	He's so smart
	I never met anyone smart like that
Max	All this time you've known Renner
Heidi	When you're smart like him
	You don't have to say stuff all the time
	You just sit perfectly still
	Your face in shadow
Max	After the fact of course it seems obvious
Heidi	I think his head is made of gold
	He sent me down to the 7-Eleven
	To give you this

HEIDI hands MAX an envelope.

Max	I'm not taking anything from you

MAX takes the envelope, rips it open.

	What is it?
Heidi	An invitation
	An invitation to his party
Max	Go now out leave

HEIDI stares at MAX. MUSIC. LIGHTS shift.

*

Scene 7

Moments later. HEIDI sitting on VICTORIA's lap. MAX as before, staring at the invite.

Max I mean
Can you imagine?
Being invited to a party at your own house?
How would that make you feel?
I mean, just picture yourself hearing about it
The rage
And imagine if you actually went
If you got the invitation and you said okay
Okay I'll go
Maybe you're so filled with longing
To look out across your old patio
To walk through those rooms
Or maybe you're just curious

And you decide to go

So then you find yourself up in your old house

You're just ruined by what they've done

The hideous alterations

The crimes of bad taste

How did he tell you?

Was he smirking to himself?

When he instructed you to bring the invitation was
he laughing?

Ha ha ha let's laugh at Max at this very moment
Heidi

I am being turned inside out by anguish and by rage

To look out across that view

And be just another invited guest

Sucking down the canapés the drinks

Handing my keys to the valet at the gate

Walking the halls—ooh look at the bedrooms

Oh the fluffy comforters very nice

HEIDI crosses to the doorway and checks the hallway.

Heidi	I asked him once if he was a murderer
	No he said no I may be a killer
	But I am no murderer you see
	He drew that distinction
Max	Is that a threat?
	Are you now threatening me?
Heidi	He told me he made it a policy
	To kill only those already condemned
Max	Were you sent here to threaten and intimidate me?

Because of what I know which could be so damaging?
Should I be looking over my shoulder
Let me tell you
So you will know and so
Everyone else will know
There is an affidavit Heidi
On file with certain parties
And this affidavit will be unleashed should Max meet
An untimely end unleashed
Unsealed for all to see
Oh I know how they work these people
I will not die an idiot with my head in a sack
And I think you should forewarn them
I think Renner in particular should be forewarned
About the affidavit
Before he sends any more of his hot ass little coozes
down here
In pajamas to issue vague threats and innuendo
Tell me something Heidi
What is it they're so concerned about
That they would stoop to intimidation
When hey they could simply buy me off
It would be simple enough I can be bought
Are you armed?
I should have frisked you
At the door

Behind the bar, HEIDI is polishing a glass.

Heidi   I'm not armed

	But there are many ways to kill a man
	When you're an angel
Max	What is it you want?
	I'm not talking about Renner
	I'm talking about you
Heidi	I only want what's mine already
Max	The bracelet
	Is that what you want
	Your brother's bracelet?
	I mean that's what you said
	Your precious brother
	As if we had anything to do with any of that
Heidi	They told me he had died
	My brother and until tonight I always half-believed them
	I don't know why you complain
	About this condo
	It's not so bad here
Max	Not so bad it's a hovel
	Look at the construction
	(Stamps foot)
	The walls shake look at that
	Somebody spent five minutes thinking about that wall
	Before it went up
	Five minutes tops and there it sits
	That *has* to mean something
	How could that flimsy wall *not* mean something
	About the *value* of the people who live here
	How could it *not* mean that our lives
	Are cheap and worthless?
	How it could mean *anything* other than that

Is a mystery to me
And this lamp
The entire social structure rests on this odious lamp
Meaning what it means—Victoria and I
We now live
Entirely
Disposable
Lives

Heidi   Oh I don't know
I think it might be just what Renner has in mind
This tacky pad
He needs a place nearby
The foot of the hill
Can't get much closer than that
He could roll out of bed
Roll right down the hill to his favorite mistress

Max   This note of bitterness
You no doubt speak of yourself
The mistress in question is no doubt Heidi
Former espresso girl
These condos let me clue you
There's quite a waiting list and you're very lucky
To have a friend on the inside by which I mean me
I'll even put in a call to my pals
In the management office I'll sing your praises
You'll get a choice unit
With a view of the summit
You and Renner can communicate via Morse code

Heidi   Oh, I already know the unit I'd need

Max   *(Beat)* Oh of course

	This unit?
	This unit here which I currently inhabit
	Along with my beautiful wife
	Not a chance I'm very sorry
	This unit is not on the market for sale or rent
	I mean think about it
	I've already given Renner my mansion
	Now he wants my *condo*
	Never
	And furthermore
	We've talked it over telepathically
	So I speak for Victoria when I tell you
	We do not care to attend this evening's soiree
Heidi	Of course I'd need more furnishing
	A comfortable couch at least
	I mean you can't have a mistress
	If you don't have a couch
Max	Very sorry
	We decline and rip up the invitation

MAX rips up the invitation and moves to the window.

Heidi	Oh, but everyone will be there
	And they all want to see you
	They all miss you and want news of you
	They're tired of getting their news of you secondhand
	They want to hear it directly from your lips
	(She crosses and slowly picks up the torn bits of paper)
	And see for themselves and hear your voice
	And there'll be wine and delectables

And everyone has gotten so damn rich
Everyone we know is just rotten with money
With power and influence
We'll have a good cry about it back by the pool
You and me
Back in the grotto you and me will have a good cry
I'll be taking all sorts of drugs I'll be armed
A dangerous combination I'll be armed to the teeth
There'll be music and dancing
A big band imported straight from the 1930s
Will serenade us into the silver light of morning
We'll grab coffee together
Just the two of us, coffee and rolls
We'll read the Sunday paper together
Laugh and sing our time together
Will live on in the annals I feel sure
I feel certain I just know

Max   What's it like?
Your thing with Renner I mean
You're what they call a side dish
Heidi the side dish
Spring Street sure he must have liked that
Quick little trips down to Spring Street sure
For a little on the side with Heidi the espresso girl
But now he wants you closer
It's too far to drive all the way
Down to Spring street that's a bad sign
I'd be worried if I were you I bet
You think I'm about to ask you
All sorts of sexual details

But see Max would never do that
Find out too much about another man's sex life
You can fall under their sway
Is he romantic?
Does he have a soft romantic side?
Does he bend his face slowly toward you?
I bet he wanted you right from the get-go
I bet he took one look at you and longing entered
his heart
Yes yes a ribbon of longing
Extended all the way over the horizon of Mars
The instant he laid eyes on you Renner
What does he like what are his predilections?
Does he like the rough stuff?
Does he beg to be smacked around?

Heidi   If you really want to know you should
Ask Victoria

Max   *(Beat)* Ask Victoria what?

Heidi   Ask her what sort of lover he is
Your friend Renner

*MAX and HEIDI watch for a moment. Then MAX turns
to HEIDI.*

Max   Oh but
How in the world would Victoria
Know the first thing about Renner
And his predilections.

Heidi   He was there the day she came to visit

Max   Renner was there?

	The love nest on Spring?
Heidi	I put the bracelet on her arm
	I went out
	I went out for the rest of the day
Max	Am I to suppose yes well
	I can't think about this right now
	They're gonna cart me off to the hospital Heidi
	I can't afford to get carted off
	Right now
	To the hospital
	They'll find me crawling
	Down the 405
	On my knees down the hill on my knees
	Unable to stand
	Unable to speak the words
	Streaming out of me the blood
	Of words pumping out as I crawl
	From the gash in my heart
	The gash you just opened
	In my head
	I have let him take everything
	I can not allow him to annihilate me completely no
	Complete annihilation is where I draw the line
	Wait a minute

Victoria exits into the bedroom.

	Something terrible is about to happen
Heidi	Yes
Max	What is it?

| Heidi | Complete annihilation |
| Max | The end of me? |

HEIDI stands and moves close.

| Heidi | The end of you |

Pause.

| Max | Did I end? |
| Heidi | Yes |

Pause.

Max	I don't feel as though I ended
Heidi	People never know when they're over
	But they are
	I probably wouldn't even know
	Except you made me an angel and an angel
	Is always on the lookout
	For this kind of thing
Max	So
	What happens now?
	Now that I've ended
	What happens?
Heidi	You become a thing
Max	A thing?
	A piece of furniture?

VICTORIA enters. She's dressed now, in party attire.

Victoria   Do I look all right?

Exploring my closet I got lost

I came to the banks of a slowly moving—

It rose up out of the water a serpent

Around my leg I felt it—

Oh

Those spangled golden eyes

I will make of the world your pillow

It whispered

Look there's Max

I never rest anymore

Max do you rest?

The highway's so close here the trucks

You know, Max

I've been meaning to tell you

You are truly a delicious man

The way you sidle up on your hands and knees

And your analytical mind

I remain so happy to have married you

When we first met straight away

I detected this thing about Max

Which is that I couldn't ever think about Max

I would try to think about Max

I would just go straight to sleep

Or else I'd get real busy

And then a day or two later I would remember

Oh

I was going to try to think about Max

But I couldn't think about him so I married him straight

away

And he has ruled over me ever since

HEIDI crosses and sits in VICTORIA'S chair. MAX is behind the bar.

Heidi	He came down to Spring Street
	Renner
	He looked around at my room
Victoria	You don't belong here
Heidi	He told her
Victoria	No, I certainly don't
	I replied
Heidi	In this hovel he said
	You belong in a palace
Victoria	Yes, that's quite correct
	I said
Heidi	And I have one for you, he said
Victoria	A palace
	Come with me

VICTORIA crosses, unsteady. Pauses.

Heidi	But she didn't come
	Because you see back then
Victoria	She still loved you
Max	She loved me?
	Don't say that
	Don't say that now
Victoria	*(Looking up out the window)*
	Some compliments a man will pay you

	Take six hours or more and are quite painful
	To be honest
	Max?
	I'm going to leave you, Max
Max	Forever?
Victoria	For all time
	Yes
	I'm in danger
	I must leave here at once
	What city am I in?
	Dallas? Los Angeles? Denver?
Heidi	At night it's impossible to know
Victoria	We own homes in all areas
	Isn't that so Max?
Heidi	Yes but
	Once the world goes dark it's impossible
	To be certain
Victoria	Isn't that so, Max?
	Don't we own homes in all areas?
	What city are we in?
	Tomorrow I'm giving orders to the staff
	In large letters to spray paint
	Across the walls the name of each particular locale
	Max?
Max	Yes?
Victoria	Max
	I will only think about you once in a great while
	The way I think about that girl we lost
	In Tegucigalpa once in a great while she crosses my mind
	I felt so hurt so betrayed the way she

Ran up from the beach screaming to our veranda
And covered in blood the poor thing
As if we could help her
As if we would want to
And I'm not sorry about what happened to her
Not at all sorry
I never think of it
Can scarcely remember it...
What was I saying?

Heidi   You were discussing Guatemala

Victoria   Guatemala
That's right well of course
This was in the time before we were poor
And there were cushions to sit on
And fruit on the table books piled high
And candles and the streets outside grew quiet
At night and we would sit together
In our easy chairs
And review together the events of the day
And what we knew of history down through the ages
Eating fruit and sometimes nuts from bowls
Laid out on tables amid books
We would look into each other's faces
Our eyes were full of wonder scarcely any fear
And the night that pressed in against the windows
Was soft like velvet
The earth warm the oceans calm
Does your mouth get sore from talking?

Heidi   Is the first thing he said to me
Mine does he said and then

Victoria	Here's another question—all this remembering
	Is it not a form of slander?
Heidi	That's what he asked you
Victoria	And have we not been warned against slander?
Heidi	It's good you don't answer he said
Victoria	It shows you're alive
	It shows respect
	Self-respect

The SOUND *of* DISTANT EXPLOSIONS, OFF.

Hear that?

More EXPLOSIONS, OFF.

	The party has begun
Heidi	Now
	At any moment
	The door could fly open
	We could find ourselves confronting a fugitive
	From the party
	In vain they would beg for their lives
	Because the nights around here have turned hard as stone
	Since Renner arrived
Victoria	And the earth is stone
	And the oceans do not speak they are swollen
Heidi	With the corpses of his enemies
Victoria	I have lost all self-respect
Heidi	Renner has enough self-respect for hundreds like
	You and me

Victoria	Oh but when Renner comes over I could have bowls
	Bowls to present on the tables I could have fruit
	And today the trees in front were all down
	How did they get that way?
	All their roots were out
	So indecent still clutching rocks
	And clods of earth the rain was not normal rain
	It was hot it was steaming as it fell
	I knew I was not supposed to talk about it ever
	It gets so hard to keep track
	Of what cannot be said
	I'm afraid
Heidi	So am I
	But I'm not worried
	We'll need help that's all
Victoria	There is no help for us in the natural world
Heidi	Maude will help us
Victoria	Do I know Maude?
Heidi	Maude is my bitter, vengeful brother
	A slave-in-business to your husband
Victoria	I don't think I know Maude
Heidi	He's right here
	Standing right here
	He's been here the whole time, resembling a lamp

The LAMP raises up, taking human form. The lamp looks at HEIDI, blinking. This is CLAUDE, HEIDI'S brother. When he speaks, VICTORIA screams.

Claude	My name is not Maude

Maude is a woman's name
For lady's only
My name is Claude, a common name in France

CLAUDE takes a step.

This is me talking
I am talking
Me
I am breaking my silence
Which began so long ago
Drawing myself up
Pushing myself out
In the form of words spoken
Syllables released into air

Pause.

I don't remember why I said nothing for so long
I don't know why I was hiding
What I was waiting for
The right sign
The right conditions
I invested in silence
On the idea
It would bring me something but it brought me nothing
And I couldn't survive that disappointment
So I kept faith with it
It was like a marriage
A codependent relationship

With evasion and silence
I was driven to do this
By despair, but still it is what I chose to do
I did it I got in the habit of doing it
I rode the doing of it right up to the end
Oh yes now I remember
I was a reeeevooooluuuutionary
I understood
The cycles of history
The circuits of time
I was
In... can... descent...

Heidi   Claude?
Do you know who you're speaking to?

Claude   Who is this man?

CLAUDE towers over MAX.

Tell me how I came here

Max   You were a gift
You never complained we assumed you were satisfied

Claude   As I speak I realize that I
Have allowed myself to become a household appliance
Partly I have done this out of perverse willfulness
But partly too I have acted out of a sense of duty
I have felt, and I still feel
That it is my duty to cripple myself
Through hatred and anger and greed
Not to mention envy and pride
Through this act of crippling

I show solidarity with my fellow man
For all of us are the same
Yes, you too are creatures of malice and vice
You too shun the light and live in shadow
And all who know and love or hate you
Blunted instruments we are
Smashed up violins and crushed pianos
Melted ore no let me go on I just woke up I've been fortified
A child with wide-open eyes, eyes that reflect the sky
Eyes full of heaven—what do we say?
What do we—I forgot what I was saying
I dropped my own thread this is what happens
When you retreat into the vile habits
Of humanity

Victoria   He's so sad
I don't think I've ever seen someone
So sad

Claude   *(His speech gradually slowing)*
The longing... for usefulness... simplicity
What's sad...?
The love... of blankness...
The simple... giving
Of light...

CLAUDE returns to life as a lamp. A pause.

Heidi   Claude?
Claude speak to me
Claude you are free

I have given you freedom

Pause.

Max	Victoria?
Victoria	What is it?
Max	I'm gonna take your lamp now, Vic
	As a gift to Renner, he can have him rewired
	So he casts a whole different kind of light
	And you'll come to realize
	Crouching in your own shadows
	You'll realize what you once had
	We'll go now the lamp and me
	Just wait while I disassemble…

Jackknife in hand, MAX approaches CLAUDE and begins to tinker beneath his arm.

Claude	YAAAAAAAAAAHHHHHHH!!!!

CLAUDE runs out into the night. MAX runs after him. A pause. HEIDI crosses to the door. VICTORIA watches. LIGHTS shift.

*

Scene 8

Lights rise on Heidi and Victoria downstage, looking up at Renner's distant hill. Great arcs of electric light flash in the sky outside the windows.

Victoria	I wake up sometimes at night
	I think about Renner
	About my encounter with Renner
	It's like someone shocked me with a wire
Heidi	Do you know that at any moment
	Our lives are complete?
Victoria	What would he do if we went up there
	And just forced our way
	Through the door and said
	Get in the pool house
	Before we drown you and stay there
	Until you choke on your own spittle
	What would he say then?
Heidi	It's what his bodyguards would say
Victoria	I can be violent
	I have violence inside me I mean
	We all know how this goes
	We've all seen the films
	Where people must you know
	Combat evil
Heidi	Oh but
	This man knows many stories
	He makes me laugh
	When he talks about the time before the war

There's almost a music to his memories
I get down on my knees of my own accord
The bodyguards are laughing over by the little fridge
Their weapons lined up against the wall
And we could talk about it
Afterwards
Discuss who's cute this one guy Brian
Is cute
I think he's the cruelest one though
I saw one woman get just so ruined forever
Her arms all hanging loose like they do
It's so easy to hurt someone
I'm sure he raped her too Brian
I never want to get raped
I never want to get winched up in the air
By my arms either
They just cuff your hands behind your back
They have this winch
They winch you up into the air by a chain
Before long your arms give way
Bust right out of your sockets
I never want that to happen to me
I never do

Victoria moves front and stands beside Heidi.

Victoria   With both arms we give away
All hope of happiness
Heidi   Eventually we'll reach a point
Where we won't mind

	His little visits
Victoria	They will bring joy to our hearts
	Instead of fear
Heidi	When it rains
	We won't even notice the rain
Victoria	We'll invent our own words
	And promptly forget them
Heidi	They'll be words only used once
Victoria	They'll have been understood perfectly

Max enters, unsteady on his feet. A pause.

Max	Look I'm impatient with all this pointless chatter
	Let's do ourselves up and go enliven that party
	Oh yes
	I've changed my mind now I relent
	And accept the invitation
	Call her "mom"
Heidi	"Mom?"
Max	Ha ha "mom"
	He'll think we've got the goods on him
	He'll come unhinged the man lives in fear
	All those enemies domestically and abroad
	During his long career as a counter-insurgency specialist
Heidi	*(To Victoria, indicating lights out window)*
	Look at what Claude is doing mom
	Now that he's free and out in the world
	All the lights in the night sky
	It's just the beginning
Victoria	*(Turning to Heidi)* What did you call me?

Heidi	"Mom"
	I called you "mom"
Max	Come with me tonight, we'll make a start of it
	Definitely the thing to do
Victoria	It sounds so nice
	To hear someone call me that
	"Mom"
Max	You can probably tell from the drift of my comments
	That my opinion of Renner is in the process of shifting
	Frankly I'm beginning to admire the man
	I mean imagine getting caught up in that whole Texan accent thing
	You grow up in the pine barrens of Eastern New Jersey
	One day you hear yourself say
	Howdy ma'am you say
	Gosh you say Howdy
	Went out walked the property line you say
	You begin to speed walk around
	Speed walk around the back forty
	Find a canyon start clearing brush
	Yonder you say over yonder
	It starts slowly
	A few words at first
	Then gradually it spreads
	The disease of a Texan accent
	It takes you over entirely ha ha
	Get along you say get along little doggy
Heidi	Mom?
Victoria	Yes dear
Heidi	I love how you stroke my hair

Victoria	She's calling me mom
Max	That's great hey
	Come with me tonight we'll make a start of it
	Definitely the thing to do
	Go to him tell him how we feel
	How much his example has meant to us how we
	Would like to follow in those footsteps
	Let our pride be the first thing we offer up
	He'll appreciate it so much
	I know the psychology as if it were my own
	(Indicating HEIDI)
	How do you think she'd feel about handing out a few
	You know intimate favors?
Victoria	Oh Max that's terrible
	Awful
Max	Back in the pool house?
	Only a few of Renner's guests would ever go for that sort of thing
	Only a select few of his guests
	Are we terrible?
	Are we heartless?
	Why are we so heartless?

VICTORIA reaches out and strokes HEIDI's hair. LIGHTS flash in the sky outside the windows. A pause.

Okay then I'll just sit I won't
Say a thing
And when Renner comes over
I'll contribute we have a good rapport

Me and Renner
I'll stay out of the way you two
Can entertain him to your heart's content
I won't watch
I'll cover my eyes pay too much
Attention to another man's predilections
You fall under their sway

HEIDI vacates the chair for MAX. He staggers to the chair and sits.

Gimme that bracelet I think it fits
Give it here

MAX takes the bracelet from HEIDI and puts it on his arm and falls silent. The hilt of the jackknife sticks out of his chest. Music. LIGHTS shift.

*

Scene 9

MAX in the chair wearing the bracelet, the knife in his chest. VICTORIA at front, looking out, waiting. Heidi there too. MAX takes the bracelet off his arm and speaks.

Max When Renner comes over to see the two of you
On one of his visits
I'll know exactly what to say
There are people I'd say who
If they knew what we're planning
They would hate us
They must be destroyed before they realize
What we're planning
I'll say
There are people they hate us
I'll tell him
And they need to be destroyed
I'll helpfully point out
Because they hate us

MAX puts the bracelet back on. A pause.

Heidi Hey ma
Victoria Yes dear
Heidi I want you to know
I will stand by your side and I will look
The devil straight in his yellow eye

VICTORIA moves slowly left, looking out.

Victoria   We will look together, we will look
And we will know

MAX takes the bracelet off his arm and speaks.

Max   I never lived I'll tell him
I was never alive I'll say
What time is it?
I think I'll go find him right now

MAX reaches up and grabs the hilt of the jack knife. He pulls the knife out of his chest and holds it up. Expires. The two women look on. A pause.

Heidi   There will be no more sleep
Victoria   We'll sleep no more

HEIDI backs toward the stool at the bar.

Heidi   We'll discover in ourselves such capacities
Not shrinking from darkness we'll discover light
Victoria   We'll discover it was there all along

VICTORIA stops STAGE LEFT and looks out. HEIDI sits on the bar stool.

Heidi   Covered over it was there
And we knew it was there

Victoria	But fear
Heidi	*(Smiling)*
	We almost let it ruin us
	It was fear

All hold. LIGHTS flash in the sky outside the window...
and then all SLOWLY FADE.

The End

Spanish Angel

A play in two acts

by John Steppling

Characters

Delphy

Haggert

Ursula

Jensen

Setting

Paint shop, Arizona desert
Motel room, Juarez

Act One

Scene One

LIGHTS up slowly...

DELPHY sits DOWNSTAGE on three-legged stool... while UPSTAGE a man, HAGGERT, watches. It's unclear if he is actually listening.

Delphy   *(To audience)* I leaned forward... speaking slowly. *(Beats)* I've always been scared of children... I don't know how to talk to them... *(Pause)* But I wanted to fucking make clear that this little shit had to clean up the fucking broken glass.

DELPHY pauses... thinking...

I wanted to scare him. And he started to pick up the glass... this was from a broken milk container... Not like the paper cartons you have now... and he was barefoot too. He cut himself, on his hands and on his feet, too, I think.

Silence.

A man walked past. I knew this guy, I mean I knew who he was. He was Ukrainian or something. He didn't speak great English. He said to me, he said, "cure me." I said, what? "Cure me, you are like the doctor." I waited, you know, cause I didn't know what to say, what he meant. Finally he says "I know you can cure me." Of what, I ask. He shakes his head, laughing. He hurried off. *(Pause)* The boy stared at me and then he went on back picking up the glass again. *(Longer pause)* Crazy guy, wanted me to cure him. I don't know what he meant. I still don't know. He had seen the boy and his bleeding feet. He saw, and he said what he said, and then he just went away.

DELPHY *turns around to look at* HAGGERT.

Haggert   I'm listening.

Pause.

Delphy   You sure I was talking to you?

Haggert   Let me ask you something.

Delphy   Yeah...

Haggert   Did this boy's father come to see you? After you made his boy pick up broken glass.

Delphy   Yeah... next day he did. He was a pussy... he was more scared than the little boy. *(Pause)*

Haggert   The world is full of weaklings.

Delphy   I might have been talking to someone else. You don't think of that, do you?

Haggert   You know, I had promise at one time... my life had promise.

Delphy   Did it?

Haggert	I was a top amateur boxer. You know that, you saw me.
Delphy	Yeah.
Haggert	Then the motorcycle thing...

HAGGERT knocks his fist against his lower left leg... it's plastic...

Not a lot I could do with my early dreams... was there?

DELPHY shrugs. Pause.

Fucking motorcycles...

Delphy	Do you get up in the middle of the night? Sometimes... I mean, with... like, you can't sleep... you look at the clock and it's like 3:00 A.M. and you know you won't go back to sleep.

HAGGERT stares at him. Silence.

Haggert	The fucking damaged world keeps me awake every night.

Pause.

BLACKOUT.

*

Scene Two

LIGHTS up... same as before except HAGGERT has moved a little closer.

Delphy   What?

Silence.

You need money? What do you need?

Pause.

Haggert   I don't wake up... I just can't go to sleep. Many times... At night... I can't go to sleep... you know?

Pause.

I think about what I have read.

Delphy   You read a lot of shit. What you read.

Haggert   I think a lot. At night. When I can't sleep.

Delphy   About race wars? About the decline of white men?

Haggert   About my lost leg. I think about that.

Silence.

Delphy   You ever dream you still got your leg?

Haggert   I dream... every dream I've had for ten years... in every one I still have my leg. That's pathetic, don't you think?

Delphy   How much money you need? What's the least I gotta give you?

Long pause.

Here...

DELPHY *takes out his wallet... peels off a couple hundred dollar bills... offering them to* HAGGERT.

Haggert   How much money you carry around with you? *(Pause)*
Is that... what... a way to impress women? *(Pause)*
I need more than that.

Delphy   Alright...

Peels off a couple hundred more.

Haggert   I can't give this back for a long while.

Delphy   I never asked you to give it back.

Haggert   Does it work?

Delphy   What?

Haggert   With women, showing them a wallet full of hundred dollar bills.

Silence.

Slowly HAGGERT *puts the money in his pocket.*

I appreciate this. The money.

DELPHY nods. Silence.

You want to come to a meeting?

Delphy What kind of meeting?

Haggert Doesn't hurt to come listen to other ideas.

Pause.

We are all good Christians, you should remember that.

Pause.

You could learn something.

Pause.

Do you dream of your ex-wife?

Delphy Why would I do that?

Haggert Because she's dead, I don't know.

Delphy I don't think I dream about dead people so often.

Haggert Do you dream the world will end?

Delphy Is this what you talk about at those meetings?

Haggert Do you? Do you dream of the end of the world?

Delphy *(Pause)* No.

Silence.

LIGHTS out.

*

Scene Three

LIGHTS up slowly ...

A woman (URSULA) on the floor. She is cross-legged. She is maybe 35... maybe a bit more. She wears old overalls and a T-shirt.

DELPHY stands upstage.

Ursula I've a headache... from the painting.

Delphy Yeah, paint is toxic.

Ursula I should hire someone...

Pause.

Delphy You could.

Ursula Except I got no money. *(Beats)* I could hire some Mexican... some illegal... have him work for me for a few days.

Delphy You don't even have that much money.

Pause.

Ursula You don't like it when I say shit like that, do you? About hiring Mexicans and shit.

Delphy I think you listen to Haggert too much.

Ursula I just fuck Haggert... I don't really listen to him. *(Pause)* I'm just young and don't know any better.

Delphy You're not young.

Pause.

Ursula I grew up on a farm... dairy farm. *(Beats)* Milk farm. This is Norway... up north... west central Norway. A small farm, in an old community, a very old culture there.

Delphy Farms, huh.

Ursula It's a dark place a lot of the year. It's dark all the time in winter... You get about an hour or so of sun. In summer it's the opposite, but summers are short. *(Beats)* My father's farm... the farm house and the barn, were built in 1814. The barn scared me... and in that area... in those valleys, a lot of farms had closed down. People died or just gave up, I don't know.

Silence.

At three in the afternoon, it was pitch black... and I had to go help with the milking, and that took a couple hours. We had maybe twenty cows. And in the barn it was even darker... and it had that strong farm smell... And the cows, our cows anyway, were mean... they kicked at you all the time. My father scared me, too. *(Long pause)* The other farms, the ones that had closed, they were close by... fifteen-minutes walk. And I would sneak over there sometimes, and go inside these old barns. They were dark, and they felt of the death of the farm, the loss of life, of living animals. Of work. *(Beats)* These were places built in the eighteen hundreds, and they were mostly all painted red. A very particular red, and it was named after where I came from... but anyway,

I started to feel that in those old empty barns, in those shadows, there was something, and maybe it was just an echo of my self... not a sound... a sort of spiritual echo. Maybe it was something that had nothing to do with me at all.

Pause.

Are you going to laugh at me?

Delphy   Why would I laugh at you?

Long pause.

Ursula   But the dark wouldn't let up... that's how I felt... as a girl... it was always there it seemed. And inside these old houses and barns, because I went into the houses too, the old abandoned ones, and in there, inside were sometimes furniture, still, and kitchen things. *(Beats)* People worked hard. My father worked hard. They tended, the men, to die young. *(Beats)* The Benedictine monks, they say that to labor is to pray. But I don't know, honestly. My father was a praying motherfucker if it's true. He died at 51. He was worn out... and he didn't give a shit anyway by that point. My brother was gone, and he knew I was going. I couldn't imagine living in the shadows of those barns... in the place of abandonment, and night. And then there was the cold. I don't know how far we were, not so far, from the Arctic circle. People further up got strange. They were too isolated. Fishing villages full of suspicious people, with pinched faces, and few words. But then my father never said much either. He loved his dog... but I doubt he loved my mother, and I'm sure he didn't much love his children. *(Pause)* We are in the dream, all of us, right now... but in those places where things are worn down, and cold and damp, and where the sun never reaches... In those places the real world exists. Among the animals, the animals that have been beaten into submission, and work, too. They work too... and man bred them to be stupid. Docile and fat and stupid. And I got creeped out when I would look in their eyes. And I didn't look if I could help it, because when I did I felt they were asking me something. I don't know what it was, but I knew I didn't have an answer. *(Pause)* But somehow, those were the conditions that allowed something to happen... a part of the mask to fall away.

Pause.

I felt that in those barns... in the forgotten ones, that I was able to see something that usually you don't or can't see... and even if it was only my own reflection, the sense of the inside of my own head, it didn't really matter. It was still something you couldn't find anywhere else. Maybe, I don't know, in caves in Nepal or some shit, I don't know... but in this old world of crippling physical work and of darkness, you could see the face... like the face of an angel... hiding in the darkest part of the barn... maybe in the loft area where they used to put hay... and you didn't really see it... not in the way I can see you

	right now... but you knew, you could see part of it, some

right now... but you knew, you could see part of it, some
kind of outline.

Delphy   Why do you think it was an angel?

Ursula   A fallen angel, maybe. A lost angel. Sent down to dwell
in dark worlds of toil. *(Beats)* Those barns were places of
deep mystery. Not secrets, see... because secrets are just
the perversion of mysteries.

Delphy   Maybe it was an evil thing... like Satan.

Ursula   *(Pause)* A lot of children in that area were born retarded.
Nobody knows why. But a lot were. Way too many.

Delphy   Environmental pollution.

Ursula   You don't believe that. I know you don't.

She laughs.

LIGHTS *fade out.*

*

Scene Four

LIGHTS *up...*

URSULA *lying on the floor.*

DELPHY *watching her.*

Silence.

558

| Ursula | You have too many secrets—you're too secretive. You scare me... that part of you. |

Silence.

If you had come to me first, before Haggert, I'd have slept with you.

Pause.

	Sex is too secretive. It's all part of this thing, this project... the human school of "not seeing."
Delphy	Maybe I didn't want to sleep with you.
Ursula	But you do now, don't you?

Pause.

Lights out.

*

Scene Five

Lights up...

Delphy by himself on stage... in dim spot. His head is down... as if asleep... and then suddenly he jerks awake... eyes wide open...

Delphy   I was watching a man being beaten. I was outside... and I was looking inside... into a warehouse maybe... and somehow I knew this man, the one whose head I could hear hitting the floor... a tile floor maybe, I don't know. *(Long pause)*

He is a bit calmer.

There was suicide in my family. I don't ever talk about it. There was violence. I don't ever talk about it. There was sexual oppression, sexual extortion... and I don't talk about it. *(Pause)*
There was an endless failure to everything. *(Pause)* The failures I talk about. This man I watched being beaten... I don't know for what reason he was being beaten... what he had done... if he had done anything. I called out for them to stop... it seemed I knew who was administering the beating... how they put it sometimes... but I'm not sure... it was all very familiar.

LIGHTS fade out.

*

Scene Six

HAGGERT and DELPHY. Both are more or less as before...

Haggert	I don't know what she is thinking. *(Long pause. He starts to sing… a heavy metal song… stops after half a verse)*

Silence.

Black Crows… I don't know. Someone like that. I think the world might be the way she says it is. We are all in someone else's dream—and that's all it is. And it's all just endless, too. I don't think you really die… you just go somewhere else to play a different game.

Silence.

You think I've been treated unfairly?

Delphy	By whom?
Haggert	No, I just mean in life. In general.

DELPHY pauses…

Delphy	I think you have, I know you have. I've known you a long while, Haggert. Jerry. So, yeah, I think you've had a lot of tough luck.
Haggert	You think I make my own bad luck?
Delphy	I don't know.
Haggert	You're not overly successful, either, you know.
Delphy	Not by anyone's standards, no.
Haggert	*(Pause)* I want you to do something for me… with me, even. *(Beats)* You want me to tell you now? Tell you what I want?

Silence. Delphy *nods.*

I want you to help me and Ursula.

Delphy Help you how?

Haggert There are people I owe money to. And there are other
people, official people... not exactly cops, but... well, and
they want me too, and if they find me they're gonna hold
me, and then I'm gonna catch a shiv in the shower room.
The people who want me, they got a lot of friends up
in that state prison.

Delphy I don't have enough money to keep giving it to you.

Haggert Did I ask you for money?

Delphy Yeah, just yesterday.

Haggert Well, I don't want any money today. That's so like you,
just assuming you know something. No, I don't want any
money from you.

Pause.

I want you to take us down to Mexico.

Delphy The fuck can't you just drive yourself down to Mexico?

Haggert First, we got no car. Not one that would make it. Second,
I know I'm gonna get stopped, so I want to ride in the
trunk... in back, or someplace...

Delphy Right.

Pause.

Haggert Do it for Ursula... if you can't for me do it for her.

Delphy	She isn't the one needing to get out of here—you are. Anyway you slice this, it's all what you need... really.
Haggert	She needs some breaks. I didn't get any breaks... but maybe that's my fault... I can see how it might be. *(Pause)*
Delphy	OK...

DELPHY starts pacing... helping himself think.

	What is my motive for helping you?
Haggert	For helping "us."
Delphy	I have no family, few friends. I live alone... I do what work I can... and run this little paint shop. Sell little things... cans of paint, brushes, and little hardware items. I'm the only guy around here who does that, so I do alright.

Pause.

	You know about this thing with the little boy. I told you about that. I didn't exactly do anything wrong. I didn't hurt the kid... but I scared him. *(Beats)* And so I'm a lot less popular around here now. And I'm going to be fifty-seven soon... and I feel even older.
Haggert	Yeah, you don't look that old at all, you know?!
Delphy	I don't expect any new women in my life. Not at this point—and that makes me feel... I don't know.
Haggert	Ursula thinks you're attractive, she even told me she did.
Delphy	Ursula is your woman... and that's not what this is about... about my loneliness.

Haggert	Look, for me... listen to me, Delphy, this is sort of life and death stuff... or life and ass-kicking stuff. But serious ass-kicking, serious put-in-ICU stuff.
Delphy	I don't want to take on your problems, Haggert.
Haggert	I just want you to drive us. I don't want anything else.
Delphy	Mexico.
Haggert	Yeah. Maybe cross over at Juarez. I don't know.
Delphy	You ever been to Mexico? You know anyone there?
Haggert	I'm fine with Mexico... with being in Mexico. And Ursula can speak a little Spanish.
Delphy	And Norwegian, which will help.
Haggert	What?
Delphy	What do you do when I leave you there, on the streets of Juarez?

Pause.

Haggert   I will find us the right street. The one right street for us to be on.

Silence.

There will be mariachi music, and there will be fat Indian women cooking, and there will be a fiesta.

Pause.

Ursula can sense things. She will know where we are.

Delphy   I leave you in Juarez. I don't care. I don't care. That's where I leave you.

Long pause.

Haggert   Are there any secrets you haven't told me? Any surprises? You can just leave us on the street... in Juarez. That's all I want from you.

Long pause.

LIGHTS FADE OUT.

*

Act Two

Lights fade in...

Delphy sits on edge of cheap motel bed. It's been slept in and hasn't been made. Upstage is Haggert. It's afternoon.

Delphy How many times is it now? *(Pause)* How many days?

Haggert For what?

Delphy Your life, it just rushes past you, and you don't notice, you don't notice until your body hurts and it's hard to get up in the morning. Then you notice but then you've missed it.

Haggert Missed what?

Delphy If I knew, maybe I wouldn't have missed it. I just know... I know when I look around me, here, that there is something fatal going on. *(Pause)* All my life has led to this?

Haggert It's just another Tuesday.

Delphy In Juarez. *(Pause)* All my life... I end up in some fucking motel in Juarez. *(Long pause)* When I was about thirty-five, I imagined I still might do this, or do that,... you know... and I remember, I had this apartment, little place and the landlady was sort of a friend, and I used to fuck her, too, sometimes, but I stayed at that dump for six and a half years. *(Pause)* I wasn't doing anything, really... no kind of job I liked or felt was leading anywhere... but I stayed at Christie's place and I fucked off six years and change. Amazing.

Silence.

I wanted to have kids. I think I wanted to have kids, I don't know really, now, looking back. *(Pause)* And here I find the road leads to you, Haggert.

Haggert   You're being mean again.

Delphy   How many times ? Do you know?

Haggert   What?

Delphy   I was to drop you off. That was what you said.

Haggert   I still am saying it.

Delphy   I wasn't to stay here... I was thinking of taking myself to a movie tonight... or was it yesterday night... if I'd have been home. But I didn't go home. *(Pause)* How many chances do you get? Or do you only get one of these?

Haggert   You're being mean.

Delphy   People have changed... since I was a boy.

Haggert   This is another fucking story that ends up being some-way mean to me.

Delphy   There wasn't so much softness... everyday working people... men weren't fat... they worked too hard to get fat. They had an edge to their face... they were hard men. Today... people are driven mad, and they slave, but it's an easy slavery—and they all look like they take some kind of medication.

Haggert	They all *do* take some kind of meds.
Delphy	I think that people are dying out. That's what I think. God is coming to take us all home.
Haggert	You a fucking Christian, now, or something? *(Pause)* Delphy—you can go, you know, you can go anytime.
Delphy	Maybe the oracle is to be found in an alley in Juarez? you think?
Haggert	The fuck...?
Delphy	I can't return, Haggert. I realized that a couple days ago. Funny how such things can hit you... there is nothing to return to.
Haggert	You think there ever was something to return to? That anyone has ever had something to return to.
Delphy	I think we must have had a home... or we wouldn't have come up with the word "home."
Haggert	When was this?
Delphy	Way before we were alive. *(Beats)* I don't know.

Silence.

	Where is Ursula?
Haggert	Maybe she went home. *(Laughs)*
Delphy	Hey, that's funny. *(He's not laughing)*
Haggert	Except, you know, maybe she did.

Pause.

Delphy	Where did she go, when she left?
Haggert	You know, she goes out... that's a thing she does... and I've never known where she goes. It can be irritating. But that's her...

Pause.

She has things that come back to her... from places—I don't know—I really don't. But shit gets to her and she goes away.

DELPHY *nods.*

Delphy	Children. You want to have children, Haggert?
Haggert	Strange moment to ask that question.
Delphy	I guess. *(Pause)* I think it's purely a thing you do to fend off death. Like if I make a child I won't really die. But you do die... so maybe it's like, well, someone will remember me because we all remember our parents.
Haggert	Go home Delphy. Really. This isn't your problem.
Delphy	Right, I got my own problems. Right?
Haggert	Yeah, right.

Silence.

LIGHTS *fade out.*

LIGHTS *come up slowly...*

Same as previous scene... except now it's night.

DELPHY *is stretched out on bed. He is awake. It's late. It's quiet. A train whistle blows in the distance.*

Delphy	Haggert?

No answer. He is alone.

Who's on that train I wonder.

Silence.

Think I could pay one of these whores down here, pay her to have my kid? You think I can even make children anymore?

DELPHY *sits up... lights a cigarette.*

Son of a Juarez whore. But he would remember me, wouldn't he.

Silence. DELPHY *stands up. Pause.*

(A little louder) Haggert?

Silence.

How long? Alone. How long... how much money is left... months... six months maybe. *(pause).*

KNOCK *at door.*

DELPHY *tenses... then steps toward door...*

Silence.

VOICE *(OS)*   My name is Jensen. Sorry to wake you up, whoever the fuck you are.

Another KNOCK.

LIGHTS *fade out.*

LIGHTS *come up slowly...*

DELPHY *sits on bed. A man,* JENSEN, *in his early sixties maybe, stands.*

Jensen   I just need to see him. Him and the girl.

Delphy   Right, well, I just don't know where they are. Haven't seen her in a day or so.

Jensen   I'm really sorry you had to get wakened—this is nothing to do with you. I'm real sorry.

Delphy   Can I ask what this is about?

Jensen   Nothing to do with you, I assure you. Nothing at all.

DELPHY *nods. Pause.*

Delphy   I'm a friend of Haggert in a way. He's not a bad person, really.

Jensen   I'm not in the judging business, ya know. Nice, not nice, it's for some sort of Destiny to sort out. Or maybe the police, I'm not sure. *(Pause)* Maybe Jesus.

Delphy   What is it you plan to do when you see Haggert?

Jensen   My friend, that is not something for you to be involved with. Mr. Haggert owes us some money.

| Delphy | Yeah, well, I'm sure he does. He owes me too. |

JENSEN nods, thinking.

Jensen	It is my belief, my firm belief, that that kind of reckless behavior, that Mr. Haggert has displayed all of his young life, that that behavior catches up with you. I believe that.
Delphy	How much do you know about Haggert?
Jensen	I am making assumptions... I know that. But I'm in the business of finding people of a certain sort... mostly they are much the same. If your friend is different, then more's the pity, ya know.

Silence.

| Delphy | Jensen, can I ask where you're from? |
| Jensen | Not far from here... across the border though. Arizona. I lived down in this shit for most of my life. I ain't done much with my life... is that what you're thinking? How do I say stuff about your friend... and whatnot... and here I am a dirtball desert rat, working border towns— doing collections. Is that what you're thinking? |

Pause.

Well, you mind if I sit down for a while... I'm tired like a motherfucker.

DELPHY nods OK, motions him toward the one chair.

Jensen	What do you do, mister... *(waits)*
Delphy	*(Laughs a bit)* Delphy.
Jensen	That a foreign name of some sort... French? Creole?
Delphy	My father was Sicilian, but the name... well, it's a long story.
Jensen	My grandfather was from Sweden, Holland, one of those fucking cold-ass places.
Delphy	You don't know?
Jensen	Died, old sucker died when I was like two minutes old. That's a long story, too.

They sit, neither really moving or looking at each other.

	Family don't really matter anyway. *(Pause)* So, what is it you do Delphy?
Delphy	I ran a sort of hardware store... back in California.

JENSEN sits and thinks about this.

Jensen	You make a living doin' that?
Delphy	Of a sort, I guess. *(Pause)* Let me ask you something Jensen, about who hired you to find Haggert.
Jensen	Now you know I can't tell you that. Don't matter anyhow... everything is all the same in the end. We die, and people slowly forget us, those few who knew us. *(Pause)* I rarely talk to normal people—from the straight world. I sort of live in the shadow world—that's just how it's turned out. And you're the same Delphy, or you wouldn't be here. We wouldn't be having this talk.
Delphy	You got children, Jensen?

Jensen	Married once, to a Mex girl. No children.
Delphy	You remember what that was like, with that Mexican girl?
Jensen	Long time ago. *(Beats)* I remember she smelled good, had beautiful black hair... cooked good and fucked all my friends.
Delphy	But do you remember yourself... who "you" were when you decided, shit, let me marry this black-haired girl?
Jensen	I remember I liked to wake up and see her next to me. All that black Indian hair, and that pretty mouth. I don't remember what was actually in my head, what kinda thoughts I had when I rolled over and saw that girl there.

DELPHY nods.

You staying here... in town?

Delphy	*(Smiles)* That's like asking, you plan to die eventually.
Jensen	*(Beats)* Is it?
Delphy	Am I staying here? Yeah... for the moment. For how long, that what your asking? How long can I take staring at these walls?
Jensen	No law you can't go out. Get a taco... buy a beer.
Delphy	I could, that's true.

SILENCE.

How long you gonna sit here?

JENSEN smiles.

Jensen	You want to sleep? I can wait out in the truck.
Delphy	I more or less stopped sleeping.
Jensen	Yeah, me too. *(Pause)* Well, Delphy, now you really don't know where Haggert might be? I looked around town.
Delphy	Check the jail?
Jensen	First place I looked.

JENSEN stands.

Delphy	You carry a gun, Jensen?
Jensen	Call me, Perry. That's the name my momma gave me.
Delphy	OK, Perry, you carry a gun?
Jensen	Yes sir, I do. Always.

JENSEN starts toward door. Stops.

I wanted that Mex girl quite badly... to be honest.
I knew she was a fucking headcase slut. Didn't matter.
That's what I remember. Knowing shit would turn
out bad and not caring. Just being carried along on
some kind of terrible need, of want. Of sexual madness.

Pause. DELPHY nods.

I'll be outside.

| Delphy | Right, in the truck. |
| Jensen | Chevy pickup. The red one. |

JENSEN turns away...

LIGHTS OUT.

LIGHTS FADE UP...

DELPHY alone in almost dark.

RECORDED VOICE OF DELPHY...

Delphy Sometimes in the middle of the night, sometimes in the heat of day, sometimes I hear a voice. I think it's my father, but I know it's just shit rattling around in my head.

DELPHY sits... on edge of bed. He stares off into space.

Sometimes I get so tired. Not sleepy, cause I don't sleep, but tired... so tired I can't lift my arm up to answer the phone. So tired, sometimes, that I'd pay someone to answer it. Sometimes I gotta sit... at night, at noon, I sit and I feel my entire body ache and tremble. I sometimes get an idea in my head, that what is making me tremble is God. God is visiting me... we're all God's children, that's how I was taught. I didn't believe it... but I still think these visits from God are what is making me so damn tired. *(Pause)* Sometimes I think that voice I hear is God's voice, and it only sounds like my old Sicilian father. And then I think, no, you damn fool, it's just the burned-out wires in your tired-ass brain... the fried and soaked and brittle old synapses and shit...

they're just firing off random electric charges and this is all God has ever amounted to. *(Beats)* Sometimes in the late afternoon shadows, in the woods where I live... in these old pines, where it's always cool, I hear the sound of small animals. And I believe if I lived there long enough I would eventually understand their language, but that humans never have lived long enough to learn those kinds of things. And I walk slowly and sadly from the dark woods into the light and I hear the sound of cars and screams and sirens and breaking glass... and I don't know if it's real and then I think it doesn't matter.

Silence.

Sometimes I want to wake up and want not to be alone. *(Beats)* And now I hear the voice of Ursula... and I don't or can't hear Haggert. And maybe this man Jensen has killed him... and I should run out and see what is going on... except I'm not sure I hear anything.

Silence.

Maybe it's someone else being hurt. Maybe Ursula and Haggert left for Oaxaca or Veracruz. Maybe they signed on a cruise ship and went to Costa Rica. Sometimes the nights are like this. Voices, cries, and absolute silence.

Silence.

Sometimes.

Silence.

RECORDING STOPS... *now* DELPHY *speaks live.*

Ursula? *(Much louder)* Ursula ??!!! You out there?... who the fuck is out there??... *(Screams)* Who is out there? Who??... Who!!?!?!

Blackout.

Finish

THE PLAYWRIGHTS

Hank Bunker's play, *The Interview,* was originally produced at Theatre of NOTE in Hollywood, where it received a Garland Award from *Backstage West.* His subsequent plays *Futon Dialogues* and *All Saints' Day* also premiered at NOTE, the latter winning *Backstage West* and *Dramalogue* theater awards. He is a co-founding member of the acclaimed Los Angeles theater company Oxblood, which originally produced his baseball noir, *The Noon of Games.* Other plays include *Lefty*, *Lemon Head*, and a radio play, *Citrus.* His plays have received productions throughout the United States. As a performer he has appeared in numerous plays, including new work by John Steppling, Neena Beeber, and Murray Mednick, receiving a Best Actor nomination from the *LA Weekly* for his performance in Mednick's *Taxes.* He holds an MFA from USC and lives in Los Angeles.

Heidi Darchuk is a writer and actor living in Los Angeles. She has written plays for Padua Playwrights, the Virginia Avenue Project and A Contemporary Theatre. Her micro-fiction has been published in the anthology *Pontoon 5.*

Murray Mednick is the founder of the Padua Hills Playwrights Festival and Workshop, where he served as artistic director from 1978 through 1995. Born in Brooklyn, New York, he was for many years a playwright-in-residence at New York's Theatre Genesis, which presented all of his early work, including *The Hawk*, *The Deer Kill*, *The Hunter*, *Sand*, and *Are You Lookin'?.* He was artistic co-director of Genesis from 1970 until 1974, when he moved to California. Plays produced since then include *Iowa* and *Blessings* (for the PBS series

"Visions"), *The Coyote Cycle, Taxes, Scar, Heads, Shatter 'n Wade, Fedunn, Switchback, Baby, Jesus!, Dictator*, and *Freeze*. Mednick's plays *Joe and Betty* and *Mrs. Feuerstein* received dual runs in Los Angeles and New York in 2002; *Joe and Betty* received the American Theatre Critics Association's Best New Play Citation in that year. He is also the recipient of two Rockefeller Foundation grants, a Guggenheim Fellowship, an Obie, several Bay Area Critics Awards, the 1997 *L.A. Weekly* Playwriting Award (for *Dictator*) and a 1992 Ovation Lifetime Achievement Award from Theatre LA for outstanding contributions to Los Angeles theatre. In 2002, Mednick was awarded the Margaret Harford Award for Sustained Excellence in Theater by the Los Angeles Drama Critic's Circle. His most recent production was *DaddyO Dies Well*, at the Electric Lodge, in May 2011. It is the fifth of the *Gary Plays*. The sixth (*Gary's Call Back*), and number seven (*The Fool and the Red Queen*), will be produced in May, 2012 at the Electric Lodge in Los Angeles.

An original founding member of the Padua Hills Workshop and Festival, **John Steppling** is a two time NEA winner, Rockefeller Fellow, PEN-West winner (for *Teenage Wedding*) and two-time *LA Weekly* winner for best play. He recently taught screenwriting at the Polish National Film School in Lodz, Poland, for six years, and has done the same in France, England and Norway. His plays include *Dream Coast, The Shaper, Dogmouth, Phantom Luck, Standard of the Breed, The Thrill* and *Sea of Cortez*. He adapted Eddie Bunker's *Animal Factory* for director Steve Buscemi, released in 2000 with Willem DaFoe. He divides his time between the high desert of Southern California and Norway with his wife Gunnhild Skrodal Steppling.

Rita Valencia is a writer and graphic designer. Her fiction has been published in numerous literary/art journals and her plays produced in Los Angeles and New York. Her essays currently appear online in the *Times Quotidian* arts and culture blog (www.timesquotidian.com). In the field of entertainment advertising, she has won numerous awards and for her design work on both mainstream and independent film and television campaigns. ritavalencia@mac.com

Sharon Yablon was a member of Oxblood, a critically acclaimed playwright/producing group. Her plays have been published in (among others) the *2008 Anthology of Best One-Act Plays* from Desert Road Publishing. She's appeared on local radio programs and had a radio play broadcast by KXLU. Her work is in the Eumenides Project, a gallery installation. She is the founder/producer of The Farm, which presents short plays around Los Angeles in old hotels, houses, pools, offices, and parks to audiences not usually exposed to theater. She is a co-writer of *Republicans In Love,* a photo-comic strip that appeared in *Bedlam* magazine. Her plays have been produced by Theater Unleashed, Bootleg, Gunfighter Nation, Padua Playwrights, Echo Theater Company, and Overtone Industries. She has taught at UCLA, Antioch, and the Playwrights in the Schools program. Her next projects are a photo comic book of monologues, and an evening of short plays set in different cafes in downtown Los Angeles.

An award-winning writer, director and producer, **Guy Zimmerman** has served as artistic director of Padua Playwrights since 2001. Under his direction, this LA-based company has staged more than twenty-five productions of new plays, including three in New York City and three abroad, that have garnered a host of *LA Weekly,* Ovation, Garland, and Los Angeles Drama Critics Circle awards and nominations. Zimmerman has edited a six-volume anthology series for Padua Press, distributed nationally by TCG. He has also produced and directed a series of digital media productions of original plays including *Girl on a Bed, Gary's Walk, Pronghorn,* and *Snout.* Previously, Zimmerman wrote for network television, including the shows *Cracker, The Pretender* and *Wonderland.* His own plays include *La Clarita, The Inside Job,* and *Vagrant.* His articles and essays about film, theater, art, science and politics have been published in the *LA Weekly, LA Theater Magazine, Backstage West,* the *LA Citizen, Cyrano's Journal, Bedlam Magazine* and, most recently, the arts and culture website *Times Quotidian.* Zimmerman received a BA in History from the University of Pennsylvania, is currently working towards an MA in Urban Sustainability at Antioch University and begins a doctoral program in Theater and Dramatic Arts at UC Irvine in the Fall of 2011. He currently lives in Silver Lake with his wife, Jenny Bright and their daughter, Eliza.

ABOUT PADUA

Padua Playwrights exists to generate, for the public, innovative, transformative plays by preserving the playwright's traditional place at the heart of the writing and production process. Padua cultivates unique voices in American theater via intensive workshops, engagement with the classics, stage and media productions of new work and, finally, publication.

Padua Playwrights began as an annual festival and workshop in 1978 when Murray Mednick invited five other playwrights, including Sam Shepard and Maria Irene Fornes to join him on the old Padua Hills estate in the foothills of the San Gabriel Mountains, just east of Los Angeles. The playwrights, as well as playwriting students and actors, were given free reign to reinvestigate their creativity, developing writing exercises for the morning, rehearsing in the afternoon, and presenting the results in he evening. Under Mednick's artistic direction, the Festival became a model that, staged annually, had a lasting impact on American theater. Among its prominent alumni are Henry David Hwang, John Steppling, John O'Keefe, Jon Robin Baitz, Marlane Meyer, Julie Hebert, Kelly Stuart, Guy Zimmerman and Wesley Walker. Since 2001, under the artistic direction of playwright and director Guy Zimmerman, the company has been offering regular seasons of new work from new and established Padua playwrights to critical acclaim. In its first nine seasons the company staged 26 productions, including three in New York City and three abroad, and garnered a host of *LA Weekly*, Garland, and Los Angeles Drama Critics Circle awards. In 2003, the company began publishing this series of new play anthologies, six to date, distributed nationally by Theatre Communications Group.

All inquiries including requests for permission to perform any of the plays in this volume, in part or in their entirety, should be directed to Padua Playwrights Productions. They will be forwarded to the individual playwright.

Padua Playwrights Productions
840 Micheltorena Street
Los Angeles, CA 90026.
info@paduaplaywrights.com

Other Padua titles available through your local bookseller and through Theater Communications Group (www.tcg.org):

Beneath the Dusty Trees
The Gary Plays
by Murray Mednick
Includes *Tirade for Three, Gary's Walk, Girl on a Bed, Out of the Blue, DaddyO Dies Well, Gary's Callback, The Fool and the Red Queen,* and *Charles' Story*
504 Pages, Paperback, ISBN 0-9630126-4-9
$16.95

Padua: Plays from the Padua Hills Playwrights Festival
Includes plays from the Padua Hills Playwrights Festival by Neena Beber, Maria Irene Fornes, Joseph Goodrich, Murray Mednick, Marlane Meyer, Susan Mosakowski, John O'Keefe, John Steppling, Kelly Stuart
504 Pages, Paperback, ISBN 0-9630126-4-9
$18.95

3 Plays by Murray Mednick

16 Routines, Joe and Betty, and *Mrs. Feuerstein.*
Murray Mednick at his darkly comic best.
"A playwright's playwright... *Mednick has spent his career at the
forefront of avant-garde theater." —Sandra Ross, LA Weekly*
300 pages, Paperback, ISBN 0-9630126-3-0
$14.95

Best of the West

Includes plays from the Padua Hills Playwrights Festival by Susan
Champagne, Martin Epstein, Maria Irene Fornes, Julie Hebert,
Leon Martell, Murray Mednick, Susan Mosakowski, John Steppling, Kelly Stuart
312 pages, Paperback, ISBN 0-9630126-2-2
$14.95

The Coyote Cycle

Seven Plays by Murray Mednick
*"...it permanently reshaped my vision of what theatre could
achieve—ritual, magic, playfulness, and respect for the playwright-
actor bond entered my creative vocabulary and have been my
resources ever since... in a day when much of the public has come to
doubt the power of theatre, Murray Mednick's* Coyote *is proof that
the best of it can still change lives."—David Henry Hwang*
176 pages, Paperback, ISBN 0-9630126-1-4
$15.95

Hipsters in Distress

Are You Lookin'? and Other Plays

by Murray Mednick

Includes *Are You Lookin'*? Scar, Heads, *Skinwalkers, Shatter* 'n *Wade, Dictator,* and *Switchback*

460 pages, Paperback, ISBN 0-9630126-7-3

$14.95

Plays for a New Millennium

New Work from Padua

Includes plays by Sarah Koskoff, Murray Mednick, John O'Keefe, John Steppling, Wesley Walker, and Guy Zimmerman

522 pages, Paperback, ISBN 0-9630126-6-5

$18.95